WASHOE COUNTY LIBRARY

3 1235 01575

THE BIG ROUNDUP

AN ANTHOLOGY OF THE BEST
CLASSIC AND CONTEMPORARY POETRY
FROM COWBOYPOETRY.COM

Margo Metegrano, Editor

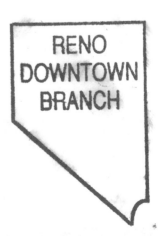
RENO
DOWNTOWN
BRANCH

New West Library
SAN FRANCISCO

The copyright of each poem in this book remains with its author.
All poems are reprinted with permission. No poem herein may be
reprinted or used in any form without the author's express permission.

Cover art: "The Best Laid Plans" Bill Anton
Oil on canvas 48 x 42, Courtesy of the artist

Design: William Braznell

©2002, New West Library
P.O. Box 330444
San Francisco, CA 94133
www.NewWestLibrary.com

All rights reserved, including the right of reproduction in whole or in part in any
form without the written permission of the publisher, except in reviews.

Manufactured in the United States of America

First Printing

LCCN 2001093094
ISBN 0-9712-5503-2

NEW WEST LIBRARY

To all those who carry on the ranching tradition
and strive to honor, preserve, and share
the cowboy way of life

Contents

And The Sky is Not Cloudy All Day

Don't Fence Her In

Strange Things Done

THE WEST THAT WAS

OLD HANDS

HOME ON THE AUSTRALIAN RANGE

Ever Faithful and Mavericks

Come Sit By My Side

Cowboy Christmas

Beat the Drum Slowly

Quiet Starlight on the Plains

About the Poets

Best of the West

Indexes

FOREWORD

Like all good poetry, Cowboy Poetry is a celebration of many things: the Cowboy way of life and the romance of the West, to be sure, but much else as well. And, like most "genre" literature, it is also burdened with common misconceptions and prejudices that the best Cowboy Poetry simply doesn't deserve.

Cowboy Poetry is not all about heavy metrical patterns and simple rhymes. Even if this were not true, exactly what would be the problem? As the massive attendance at Cowboy Poetry festivals attests, this is just as much "people's poetry" as what you would hear at any urban poetry slam, where strong meter and in-your-face rhymes win prizes, not criticisms. The success of Cowboy Poetry is dependent upon its oral tradition, and that tradition depends on attention to precisely these poetic devices.

The themes of Cowboy Poetry are universal. There is a heavy emphasis on nature, history, folklore, family, friends, and work (especially danger and tedium) as well as delight in the language itself. Even though Cowboy Poetry tends not to take itself too seriously, it is in fact worthy of serious study.

Cowboy Poetry is inclusionary. The Cowboy Poetry tradition includes women, Mexican American Cowboys, gauchos, Cowboys and loggers of the Pacific Northwest, and the poetry of the Australian bush.

Happily, scholarly and popular texts attest to these truths, which are amply illustrated by the poems in The Big Roundup. These selections illustrate and celebrate the diverse, vibrant current state of Cowboy Poetry. That they were gathered in a most modern "virtual gathering" on the Internet is proof of the enduring popularity and relevance of the genre in this new millennium.

TOM MAYO
POETRY COLUMNIST
Dallas Morning News

INTRODUCTION

Cowboy Poetry is a living chronicle of people, places, and events.

The earliest American tunes and poetry came from the trails of the working Cowboys, influenced by the spirit of the songs and poems of their ancestral balladeers. During the era of the great trail drives—which lasted for fewer than three decades in the last part of the nineteenth century—Cowboys sang songs as they worked and told tales for entertainment, to relieve boredom and loneliness, and to pass along their experiences.

As more of the western range was fenced, "progress" gave way to smaller ranches and fewer Cowboys, and Hollywood added its romantic visions. Cowboy Poetry themes evolved: the Chisholm Trail wound its way into the Dust Bowl, hopped on to a Massey-Ferguson, rode on to the rodeo and Melody Ranch, went up against government bureaucracy and the changing landscape, and pulled into the Kmart parking lot.

Now entering its third century, this rich tradition continues to tell the past and present stories of Cowboy and ranching life both in recitations and in written form, at gatherings and on recordings, and in books and on the Internet.

Cowboy Poetry's current popularity attests to its enduring relevance. A small gathering of Cowboy Poets in Elko, Nevada in 1985 sparked a renewed interest in the form, and today there are hundreds of gatherings across the globe. Now nearly ten thousand fans gather annually at Elko and—in a most modern venue—many hundreds of poets take part in a continuous, "virtual" gathering at *CowboyPoetry.com's* internet BAR-D Ranch.

No other way of life has spawned so many poets, and that nearly organic component of Cowboy and ranching life comes through in the authenticity of experience imparted in the classic and contemporary poetry in *The Big Roundup*, a selection of the best poetry from *CowboyPoetry.com*. Each chapter's initial classic offering reflects the general theme of the poems that follow.

Where the Handclasp's a Little Stronger takes its name from Arthur Chapman's "Out Where the West Begins." Chapman wrote the poem in 1917, dashing it off for his *Denver Republican* column when the Western states' governors were arguing about where the West began. For years it remained a popular poem throughout America. It hung in the office of the

Secretary of the Interior in Washington, was quoted in Congress, and was used as campaign material for at least two governors.

Other poems in *Where the Handclasp's a Little Stronger* go on to speak of the "where" as well as the "who" and "what" that goes into the makeup of the West's Cowboys and ranchers. Red Steagall's forceful statement tells where his own West begins, in "Born to This Land." Generations of pride stand solidly in this very personal and moving poem, which begins:

> I've kicked up the hidden mesquite roots and rocks
> From the place where I spread out my bed.
> I'm layin' here under a sky full of stars
> With my hands folded up 'neath my head.
>
> Tonight there's a terrible pain in my heart
> Like a knife, it cuts jagged and deep.
> This evening the windmiller brought me the word
> That my granddaddy died in his sleep.

From Missouri's Leroy Watts' "Gateway to the West" to Oklahoma Cowboy Poet Laureate Francine Roark Robison's "North to Abilene," the chapter's poems further define people and places of the West, and beyond. We learn the histories of the Hawaiian "Painolo" Cowboy; the Florida "Cracker" Cowboy (so-called for cracking sounds made by his whip as he herded cattle); and of one of the thousands of Black American Cowboys who rode the early range. And from across the ocean, Liverpool's Thomas Vaughan "Melancholy" Jones' lilt carries through to his poetry now as it likely did in the songs and poetry of his emigrant ancestors in their own time, men he writes about in his "The Immigrants, 1858":

> They paved the roads of Texas,
> Through the prairies and the plain.
> I doubt if we will ever see
> The likes of them again.
>
> God Bless you Jimmie Currie,
> and God Rest you, Uncle Bill
> We never yet forgot you,
> And we swear we never will.

Along with the love of the land present throughout many of these verses, there are respects paid to the more forbidding landscapes as well. In other poems, modern Cowboys survey the land and the big sky and kick up some fun. Throughout the tales of hardship and struggle, in homage to the land and those who made their way, as the past merges with the present, a vision of the West takes hold. Chapman had it right:

> Out where the world is in the making,
> Where fewer hearts in despair are aching,
>   That's where the West begins;
> Where there's more of singing and less of sighing,
> Where there's more of giving and less of buying,
> And a man makes friends without half trying —
>   That's where the West begins.

Poems about the "real Cowboys" comprise *Git Along, Little Dogies*; named for one of the most well known traditional Cowboy songs, "Whoopee To-Yi-Yo, Git Along, Little Dogies," which is included in *The Big Roundup*. The song evolved from a sixteenth century Celtic ballad, "The Old Man's Lament," the story of an old man left to raise a child that is not his own:

> I was out walking one morning for pleasure
> Down by the river I rambled along
> I met an old man making sad lamentations
> Rocking a cradle that's none of his own
> ...
> It's my misfortune but none of your own

To hear the old ballad followed by the Cowboy version:

> As l walked out one morning for pleasure,
> I spied a cow-puncher come all riding alone
> His hat was thrown back and his spurs was a jingling,
> As he approached me a-singin' this song,
> *Whoopee ti yi yo, git along little dogies,*
> *It's your misfortune, and none of my own.*

is to appreciate the threads of history that stitched the tapestry of the West.

Git Along, Little Dogies includes tales of the hard trails and poets with much to say about what makes a "real" Cowboy and how he's different from the "reel" version.

Contemporary life figures in many of the poems, from Rod Miller's intricately amusing "The E. S. L. Ranch," where a Cowboy struggles to understand the working lingo, to Sam Jackson's on-target contrast between the picture-perfect Hollywood Cowboy "Tall, lean and disgustingly handsome" and the "real" item, in his "Reel vs. Real Cowboys":

> Now—picture this work-a-day feller;
>   five-eight, and he's built sort'a slight.
> Boots decorated with cow-salve,
>   and clothes that ain't fittin' just right.

When it comes to rancher Paul Bliss, it's not clear where the Cowboy ends and the poet starts: in January of 1999 he rode his own horse over 300 miles through blinding snow and sub-zero temperatures to the Elko Cowboy Poetry gathering. His "Cowboy Poetry in Motion" takes the reader on another exciting trail ride, and despite his assertion that words can't portray the experience, few do better than he as his ride comes to a close:

> The sun it tops a ragged ridge, un the rays come bustin' through,
>   Un ya watch the herd snake down the trail, in solemn overview.
>
> It's a picture that can't be described by anybody's notion,
>   'Cause pardner it's a feelin', "Cowboy Poetry in Motion."

In 1873, when Brewster Higley and others improved upon a poem Higley had written, a Western anthem and the makings of "Home on the Range" were born. Higley's partners talked him out of lines such as "Where life streams with buoyancy flow" and convinced him that "the skies are not clouded all day" needed just a bit of work. This book includes the early song, "The Western Home"; the original poem is posted at *CowboyPoetry.com*. Today "Home on the Range is the state song of Kansas, a tune recognized the world over.

Higley's song compares the natural beauty of his Western world to the heavens above:

How often at night
When the heavens were bright
By the light of the twinkling stars,
Have I stood here amazed
And asked as I gazed
If their glory exceeds that of ours.

The air is so clear,
The breeze so pure,
The zephyr so balmy and light;
I would not exchange
My home here on range
Forever in azure so bright.

But in the real world, the land and the weather are opponents as well as inspirations, as some of the other poems in *And The Sky is Not Cloudy All Day* address.

The rancher's calendar is measured in seasons, not days. An old Larry Chittenden poem refers to a cowman who "scanned the books of nature, as the seasons turned the leaves." Written a hundred years later, Jo Lynne Kirkwood's elegiac four-part "A Cowboy Season" encapsulates a year of ranching life. In her description of Spring's calving, the weather is cursed:

You were gruntin' and gaspin' and covered in sweat,
cussin' to drown out the pain,
Neck deep in muck and cursin' the sky,
though you knew in July you'd need rain.

and then a change of spirit occurs, as it often does for those who live their lives hand in hand with Nature and witness her miracles:

Then a little feller you'd thought was left dogie
answered the bawl of his ma,
and thrustin' his head 'gainst that cow's achin' udders
he sucked life from that muddy spring thaw.

And awareness come hard, like the thunder,
with that power that deep knowin' has.
There was no other place you would rather be
than right here, in the spring, birthin' calves.

Fellow Utah poet Michael Sorbonne Robinson paints a vivid picture of a drought and "starvin' stock" with "lips all parched and dry." He's convinced "ol' Mother Earth's a brazen, teasin' flirt" in the long wait for rain described in his "The End of the Drought." And when Nature does come through, once again the event is met with awe:

> The land's all soaked and clover-cloaked;
> I'm wet, right to the core.
> It's like the bliss of my first kiss,
> to feel the rain once more.

Other lives and other seasons round out *And The Sky is Not Cloudy All Day*, which closes with Mickee Cheek's observations on the Nebraska sandhills, where "work gets done when it gets done with the changing of the seasons."

In today's West, where men and women work shoulder to shoulder and a good number of women run their own ranches, it follows that the stories of Cowboy life are well told by both male and female poets. In *Cowgirl Poetry* (Gibbs Smith, 2001), an excellent compilation edited by poet Virginia Bennett ("All That is Left") some classic female poets were anthologized for the first time. Bennett's inclusion of Canadian Rhoda Sivell's work led us to Sivell's 1912 book, *Voices on the Range*, which includes her poem, "The Cow-Girl," that heads our *Don't Fence Her In* chapter. Behind what appears to be romantic verse about "the cow-girl of my dreams," we find a girl "With the look of a half-broke broncho / Half fearful yet trusting inside," who is "as wild as the silver sage brush / That grows by the grey wolf's lair." Then as now, the Cowboy and his Cowgirl "lope o'er the shadowed prairie," side by side.

Common themes in the autobiographical poems in *Don't Fence Her In* include the Cowgirl's mentors—often brothers, Dad or Grandad—and how these women, too, felt "born to this land" and way of life. Texas poet, performer, and rancher Linda Kirkpatrick, who often writes poems about historical female Western figures, tells her own story in "My Cowgirl Life":

> I toddled out behind my Dad 'cause I thought I was a hand
> Just a regular 'ole cowpuncher riding for his brand.

Oklahoma rancher and poet Debra Coppinger Hill weaves a beautiful tribute and tale in her "Wild Stickhorse Remuda." The poem is a story of her grandather Ralph W. Gass, "Papaw," who she says taught her "who I was and gave me my love of the West." It speaks of a simpler time and a devoted man whose gentle guiding hand whittled a collection of stick horses (each with her own brand) while he passed along the history of the West. She learned as much about the Cowboy Way as any boy who rode fences and roped mavericks with Dad or Grandad, as these excerpts tell:

> Along our trails together
> There were many lessons learned,
> Like bein' a cowboy through and through
> Is something that you earn
>
> ...
>
> Sometimes you have to let things go,
> Sometimes you stand and fight,
> And anything worth doin',
> Is still worth doin' right
>
> ...
>
> I still have his sweat-stained Stetson,
> His boots, and his old knife,
> Sometimes I take them out
> Just to measure up my life.

"Wild Stickhorse Remuda" was adapted as a song and recorded by Devon Dawson, the voice of Cowgirl Jesse in Disney's "Riders in the Sky Toy Story II."

Don't Fence Her In includes poems written in honor of two of the world's most notable Cowgirls. Oklahoma dairy farmer Paula Sisk writes about Lucille Mulhall, said to be the first woman ever called "Cowgirl," in 1905, possibly by Teddy Roosevelt, from whom she won a bet when she roped a coyote, or by Will Rogers. Who originated the name is a detail more in dispute than her billing as the first woman who could rope, throw, and tie a steer.

There is no argument about Dale Evans being the world's most recognizable Cowgirl, and Arizona poet Janice Mitich combines autobiography and modern cultural history in her poem "Queen of the West," which she wrote after Dale Evans' death in 2001:

> We knew our lives were different from the rest of the girls at school,
> 'Cause, in town, they all wore dresses while we broke their
> cardinal rules

By wearing jeans, long-sleeved shirts, and high heeled, cowboy boots.
   All their teasin' and finger pointing just made us more resolute.

'Cause, you see, we had our hero, too, up on that movie screen.
   In all those Saturday serials, she was the only Queen.
In fringed skirt and rhinestone shirt, on Buttermilk she'd ride,
   To do right by all with Roy Rogers by her side.

She was the voice of wisdom and showed us girls we had a right
   To fight wrong and injustice, to be fair, good, and forthright,
To find within ourselves the courage to always do our best.
   She became our hero, Dale Evans, the Queen of the West.

Hard-living Cowboys are often the protaganists in *Strange Things Done*, and though Robert Service's "The Cremation of Sam Magee," from which our chapter title is taken, is set in the Yukon, Service's internal rhymes and themes of endurance have long appealed to Cowboy Poets. There are few who can't recite from memory:

There are strange things done in the midnight sun
   By the men who moil for gold;
The Arctic trails have their secret tales
   That would make your blood run cold;
The Northern Lights have seen queer sights,
   But the queerest they ever did see
Was that night on the marge of Lake Lebarge
   I cremated Sam McGee.

Many of the strong rhymes, ironic humor, and intriguing stories in the other strange tales in this chapter seem to owe a nod to Robert Service.

Occasionally a poet is the instrument of some long-ago Cowboy, such as Brad Smith, who serves as a sort of channel for "French Camp Red" and his partner Earl, who travel the Old West meeting with adventure and an assortment of odd characters. Somehow French Camp Red captivates his readers while simultaneously making them grateful they themselves weren't, as on the foggy night that he and Earl encounter "The Dog Swamp Stranger":

Now it happened to be that eventually
Me an' Earl found ourselves overlookin'

A poor man, we agreed, what's appearin' to be
Down a path that he shouldn'a tookin'.

That cowboy was sittin' there under his hat
And he'd made it to maybe mid-bog.
Then he sunk to his waist in a sneaky mud flat
No doubt hidden by darkness and fog.

We both told him, "Hey," and he said, "Howdy do."
And we offered to toss him a rope.
But to our great surprise he just sat in the goo.
He just sat there, then spit, then said: "Nope."

We won't spoil "the rest of the story."

Gold prospectors figure in some of the these tales. Wyoming Deputy
Sheriff Verlin Pitt's poem, "Desert Rat," delivers the undeniable wisdom
that "True security lies not in what you have, but what you can live with-
out." And in Debbie Burdic's "The Rat Pack Mine," more gold lore is passed
along, accompanied by a playful explanation for the origin of snake medicine.

The strange characters and tall tales in *Strange Things Done* would make
for the perfect long winter's night of recitations.

Few poems are more widely known than Gail I. Gardner's rollicking
"The Sierry Petes (or Tying Knots in the Devil's Tale)," a poem that became
an "immediate classic" after it was written in 1917. Because it seems and
sounds like a poem written much longer ago, it was adapted by many poets
and singers, and its origins have often been cited as "anonymous" or "tradi-
tional." Gardner spent much effort defending his authorship, and in a 1977
article in the *Journal of Arizona History*, folklorist Katie Lee tells of a particu-
larly illustrative episode: Gardner was extremely displeased with Alan
Lomax, whose first edition of *Folk Songs of North America* "contained a new
printing of 'Sierry Petes' with no credit, plus an inference of plagiarism"
implying it was based on a poem by Badger Clark. Gardner dashed off a let-
ter to Lomax that included a memorable line that would put any editor on
notice: "Professional singers of cowboy songs and editors have much in
common, neither knows which end of a horse the hay goes in or which end
of a cow gets up first ...." We thank the Gardner family for permission to
include this poem in *The Big Roundup*.

Humor comes naturally to Cowboys, and their traditional rhyming verse
is a perfect vehicle. The poems in *Kickin' Back* display a wide range of

Cowboy humor, with poems about the ways Cowboys look and act, amusing failures to communicate, and other glimpses of the lighter side of Cowboy life.

Several of the chapter's poems find Cowboys at odds with the modern world. The Cowboy in Neal Torrey's "Western Wear" explains each part of his working Cowboy's clothing to an inquisitive tourist, and then can't resist commenting on her own getup. Torrey is the author of many more serious and historical poems, and when asked why he writes Cowboy Poetry, he answered in part, "If you study the hymns and the songs of the cowboy, you see that for the most part, he was a man of honor, integrity and faith. That story is one that needs to be told, and I have taken it upon myself to tell it."

Wyoming's Michael Schroll finds himself at the mercy of steel-toe sensitive security machines in his "At the Airport":

> She probed me with that wand up close
> Went off just like a bell.
> "It's jail for you and no way out,
> You terrorist from hell!"
> "It's just them steel shanks in my boots."
> I pleaded for my life.
> "Take 'em off and walk back through."
> Her heart was cold as ice.

And in Diana Wray's "A Cowboy's Computer" the Western shopper is all confused about modern terminology:

> A keyboard hangs next to the door for my keys
> To my truck that takes me on the hard drive
> Through Wyoming snows to get me some wood
> That then I hafta download so's we can survive.
>
> I log on when I want my fire hotter
> And log off when it's plenty hot
> Prompt is what the mail ain't in the winter
> When it snows and it blows a whole lot.

Award-winning humorist Jeff Hildebrandt has his own problem with terminology, as explained in his "Nadacowboy":

I am not a cowboy, though I wear a cowboy hat
and the boots I wear have pointed toes and heels that ain't near flat.
I want to be a cowboy, but I'm stopped by one condition
I just can't get a handle on those cowboy definitions.

When you say Chaps, I think cologne, and that's not all, there's more
a Quarter Horse is what kids ride outside the Kmart store
A Bull is the just first part of an expletive deleted
and Pony's just a little keg of beer, too soon depleted.
I'm not sure what a Cayuse is, but, it's my recollection
that the Spurs play basketball and Red Eye's an infection.

Another light poem in *Kickin' Back* has just a few short lines, but the story behind it is rich and deep. Arizona poet Rusty Calhoun ("The Appaloosa") and fellow poets bring their "Write 'em Cowboy" program to their local schools, where many of the students in agricultural areas are from low-income minority families. The program uses Cowboy Poetry to teach students about their history and encourages them to write their own poetry. The top award winner from a recent competition, "I Seen John Wayne," by Jesus Cervantes is included here. Rusty Calhoun told us about the poem's author: "He is in the first English-speaking generation of his family of migrant farm workers and is from a proud Sonoro, Mexico vaquero background...Jesus works long hard hours in the fields and holds a second job as a dishwasher in a local cafe (remember he is only twelve years old) as well as going to school and playing sports." More about the program and more poems are posted at *CowboyPoetry.com*.

Roundups led to the competitions that today are called stampedes, tournaments, contests, and of course, rodeos. The temperaments of horses and bulls, the rodeo clowns, and the character and bravery of the riders are represented in the poetry about rodeos in *Bronc Bustin'*. The excitement of the rodeo fills the best of these poems, such as rodeo rider and poet Curley Fletcher's 1915 "The Strawberry Roan," the classic man-versus-beast bronc tale, where the beast is always the bad guy:

He was spavined all round and he had pidgeon toes
Little pig eyes and a big Roman nose
He was U-necked and old with a long lower jaw
You could tell at a glance he was a regular outlaw.

The rider and reader get a run for their money:

> He bowed his old neck and I'll say he unwound
> He seemed to quit living down there on the ground
> He went up to the east and came down to the west
> With me in the saddle, a-doing my best.
>
> He sure was frog-walkin', I heaved a big sigh
> He only lacked wings for to be on the fly
> He turned his old belly right up to the sun
> For he was a sun-fishin' son of a gun.
>
> He was the worst bronco I've seen on the range
> He could turn on a nickel and leave you some change
> While he was buckin' he squalled like a shoat
> I tell you that outlaw, he sure got my goat.

Move the clock ahead seventy five years or so, and Dennis Gaines' foe hasn't been tamed much in his poem, "Ty Murray—Eat Your Heart Out":

> The saddle slipped to left and right, then underneath the brute.
> The sun was burnin' blisters on the bottoms of my boots.
> He bucked right through the riggins, shucked the saddle off his head;
> My oratory blasphemies are better left unsaid.
>
> My feet was in the stirrups and my buns was in the seat;
> With a death-grip on the bridle-reins, I'd not concede defeat.
> Rockin' like a metronome, he slapped me back and forth,
> North, then South, then North, then South, then North, then South,
>   then North.
>
> Centrifugal convulsions caught the early mornin' light.
> Seven hundred tourists died from nothin' more than fright.
> The Terminator's afterburners fortified his motor;
> I was sailin' like a monkey on a helicopter rotor!

The dust flies, there are more losers than winners, more bruises than buckles, and K. T. Etling's poem title, "Temporary Insanity," probably characterizes the events best. But the participants are of a determined breed, and L. M. Larson sums up a rider's character and philosophy in "The Bull Ride":

I can feel the rope start to release from my fist
Six seconds, seven seconds; "Please don't let me miss."
I hit the ground running, gettin' gored ain't no fun
The judges say, "Sorry kid, it's over and done."

Back to the truck and out the gate I go
There's another rodeo tomorrow, I'll give 'em a show
Tomorrow I'll put on my gear and ride
Ain't no bull goin' to take away my pride.

"I knowed he was a Westerner, I knowed it by his talk; I knowed it by his headgear, I knowed it by his walk." That's what E. A. Brininstool had to say in 1914 in his poem "The Westerner," and that vanishing type and other similar subjects make up the poems in *The West That Was.*

Many of these poems are the work of Cowboy Poets devoted to preserving a very personal and local heritage, mixing pride and history with loss. Dave Rhodes, a Pony Express expert, draws on his own ancestors' experiences in "Out Here at Butte Station." Jim Hoy, English professor, Great Plains folklore historian and rancher, puts the daily lives of the old working ranchers of his native Kansas Flint Hills region to poetry in "The Days of Granville and John," days "never to come again." The stories of multi-generation Texas historian and writer Jim Fish's family and others find their way into the lines of his poem, "Heritage":

Well, now our home is long since gone; the ranch is laid to rest,
Divided, sold an' fenced in lots; the owner thought it best.
...
The land has been the legacy we cultivate an' reap,
The life has been the heritage our fathers fought to keep,
An' we are bound throughout our time with those who came before,
To give our hearts and souls to it, and make it something more.

The old home is a recurring theme in *The West That Was,* often serving as a stage for the tales of the purposeful lives that once filled the now deteriorated structures. Roger Traweek's "The Home Place" brings the old home place alive, offering pictures as vivid as a scrapbook of the three generations who worked, celebrated, laughed, loved, and lived and died within its walls. The prairie wind moans through the old empty bunkhouse, the calving shed is falling down, and the entire physical and emotional landscape is expressed in another outbuilding:

> The horse barn stands in protest and with false hope bravely waits
> For return of horse and rider through the sagging corral gates.
> In muffled cadence hoofbeats mark the life I left behind,
> Where now Champ and Snips and Rocket gallop only in my mind.
> Today I stand between two worlds, as different as white from black;
> One beckons me to turn around; the other calls me back.

Traweek and others write of the Dust Bowl's effect on peoples' lives, and nowhere does that devastating force of nature come more alive than in Barbara Bockleman's "Black Sunday," when she weaves quotes based on her interviews with those who lived through that tragic Easter Sunday in 1935. Bockleman arrived in Oklahoma with her grandparents shortly after Black Sunday, and the old home place has an important part in her memories as well. She tells us "In 1936 my family moved into a sod ranch house built in 1895 located on Kiowa Creek in the eastern Oklahoma Panhandle... Eventually the soddie began to deteriorate...and the walls were returned to the sod in the west pasture from whence it came." She raised her family on that same ranch land and she still lives there today.

Poet, singer and songwriter Richard Elloyan writes about another vanishing icon in "Windmill Man." Before the Rural Electrification Project in the late 1930s, more than six million windmills populated the American West, pumping irrigation water and helping run locomotives. Elloyan's windmill man laments "I creak and groan like an old cowboy's bones."

Along with houses and structures, strong sketches of people define *The West That Was*. Jane Morton, too, grew up in the midst of the drought and the Depression and writes about the Colorado farm her great grandfather started in 1911. She creates busy and lively images of the townspeople lured out to the ranch to help in "Branding." She tells how she and her siblings worried that their gruff and exacting father would offend the greenhorns and leave them short handed. But in fact, his manner had the opposite effect:

> That worked as in the story of Tom Sawyer and the fence.
> Folks vied for invitations to the branding day events.
>
> From Canada and Cayman Isles they came by car and plane.
> Some came by bus from Littleton. Some came to entertain.
>
> They even came to like our Dad. They said that he was real.
> I guess that being tactless was a part of his appeal.

All those who helped year after year had gotten pretty good,
Although in the beginning nobody thought they would.

It doesn't happen anymore. Dad's gone. The ranch is leased.
But this is how it used to be before the brandings ceased.

In Virginia Bennett's "All That is Left," a moving poem about the power of Nature, the sad remnants of a homesteader's tree also hold the hopeful lesson of the cycle of life:

But drought sucked the life from the homesteader,
Who eventually had to move on.
And within a few years, the tree had also withered
When its daily washwater was gone.
So, today, she stands guard in the canyon
And each storm brings a new limb to the ground,
And every spring, during the desert roundup
Weary cowboys delight in the kindling they've found.

The inherent respect that Cowboys and ranchers have for those who came before makes "old hands" a natural theme for Cowboy Poets. *Old Hands* begins with the traditional "I Ride an Old Paint," a slow waltz that was often played as the last song at Cowboy dances. Despite the hardships in his life and work, the old hand's love of the Cowboy life endures:

When I die, take my saddle from the wall,
Put it onto my pony, lead him out of his stall.
Tie my bones on his back, an' turn our faces to the West,
We'll ride the prairies that we loved the best.

I've worked in the town and I've worked in the farm,
All I got to show's just this muscle in my arm,
Blisters on my feet, callous on my hand,
And I'm a-goin' to Montana to throw the houlihan.

Other poems in *Old Hands* pay their respects to these tough oldtimers. Ezra Spur introduces the theme well in his "The Old Man":

Every waddie's had an old man,
in his younger days.

That's how he came to learn the truth,
about the cowboy's ways.

Even when time passes some old Cowboys by—as in Steve Dirksen's
"An Old Hand" who is "working in the kitchen of a little cafe" and in Dan
Faught's "Bankin' With an Old Cowboy," where the challenges of modern
technology overwhelm a man who knows "about cattle and horses and
keeping pastures green"—the dignity and wisdom of these men prevail.

Paul Harwitz's "Ride for the Brand" tells of an old hand who passes
along the traditions and values as he defines the title's term:

"It means a lot of different things, son.
It has a lot to do with what's lost and what's won.
I ain't talking about gambling, but earning a living,
Hard work, trust, respect, taking, and giving.

"It means you don't never foul up the land,
And you don't take unfair advantage or rob.
You work hard, even when the work's rough as a cob.
That's part of what it means to ride for the brand.

And as Ezra Spur so well introduces the subject, his last words also neat-
ly sum up the feelings that solidify this connection between the young and
the old:

When a young man comes along,
who's what I used to be.
I hope I leave, something behind,
like my Old Man left for me.

The Australian "Cowboy" goes by the name of Ringer or Stockman,
while an apprentice might be called a Jackaroo or Jillaroo. Australian
"Cowboy Poets" are known as "Bush Poets." The Stockmen's history paral-
lels that of the Cowboy. Poet Graham Dean writes of the Stockmen's begin-
nings in an essay at *CowboyPoetry.com* entitled "The Dying Breed": "In the
dawn of the 1800's and even up to the 1900's, fences were rare and proper-
ties were measured in hundreds or even thousands of square miles.
Boundaries were many days' travel from the homestead and the stockmen

would camp out, sometimes in permanent outbuildings and sometimes just under the stars."

Few Australian Bush Poets are as well known as A. B. (Andrew Barton) "Banjo" Paterson (1864–1941), author of the famed "The Man from Snowy River" and "Waltzing Matilda." Beloved by Australians (he is featured on the $10 bill) his bush ballads celebrate the beauty of the outback and the courage and spirit of its inhabitants. *Home on the Australian Range* begins with Paterson's "The Man from Snowy River," a historical tale with the underlying universal theme of triumph over adversity.

A patriotic love of the land runs through classic and contemporary Bush Poetry. Poet Graham Dean's "I Have Seen the Land" exemplifies such poetry in his eloquent stanzas:

> I have been to where the sun sets with a vengeance,
> And burns the sky with red and ochre hues.
> I have lived where man and his dependents
> Take solace from the best of nature's views.
> ...
> I've watched the summer storms create the fires
> That glow as night-time falls upon the land.
> I've walked the blackened ground where man aspires
> To forge a living where the ant-hills stand.
> ...
> I've flown across a landscape etched with beauty,
> Where rivers snake their way towards the sea.
> I've watched as waves sweep clean the endless beaches,
> Fuelled gently by the early evening breeze.

that end with a pride-swelling tribute to Australia:

> I've been to where the wedgetail soars intently,
> Watched as they, for movement on the ground.
> And as I've floated high above Australia,
> I've come to know this country's glory bound.
>
> And I am everything they call Australian,
> For I am every soul upon this land.
> And for all time, as nature is my soul-mate,
> For my country proudly will I stand.

Jack Sammon grew up on the cattle stations and vast open range of Northern Australia and worked as a Stockman and Drover. His poem, "After the Wet," includes a Stockman's thoughts as he works in the mines during the wet season, his thoughts never far from the range where he yearns to return:

> Where branding fires are glowing in the yards at Eight Mile Camp,
> they're pulling up big micks to the bronco-branding ramp,
> mixing in with smoke and dust and the smell of scorching hair,
> the sound of bawling cows and calves comes floating on the air.

Artist and poet Louise K. Dean offers a look at the lighter side of Australian life in her poem, "Just a Dance." The setting and characters are as recognizable to readers in West Texas as they are to those in her native Queensland:

> I saw him at a local dance in an outback country place,
> And was immediately attracted to his strong and sunburnt face.
> A stockman, tall and rugged, in his brightly patterned shirt,
> A contrast to his jeans and boots with a touch of outback dirt

Henry Lawson and "Banjo" Paterson worked together at Sydney's *Bulletin* newspaper where they often wrote lively columns critical of each other's work and the work of other writers and poets. Lawson accused Paterson of being too romantic, and Paterson in turn criticized Lawson's gloomy outlook. Both were attacked by conservative critics, who questioned the value of literature about bush life. But their writing was embraced throughout Australia, and their innovative works helped define the "Australian character" and inspired generations of writers.

The poems in *Ever Faithful and Mavericks* examine relationships among people and animals, and Lawson's "Ballad of a Drover" is the exciting and tragic tale of a man and his faithful dog.

Horses are central to many of the poems in *Ever Faithful and Mavericks*, and those essential partners to working Cowboys are given due respect and are often portrayed with with personalities as complex as any human's. Rusty Calhoun writes of "The Appaloosa," so fiercely independent and wild that he seems possessed of an ancient spirit. Other poems speak of horses' hard work and rewarding companionship.

Laced with humor, David Dague's "Backward R Double Bar D" is a sort of a modern-day "Git Along Little Dogies" verse that echoes that poem's "It's your misfortune, and none of my own":

> There is a rancho way out West,
> that's where I want to be.
> It's a spread that's like no other,
> and it was made for you and me.
>
> There the water's pure the grass is sweet,
> and the hay always newly mown.
> You'll never have to leave this ranch,
> until you're fully grown.
>
> Yep, that's what I tell all the dogies,
> so they're happy while they're here.
> Just drink the water, eat the grass,
> and forget that you're a steer.

Other creatures great and small figure in the poems of *Ever Faithful and Mavericks*, including donkeys, buffalo, and Texas Longhorns. Still other poems reflect the complex relationships between ranchers and livestock.

Margo Udelle Imes examines the fate of a calf in "The Good Mother," with poignant lines that ring true to anyone who has been in hearing range of distraught cow:

> All night she stood and bawled
> Her grief 'till it would break your heart:
> It didn't take a genius
> To know we'd torn a pair apart.

Another calf plays an essential part in a poem from Bobbie Gallup, whose poetry is often inspired by the journals, diaries, letters and other original sources she comes across in her work as an interpretive naturalist. The documented story of a Nebraska woman trapped in an 1888 prairie blizzard is the basis for "Blizzard Calf":

> late spring storms are deadly
> much like a loaded gun
> clouds burdened like a pregnant cow

before her birthing's done
snowflakes fell at a frantic pace
rushing headlong to the earth
when we looked out we realized
there was little cause for mirth

trapped as we were in my hideaway
this tiny dugout made of sod
two miles from the safety of our parents' home
at the mercy of the hand of God
the fangs of the storm that day snuffed out
the life of many a Two Bar cow
as the wind's bitter snarl
chased them off the cliff at Mitchell's Brow

Cowboy love poems are collected in *Come Sit By My Side*. The chapter title comes from the traditional "Red River Valley," a song that evolved from a popular sentimental eastern American tune, "In the Bright Mohawk Valley," written by James Kerrigan in 1896. In his book, *The American Songbag*, Carl Sandburg describes the many changes to the song as it traveled south and west, including "I have heard it sung as if bells might be calling across a mist in a gloaming."

One of this chapter's most endearing poems is Don Gregory's "She Tied Hearts to Tumbleweeds." He artfully tells his story of the grieving widow:

She started stitching little hearts,
For hers was aching so.
She tied those hearts to tumbleweeds,
And then she let them go.

and the Cowboy:

Rafe, worked for the Rafter 7,
Building fence, and riding line.
Nothing in his life to prepare him for,
What he was about to find.

...

For several months he searched,
Every canyon, every draw.
Searching hard for little hearts,
On every tumbleweed he saw.

The story of "tying hearts to tumbleweeds" is a part of American folk-lore. In his book, *The Fence That Me and Shorty Built*, Red Steagall uses a similar story in his song "Red River Rose," and he writes "there is a story about a lady in the northeastern corner of New Mexico or the Texas Panhandle doing the same thing in the early part of the 20th century." In these modern versions of the tale, everyone lives happily ever after, and indeed Red Steagall says he and his collaborators (brother Danny Steagall and Ace Ford) particularly wanted their song to end that way. A similar idea is employed in "The Ballad of Hard Luck Henry," by Robert Service, in which he writes about a message from Peg written on a Yukon egg, seeking a Klondike miner. But that poem has a twist fit for a Nashville country song: Henry arrives too late, and the formerly lonely Peg invites him in to "see the twins."

New Yorker Larry Chittenden wrote about a Cowboy Christmas dance he attended in Anson, Texas in 1885, and the event he made famous still takes place annually. His description of "The Cowboys' Christmas Ball" is so vivid, you can almost hear the fiddlers and feel the floor boards move:

The leader was a feller that came from Swenson's ranch,
They called him "Windy Billy," from "little Deadman's Branch."
His rig was "kinder keerless," big spurs and high-heeled boots;
He had the reputation that comes when "fellers shoots."
His voice was like a bugle upon the mountain's height;
His feet were animated an' *a mighty movin' sight*,
When he commenced to holler, "Neow, fellers stake your pen!
"Lock horns ter all them heifers, an' rustle 'em like men.
"Saloot yer lovely critters; neow swing an' let 'em go,
Climb the grape vine 'round 'em—all hands do-ce-do!
"You Mavericks, jine the round-up—Jest skip her waterfall,"
Huh! hit wuz gettin' happy, "The Cowboys' Christmas Ball!"

The boys were tolerable skittish, the ladies powerful neat,
That old bass viol's music *just got there with both feet*!

That wailin', frisky fiddle, I never shall forget;
And Windy kept a-singin'—I think I hear him yet—

The modern poems in *Cowboy Christmas* range from humorous to reverent. David Kelley's "My Cowboy's Night Before Christmas" is the former:

'Twas just before Santy came, the story is told.
Cattle weren't stirrin', fact they's bunched against the cold.
The tack was hung near the chuckwagon with care.
Why, we didn't know Santy was close anywhere.

Cowboys on the ground were wishin' for their beds
While nightmares of wild steers ran through their heads.
'Tween now and the next gather, we needed a nap.
Cookie had just finished, and tied down the flap.

When out past the cavvy, there rose such a fuss,
I sprang to my feet, leavin' the bedroll a muss,
And grabbin' my shotgun and my ragged ol' hat
I run t'ward the racket thinkin' "...what'n thunder's that?"

Charlie Sierra surveys the scene in "A Christmas Poem,":

The Sally Army's out in force,
A-tunin' up their band;
I always drop a dollar,
'Cause they once gave me a hand.

There's some who say we've lost the track,
'N' don't know rhyme or reason,
That all this hooraw overlooks
The spirit of the season.

and plans his own sort of worship:

I'll ride west outta Reno,
A-followin' the river,
'Way up into the mountains
Where the air's so cold it shimmers

The Cowboy's individual style and method of worship appear in the other selections as well. In Gail T. Burton's "A Christmas Prayer," his Cowboy's preparation has a solemn sense of almost clerical ritual:

> The worn and wrinkled cowboy
> slowly shaved and combed his hair.
> He picked the finest clothes he had
> and then he dressed with care.
>
> ...
>
> He stepped out of the bunkhouse,
> and pulled his hat down tight,
> Then climbed aboard his private horse
> and rode into the night.

For these Cowboys, the sky is their church's roof and their faith is found on the range. In Lanny Joe Burnett's "Nightwork," Jonesy gets sent out on a cold Christmas Eve to find a missing cow and her calf. His disappointment at missing the barn dance and festivities is replaced by reverence as he comes upon the missing mother and calf:

> My throat got a lump; my eyes got a tear
> I'm lucky, I thought, to have ended up here
> Where hardships are many, but blessings are, too
> Where a short draw can lead to a soul-shaking view

Francis Henry Maynard's classic "The Cowboy's Lament" (also known as "Streets of Laredo") borrows its tune from the "The Bard of Armagh," which dates to the turn of the seventeenth century, itself the echo of other Celtic tunes from centuries earlier. "The Cowboy's Lament" begins the *Beat the Drum Slowly* chapter, named for the work's most famous lines:

> ...
> "Oh, beat the drum slowly and play the fife lowly,
> Play the dead march as you carry me along;
> Take me to the green valley, there lay the sod o'er me,
> For I'm a young cowboy and I know I've done wrong.

Death could be a lonely event in the solitary life of the range, and in "To the Boys at Cutter Bill's Bar," Texan Rod Nichols tells of the hush that comes over the saloon as a note arrives from a now-dead Cowboy, and its effect:

The talkin' and music came back then
but none of us boys was the same
a cowboy no doubt
from some whereabouts
had died all alone with his name.

Cowboy songs and poems take varied views of the Great Beyond, exhibited in the selections in *Beat the Drum Slowly*. On the lighter side, David Dill has a unique plan in "The End," which involves skinning and tanning and his own idea of living happily ever after.

On the dark side, in Jeff Streeby's "The Wild Crew," a poem sizzling with action, four horses wear the Devil's brand as they mark the trail toward Doom:

And a killer rides the red horse
And the horse's name is War.
That buckskin mare, she's Famine,
That the Second Rider bore.

The Third, He topped Black Pestilence,
Vile sickness and disease.
The Pale Rider on the fleabit gray
Pinched Death between His knees.

In an entirely different vein, Bette Wolf Duncan's character in "I Like it Fine Down Here" argues with the "distant voice" that he's just not ready, and octogenarian poet Mary A. Gallagher Kaufman needs an important question answered first, in "Are There Horses in Heaven?":

I have no wish for Paradise
if horses are forbidden there
and golden New Jerusalem
is a city thoroughfare.
Though I'm now bound and restrained by
nature's law of gravity,
my soul, at times, takes wings to soar
and heaven means a horse to me!

South Dakota's Poet Laureate Charles "Badger" Clark celebrated Cowboy and Western life in his poems and songs. His "A Cowboy's Prayer," written in 1906 and dedicated to his mother, is perhaps the most frequently recited Cowboy prayer. The opening line "Oh Lord, I've never lived where churches grow" leads into a beautiful exposition of a love of the land and his feelings of closeness to God "In this dim, quiet starlight on the plains," those beautiful words from which the final chapter of *The Big Roundup* takes its name. Texas' Lloyd Shelby echoes a reverence for the beauty around him in his own "A Cowboy's Prayer":

> So he listened to the gentle wind, that rustled through the trees,
> And watched a deer go runnin' by, as pretty as you please.

> He marveled at the hawk up high, a ridin' in the air.
> Removin' his hat, he bowed his head, and spoke this simple prayer:

> "Sir, I don't know much about, how this ol' world came to be,
> I just know you made a place, for cowboys just like me."

> "So thank you, Sir, for givin' me, a place to work and ride,
> Where I can see your handiwork, with you right by my side."

Quiet Starlight on the Plains ends with "A Prayer for Man and Horse" by HJ "Hoss" Peterson of Wyoming. He tells that he wrote the poem while "laying, exhausted, in the bunkhouse with the thoughts of the day's activities running through my brain. The day's activities turned into thoughts of the week's then the month's, and finally into thoughts of life and all that I'd seen and was wanting to see. Before sleep caught up to me, I began to think about what was in store for me at the end of the trail." He says he wrote his poem then and, "I believe it captures everything I stand for, everything I wish for, and everything I hope for. My belief and faith in the Lord, Heaven Above and the way I live my life all come out in these words." And with that inspired poem, the collection of poems in *The Big Roundup* ends as Hoss Peterson ends his poem: *Amen and Goodnight.*

Following the poems, there are brief biographies of the classic and contemporary poets. A "Best of the West" appendix includes information for some top museums, events, organizations, and publications.

I acknowledge, with gratitude and respect, all the poets who take part in the on-going gathering at *CowboyPoetry.com*'s BAR-D Ranch to celebrate and keep alive the deep and rich Cowboy Poetry tradition—and those who went before. Even in all of these many pages of this introduction, it has been impossible to cite all of this book's excellent poetry. It is my hope that readers will find the same enduring source of entertainment and inspiration in reading these carefully selected poems that I have found in the pleasure of working with *The Big Roundup*'s contributors.

Margo Metegrano

WHERE THE HANDCLASP'S
A LITTLE STRONGER

OUT WHERE THE WEST BEGINS

Out where the handclasp's a little stronger,
Out where the smile dwells a little longer,
    That's where the West begins;
Out where the sun is a little brighter,
Where the snows that fall are a trifle whiter,
Where the bonds of home are a wee bit tighter,
    That's where the West begins.

Out where the skies are a trifle bluer,
Out where friendship's a little truer,
    That's where the West begins;
Out where a fresher breeze is blowing,
Where there's laughter in every streamlet flowing,
Where there's more of reaping and less of sowing,
    That's where the West begins;

Out where the world is in the making,
Where fewer hearts in despair are aching,
    That's where the West begins;
Where there's more of singing and less of sighing,
Where there's more of giving and less of buying,
And a man makes friends without half trying—
    That's where the West begins.

Arthur Chapman, 1917

⚘ BORN TO THIS LAND ⚘

I've kicked up the hidden mesquite roots and rocks
From the place where I spread out my bed.
I'm layin' here under a sky full of stars
With my hands folded up 'neath my head.

Tonight there's a terrible pain in my heart
Like a knife, it cuts jagged and deep.
This evening the windmiller brought me the word
That my granddaddy died in his sleep.

I saddled my gray horse and rode to a hill
Where when I was a youngster of nine,
My granddaddy said to me, "Son this is ours,
All of it, yours, your daddy's and mine.

Son, my daddy settled here after the war
That new tank's where his house used to be.
He wanted to cowboy and live in the west
Came to Texas from east Tennessee.

The longhorns were wild as the deer in them breaks.
With a long rope he caught him a few.
With the money he made from trailin' em north,
Son, he proved up this homestead for you.

The railroad got closer, they built the first fence
Where the river runs through the east side.
When I was a button we built these corrals
Then that winter my granddaddy died.

My father took over and bought up more range
With good purebreds he improved our stock.
It seemed that the windmills grew out of the ground
Then the land got as hard as a rock.

Then during the dust bowl we barely hung on,
The north wind tried to blow us away.
It seemed that the Lord took a likin' to us
He kept turnin' up ways we could stay.

My daddy grew older and gave me more rein,
We'd paid for most all of the land.
By the time he went on I was running more cows
And your daddy was my right hand man."

His eyes got real cloudy, took off in a trot,
And I watched as he rode out of sight.
Tho I was a child, I knew I was special
And I'm feelin' that same way tonight

Not many years later my daddy was killed
On a ship in the South China Sea.
For twenty odd years now we've made this ranch work
Just two cowboys, my granddad and me.

And now that he's gone, things are certain to change
And I reckon that's how it should be.
But five generations have called this ranch home
And I promise it won't end with me.

'Cause I've got a little one home in a crib
When he's old enough he'll understand,
From the top of that hill I'll show him his ranch
Cause like me, he was Born To This Land.

Red Steagall

❧ NORTH TO ABILENE ❧

From Texas up to Abilene
Th' Chisholm Trail had run
As we pointed longhorns northward
An' cattle drives begun.

We crossed th' open prairie
With prickly pear an' chips—
We crossed th' Colorado
An' th' Brazos on these trips.

We rode into th' Territory
From Texas 'cross th' Red;
Th' cattle grazin' 'long th' way,
Three thousand longhorn head.

Th' dust hung high in th' summer air—
For endurance they were bred;
Two miles to th' south, another bunch
Followed where this one led.

Th' tallgrass tickled th' bellies
As great herds plodded an' grazed—
It made up for bone-dry prairies
When they were thirsty, an' crazed.

We rode through sunny weather
An' storms while lightnin' flashed—
We held th' herd together
As 'round us thunder crashed.

For hours that night we had circled
Cattle unwillin' to bed—
Th' bawlin' an' beller'n incessant
From th' whole three thousand head.

We sang "O bury me not" an'
"Yippy ki yo, ki ya"—
We sang to soothe the longhorns an'
To keep th' night at bay.

Th' river crossin's cost a few—
But mav'ricks evened the score;
Then Trail Cutters dropped in casual-like
An' cut out sev'ral more.

We saw th' silent Plainsmen
Who watched th' white man pass;
Th' Red Man sensed disaster—
His culture could not last.

Th' Government in Washington
Made treaties 'bout th' herds,
But th' Kiowa an' Comanche
Knew they were empty words.

We saw th' moon when th' coyotes howled
An' heard th' wind blow free;
We saw th' rustlers gettin' hung
From a lonely cottonwood tree.

We smelled th' coffee boilin'
In Cookie's blackened pot—
Still had th' dent where he'd throwed it
When Jake an' him had fought.

At times we passed a soddy
Carved from unyielding earth—
Alone, with no one to help her,
A woman might die, or give birth.

A woman had an arduous life
Out on th' endless plains:
Desolation claimed her heart, while
Loneliness twined its chains.

We sang "Yippy yi yo, cattle"
An' watched th' tumbleweeds roll—
We sang to fill th' empty nights
An' spaces in our soul.

Past th' Washita, Canadians,
An' Cimarron we drove;
Those horns went clackin' through th' air
An' threads of history wove.

Across th' Arkansas now to
Th' railhead just beyond,
A market for Texas cattle—
An era newly dawned.

We loaded on th' cattle cars,
Those horns poked through th' rails—
Our pay had been collected, an'
We'd twisted our last tail.

North an' South had sacrificed an'
Lived on War-time ration—
Texas beef was makin' history
An' now would feed th' Nation.

With no regrets, we sent 'em East
By steam locomotion—
Th' lonely whistle in th' air
Hung on our emotion.

We'd sung "Git along little dogies"—
Survived th' heat an' hail;
We'd moved 'em all, an' lost but few
Along th' Chisholm Trail.

Francine Roark Robison

❧ IMPRINTS ❧

Today, the vogue is to "imprint" a colt with a human,
So he will grow up trusting the imprint as Maw.
Well, I think of that when people don't understand how
I can love West Texas, when empty desert is all they saw.

Sure, I've read the account of "Trail Blazers" saying,
This was the only uninhabitable portion of Texas.
And I've seen the scars they left in the ruts of the Santa Fe,
As they rushed across making their quick exits.

But I've also read that the stone rejected by the builder
Will be chosen for the capstone, mighty and bold.
That could have been written about these plains
Hurriedly cast aside in a rush to some motherlode.

Plains, Just the sound of the word inspires visions of
Vast, boundless vistas, with fiery sunsets against cobalt sky.
Its power to throw man back upon himself, feeling alone and small,
Is mingled with a feeling of freedom to those who pass by.

For I remember standing in silent awe of a moon rising,
To gentle evening breezes, after a windy front had passed.
Then feeling I was not alone, that the plains were filled
With kindred spirits who by choice lingered, free at last.

I know this land imprints people for I have watched
Many of them fight and struggle, vowing to leave;
Swearing never to return, only to discover too late,
That what they sought was here all along and was free.

How many times I have watched a sleeping brown pasture
Awaken—overnight, by spring rain, into brilliant kelly green.
Then felt tightness of throat as the sun broke over grazing
Mamas as their babies played and bucked at things they'd seen.

Or watched a steaming colt being urged to uncertain legs
And silently praised God on a chilly winter night;
While holding the lantern, and shaking uncontrollably
From a mixture of cold, amazement, and delight.

Yes, these plains imprinted me, yet some will never understand;
The peace I feel knowing, when I'm planted beneath the sod,
It will be on these wild and wind swept plains,
Where I can spend eternity in this land free and blessed by God.

Jim R. Anderson

❧ THE IMMIGRANTS, 1858 ❧

Tell of the men of Texas
Who tamed that savage place.
Who rode beside the devil,
Met their Maker face to face.

Of how they made a fortune
Costing sweat and toil and blood,
Then lost it at Ben Ficklin
When the town died in a flood.

Of how they bred Rambouillet sheep
On Edwards Old Plateau;
Then sold the wool and mutton
Somewhere in San Angelo.

They herded sheep and cattle
With no shelter but a poncho,
Along Dry Devil's River
Where it meets up with the Concho.

They built a town named Christoval,
And civilized the West;
And none could say no other
Than they tried and did their best.

They paved the roads of Texas,
Through the prairies and the plain.
I doubt if we will ever see
The likes of them again.

God Bless you Jimmie Currie,
and God Rest you, Uncle Bill
We never yet forgot you,
And we swear we never will.

Thomas Vaughan "Melancholy" Jones

❧ GATEWAY TO THE WEST ❧

In the river city of St. Louis
On the bank of the Mighty Miss
There stands a giant archway
A symbol of "The Gateway To the West."

For Missouri was the gateway
Through which the settlers came
And this is the story
Of how Missouri got the name.

John Sutter ran a general store
In the Missouri city of St. Jo'
Then he moved to California
To a place called Sacramento.

There on the American River
Sutter built his famous lumber mill
Then he hired a Missouri carpenter
And James Marshall filled the bill.

It was there in the sawmill tail race
Where the mill driving waters ran
James Marshall found a bit of gold
In the American River sand.

When the story reached St. Joseph
The news was printed as it was told
And that story in the St. Joseph paper
Spurred the rush for California gold.

Then many came to seek their fortunes
Others came looking for new land
Where they might find a brand new start
And Missouri is where it all began.

Some came up the Mississippi
From the town of New Orleans
Some came down the Great Ohio
Searching for their land of dreams.

Some, who hired the river boats
With the likes of Mickey Finn
Headed up the Wide Missouri
And were never seen ag'in.

St. Louis was the river port
Where the crowded steamboats came
With families seeking new beginnings
As the wild, wild West was tamed.

They debarked there at St. Louis
Bought supplies, a horse, and wagon
Then pushed on toward the sunset
Women walkin', skirts a'dragin'.

Drawn to the west Missouri border
To the towns of Westport, and St. Jo'
Where the wagon trains were gathered
And headed westward, movin' slow.

But for some the search had ended
When they found their land of dreams
On these wide Missouri prairies
And on the Ozark mountain streams.

This caused a brand new problem
Of getting mail from here to there
As families divided by the savage miles
Sought for answers to their prayer.

Then William Russell, of St. Joseph
Ran a newspaper "ad" one morn
For young, hard riding horsemen
And the "Pony Express" was born.

Binding East and West together
By couriers riding hard, and fast
Just to bring some welcome word
From family, and friends at last.

And so, the West was settled
By those just passing through
The land they called Missouri
To the dream-land rendezvous.

That, my friends is how Missouri
Became "The Gateway To The West"
Where settlers moving westward
Came to start their westward quest.

Leroy Watts

❧ LONE STAR ❧

The night was bright with rhinestone stars.
The wind, it cut to bone.
He saddled up his cuttin' horse
To look for steers long gone.

He headed north into that wind,
His chin against his chest.
His saddle creaked an awful song.
His gelding wanted rest.

Its hooves clacked hard against the rocks.
Its nostrils flared with steam.
He clenched his fingers in his gloves
Though warmth was but a dream.

At last he saw them on the rise
Like ghosts against the sky.
Their breath trailed snakelike from their heads.
That wind, it burned like lye.

He got them home real late that night.
His cabin's windows shone.
He gave his thanks, turned out the light,
This Texas star, alone.

Larry D. Thomas

❧ A TIME TO THAW ❧

It hit bout 40 below
During the 80s big blow
That swept Wyoming's Plains.
A lonesome old Texas hand,
Who had come seeking land,
But found his greatest pains.

With head that was worn bare
He had nary a prayer
To live a life of ease.
As the ice and snow did form
Even worse than the norm,
He thought of the Gulf Coast Breeze.

Where thick angora wool chaps
And brimless fuzzy furry caps
Would never be in need.
Where your cows and calves stay warm
And oh how they would swarm
When you brought winter feed.

So he said Lord take me back
On down that southbound track
That leads to my Texas home.
Where the sun gets mighty hot
And I promise that I'll not,
Evermore northward roam.

Scott Hill Bumgardner

✺ MISSOURI COWBOY ✺

Some think of me as a cowboy, when they see my western clothes.
Some they laugh, others grin, some look down their nose.
Of my raising they know not, nor of my family roots.
But make no mind, I'll be sticking to my Stetson hat and my cowboy boots.

Oh, I don't wear the stove pipes that come up about knee high.
Those handmade boots I can't afford, they cost too much to buy.
Just give me a pair of peewees, with pull holes on each side.
A Pinto horse with Angel wings and to Heaven I will ride.

With my old hat and boots I care not how you feel.
Inside this ole Saddle tramp, you'll find someone that's real.
Not an imitation you can't see what's inside.
I'm a Missouri cowboy but I walk with a Texan's pride.

Now I'm not downing Texas, that's the lone star state you know.
But Missouri has cool, clear water, a state where the rivers flow.
And Missouri cowboys are just as great, not one of them is a fool.
Strong of heart and just as stubborn as the ole Missouri mule.

So give me a pair of Peewees, and an ole Stetson hat.
Even tho Texas is a wondrous state, I'll stay right where I'm at.
So it matters not that you smile, I'm a Missouri cowboy with pride.
And that I will always be until that part of me has died.

Johnny D. Eaton

HELL'S HALF ACRE

Gather round all pardners,
    There's a story I must tell.
'Bout a place up in Wyoming,
    I myself call cowboy hell.

They were pushin' little dogies,
    Down the sage brush covered trail.
They were headin' up to Casper,
    Where they'd send 'em down the rail.

They were movin' sorta northeast,
    In the early mornin' sun.
It was maybe half past seven,
    When they all heard someone's gun.

They rode on through the sage brush,
    Where the prairie rattlers dwell.
Then they came upon a stretch of land,
    That truly looked like hell.

As they looked across the prairie,
    Not a cowboy made a sound.
It was pretty clear to all of 'em,
    They'd have to go around.

The trail boss rode up to the edge,
    With shock upon his face.
Never in his life had he seen,
    Such a Godforsaken place.

It's a place of desolation,
    Way out in the prairie sand.
And it looks like it was carved there,
    By the devil's own right hand.

The point man spotted somethin',
    And the trail boss gave the word.
He said ride on up an check it out,
    So it doesn't spook the herd.

Well the thing that he'd seen movin',
    Was a boy packin' a saddle.
The kid he really looked like hell,
    Like he'd fought a losin' battle.

As the boy told 'em his story,
    He would start to shake an shiver.
He said he was headin' west,
    To some kin in Powder River.

He said this wasn't his country,
    That he'd had a chance to roam.
But he'd fought with his ol' pappy,
    So he'd ran away from home.

He said he was just ridin',
    When he felt a sudden jolt.
Said he thought it was a rattler,
    That'd caused his horse to bolt.

Said he'd tried to hold 'em back,
    But the bronc was movin' fast.
When they dove into the hell hole,
    Said he thought he'd breathed his last.

When he came back to his senses,
    On the jagged rocks below.
Started lookin' for his pony,
    Where he was he didn't know.

He crawled down a little further,
    Then his face formed in a frown.
Cause he knew his horse was hurt bad,
    And he'd have to put him down.

Well they put him in the wagon,
    And they took him on back home.
And they knew that he'd be wiser,
    'Bout the places that he'd roam.

All the cowboys they were happy,
Cause he hadn't met his maker.
    In that hell hole on the prairie,
That they now call Hell's Half Acre.

Rickey Dallas Pitt

❧ THE HORSEMAN AND THE COWBOY ❧

This tale is about my brother when he came to visit me
It's a long way across the ocean to my home in Hawai'i
He'd always been a cowboy, albeit a weekend one
So on this trip we set out to ride and have some fun.

Well, I ain't no cowboy but I like to fork a horse
Rodeos and trail rides and some cattle work of course
We have some friends with ranches, they can usually use a hand
When it's time to work them dogies they are often undermanned.

A cowboy in Hawai'i? You think I'm funnin' you?
Sit back and learn some things about us that I'll bet you never knew
Cattle arrived with Capt. Vancouver in 1793
Many days by sailing ship, their journey 'cross the sea.

Our cowboys are a special breed, we call them "Painolo"
Trained 'bout 1832 by Mexican Vaquero.
And in case your history needs a boost, that's about three decades longer
Than the first cowboys who rode the range in Texas or Montana.

A fair amount of ranches still grace our hills and shores
Over a million acres in cattle, for Hawai'i, that's one in four.
That day we worked one corner of a 24,000 acre spread
Moseyed moms and babies down to work them in the pen.

My brother covers a lot of miles as an Oregon Buckeroo
But up until this day I must say I never knew
That working cows was new to him, he'd always ridden trails.
He learned fast from ten cowboys, and only four of them were males!

"The bawling of the cattle." It ain't just an pretty phrase
It sounds peaceful in the song, but it's different in the craze
Of a couple hundred head milling round in small corrals
With mamas calling babies calling mamas 'cross the walls.

Upper cut or under cut or swallow fork their ears.
Left if it's a heifer, on the right for bulls and steers.
Branding and ear tags, there's a separate pen for culls
Worm, dehorn, and vaccine, and the knife for little bulls.

The day's end finds you tired but you know your job's done well.
You're still caring for your pony when you hear the dinner bell
Fellowship with ranchers, proud stewards of their brand
Who walk the walk and talk the talk of cowboys cross the land.

At the ranch that night, my brother lay upon his bed.
Considering the day's events a'spinning through his head
He'd always thought he was a cowboy, at least a bit of one
But by working cows this day he'd learned that title is hard won.

It bothered him to think that "cowboy" is a compound word that means
This boy works with cows and that's how he earns his beans
He turned to me and said, as he let the thought sink in,
"I can't call myself a cowboy, when a Horseman's all I've been."

Jody Fergerstrom

THE ORIGIN OF A GOOD COWBOY

You hear all kinds of stories...some are true and some contrary,
but those about GOOD cowboys will hardly ever vary.
One thing most folks agree upon with hardly any doubt
is the origin of good cowboys. That's what this tale's about.
Good cowboys hail from Texas, or one of them states out west.
There's somethin' 'bout the "big sky" that naturally makes a man his best.
They say there's somethin' on the prairies and the mountain ranges too
that establishes the paces that a cowboy gets put through.
So a cowboy grows up fast and tough...learns to ride and stand up tall,
and learns to rise and ride again after each and every fall.
He learns quick to rope and ride and brand the wildest stud,
'cuz wild places, horses, and cattle just run naturally through his blood.
Dawn to dark he rides the range on the seat of a mustang's saddle.
Day in and day out, lays life on line for a herd of maverick cattle.
Rain or shine, and heat or snow won't stop him in his tracks.
Remember, he's the kind of guy who rodeos to relax!
Yes, the cowboy is a rare breed, an exception to most rules
who comes by profession naturally. It ain't something taught in schools.
Few ever reach the worldly fame of the cowboy's rank and station.
Down through the years the cowboy's earned a world-class reputation.
I earned my reputation tellin' tall tales, but not tellin' lies,
so the tale that I'm about to tell may come as some surprise.
I'm talkin' 'bout a cowboy who could ride with the very best.
I'm talkin' 'bout a cowpoke history somehow suppressed!
He rode the trails of Arizona, Utah and Texas too.
New Mexico, Colorado, and Nevada to name a few.
He dragged his horse and pack mule through deep Wyoming snows,
and wound up in Montana. How he got there, Heaven knows.
The cowboy's life and lifestyle is one most sane men wouldn't choose.
The trails he rides are not often kind and will make him pay his dues.
So why this cowpoke stuck it out and rode against all odds
is mystery that's left to guess and understood by only gods.
His skin was wrinkled-leather brown and his hair was winter-white.
His body showed the wear and tear and the scars of many fights.
Two scars were made by bullet wounds. But a bad one from a knife,
he got tryin' to take a Cheyenne warrior's daughter for his wife.
One scar seemed most to bother him more than any caused by lead.
Deep in his hip and bothersome was an Apache arrowhead.

There were wounds of almost ev'ry kind and ev'ry form of attack
including those of a bullwhip laced deep across his back.
The battle scars on chin and cheeks made his face almost a mask.
How, where, and why he got his scars, we knew better than to ask.
Some things are better left unsaid, and some things best left unshared.
To demand to know his secrets none of us were well prepared.
So we left him pretty much alone in camp and on horseback.
The only thing we knew for sure, he said his name was "Jack."
Through history we've been challenged by men and women who've
been spurred on by the notion that there's something they must prove.
It wasn't long before Jack had proved his merit and his worth.
He proved he was a cowboy and a "natural" from his birth.
The more he did, the more we saw the very best of man
is not always predetermined by just where his roots began.
Jack set the standard on the ranch the rest of us strove for.
He wore us out in our attempt to do as much or more.
And so Jack became our hero and few will disagree,
he was a REAL genuine cowboy...not some Eastern wannabe.
He could ride and shoot and rope and brand among the very best.
He was, no doubt, Top Hand cowboy in his part of "The West."
But it wasn't until forty years had crossed that big Montana sky,
the day God called the cowboy Home, and Jack's turn came to die.
Cowboys rode from miles around to mourn, and to console each other...
to bury a REAL cowboy...Jack, their best friend...Jack, their brother.
A cowboy is a tough-skinned kind of man with great sense of pride,
but that day beneath a cottonwood tree, a hundred cowboys cried.
Something rare and special had been taken from their ranks.
They were honored to have known him and their tears were words of thanks.
There's no need to reopen old wounds of a cowboy when he's dead.
So the pinewood cross upon his grave said all that needed said.
"Jack" was what we called him. "Jack" was all we ever knew.
And the story that unraveled from his gear I won't tell you.
I gave him the name he earned and the one most cowboys know.
"Black-Jack-Elkins" seemed to fit and seemed most apropos.
When you see his grave, remove your hat, and with all the respect that's in ya,
salute the Cowboy known as "Jack"...from Elkins,...West Virginia.
I carved as much as I will tell on the cross above his grave
out of respect for a GENUINE Cowboy...who started his life as a slave.

Dan Blair

A PRAIRIE KING

When I unroll my tarp at night
and spread my sougins out,
I look up at the starry sky
and know what life's about.

It's havin' peace and breathin' free
and havin' my own space.
It's lookin' up at God's great sky,
close enough to touch His face.

I have a kinship with His creatures
that poke around and prowl,
and even like to hear the sound
of a lonesome coyote howl.

The night birds sometimes sing to me
a restful lullabye.
and I hear willows by the creek
when a stiff wind makes 'em sigh.

When irritations of the day
have all been laid aside,
then I look at this world of mine
and nearly bust with pride.

I count my blessings one by one
out on this great prairie,
and realize that I am rich;
in fact, I'm royalty.

Tex Tumbleweed

❧ BROTHERS AT HEART ❧

Tourists in a Western state,
we were far from hearth and home
when we met a cowboy driving cows
beside a field of brome.

From fence to fence, they filled the lane,
fat Herefords, fuzzy and sleek
Cows and calves, a few bulls, too,
they were at their summer peak.

We began to talk, that cowboy and me
about the things we knew.
And though I maybe didn't look the part,
he could tell I'd herded a few.

"I've been out since 5 gathering these cows,
driving them out of the brush.
It's no easy job, I guess you know,
but now I'm in no great rush."

"Tell me, what's it like in Florida
to gather a herd of cows?"
He asked me as we dawdled along,
as a cow here and there paused to browse.

I looked at the hills faded all blue
the yellow fields tilting far away
and wondered just how to best describe
how a Cracker passes his day.

"The hours are about the same," I said,
"And our rigs aren't a lot different either.
But we breed some Brahman into our herd,
to stand up to the heat and the fevers.

"You can't see for miles like you can out here
'cause the trees and the vines get in the way."
And I added as I glanced at his dry saddle girth,
"Sometimes we'll use two horses a day.

"For when you jump those Cracker cows
in a horse-head-high clump of myrtle,
they'll scatter like a covey of quail,
lie low...and then turn turtle.

"Or they'll paddle across a mucky swamp,
and lie up in a thick bay head
ringed by palmettos with roots knee-high
And pricker vines every cowboy dreads.

"There's snakes in there and skeeters, too,
and the muck can bog your horse down,
but the day's not done 'til you drive 'em out,
so you go at it with shouts all around.

"You have to get off and wade right in
and throw in a dog or two,
and like as not when they run 'em out,
they'll run 'em right over you.

"Finally you get them headed for home,
strung out down the crevice or lane,
and after you finally shut the gate on the pen,
your horse gets a good cup of grain.

"Then you dip 'em or spray 'em,
according to your plan,
and part out the beeves going to town.
Turn out the rest and load the best
on the waiting trailer van.

"Finally the auctioneer sings and the buyers bid
and some money changes hands.
But prices are never what they were last week,
and you only hope your banker understands.

"For the Cracker never gets rich, they say
'til the day he sells the farm,
for he buys retail and sells wholesale
and prays that he comes to no harm.

"No, it's about the same as out here, I'd say,
though John Wayne never played a Cracker part.
But it gets in your blood
when you live that way and I'd guess,
we're all really Brothers at Heart."

Allan H. Horton

✒ WHEN THE OLD YELLA BUS COMES DOWN THE LANE ✒

The ol' school bus was painted yella,
Pulled through the front gate;
The school marm dismounted and
Was sorry she was late.

Behind her on the bus I spotted
Children everywhere!
Jumpin' from those seats and screamin';
Joy filled the air!

Their faces were just like a rainbow;
Each hue a gift from God.
Boots and tennis shoes and sandals
Trippin' over clods.

Not one of them had ever seen
A donkey layin' down;
They'd only seen a horse parade
Down main street in the town.

They thought that milk was bottled in
Containers in the store.
They'd never seen one on a cow...
Or seen those "spouts"...all four!

They'd never seen a baby foal
Stand up and nurse a mare.
They'd never had to wash manure
Odor from their hair.

Their pastures near their homes are concrete;
Gutters are their ditch;
Fields there are fertilized
With garbage that was pitched.

If any had a barn at all,
It housed a dog or cat;
And many of those children had
At home their own pet rat.

Too often their adrenaline
Was triggered by their fear.
Too often they had no one there
To hold them close and dear.

But they crawled into ol' barn loft
And danced across the floor;
They found a fascination with
The split-in-two barn door.

They sat their hindsides on the rail,
And watched the cowboy ride.
Their exultation o'er his courage
Much too strong to hide.

They held a tiny cube of sugar
On their palm for horse.
When that warm nose touched on their hand
Their joy ran its course.

They sat upon three-legged stool,
Pulled those "spouts" and milked.
They knew that all the stories heard
Meant their minds were bilked.

They scraped manure from their soles
And headed for the lake.
They filled their pockets there with rocks
And snails, both to take.

Those shoes came off and little toes
Sank in the soft, wet dirt;
And if they stepped upon a cactus,
Didn't even hurt.

Finally as the day was fadin',
On that bus they climbed.
Wild turkey feathers in their hands
Were firmly intertwined.

The old bus cranked, the teacher waved,
And they were on their way.
They left with memories in their mind
To warm a troubled day.

A cowboy and a rancher take
For granted all they love;
Although they often kneel and thank
The good Lord up above.

If they could watch the little eyes
Of children who know not
The value of the joys we share
They'd learn an awful lot.

If you are a cowboy from
Chicago or LA,
You may have chosen western life
To leave and go away.

But when you enter coliseums
Filled with urban folk,
Do not forget the joy you bring
Is not a silly joke.

You are the hero read about
In books by little kids.
And most of them have never seen
Or done the things you did.

Too many there will never touch
An animal so strong;
So much of all their little lives
Consumed by things gone wrong.

Cotton candy and balloons
Sweeten sight for them,
But they are there to share your life;
Rebuke a life condemned.

For just 8 seconds you may ride
That buckin' bronc that day.
But for a glimpse into your life
Those throngs would gladly pay.

So when you're ridin' out of town
Reach down and touch that hand
Of some small child who's sittin' near.
Forget the blarin' band.

And if you're not too tired and worn
When you get home at night,
Perhaps you'll take the time to show
A child all that's in sight.

Show them the moon when it comes up;
A sunrise in the morn;
And let them sit in your old saddle,
Grab onto that horn.

For I know God is watchin' us
And hopin' we will share
The life He lets us live together;
All the beauty there.

Be thankful for jack-rabbit stew;
And water gravy, too;
Be thankful for the thunderstorms;
The sun that shines on you.

However poor the crop this year,
Remember it won't grow
In concrete jungles that are all
These little children know.

Rose Mary Allmendinger

❧ THE NIGHTINGALE ❧

She was young and pretty
A very attractive miss
So what was she doing singing
and playing in a saloon like this?

Cowboys at the tables
Cowboys at the bar
Starting to get rowdy
You know how cowboys are.

Let's hear something from the piano, boys
Play the one about the silver fox
Got to warm this crowd up
Before the songbird squawks.

Cowboys at the tables
Cowboys at the bar
Drumming with their hands and feet
You know how cowboys are.

Those boys were so delighted
Excitement at fever pitch
Glasses high, they started mooing
Shaking cowlike, scratching fence.

Cowboys on the tables
Cowboys on the bar
Going cowboy crazy
You know how those boys are.

She sang of kings, queens and courtiers
Men of every stripe, Gallant deeds and
Honor won, Fair maidens in their time.
Lyrics of redemption, no exemptions
Kept this cowboy crowd sublime.

Cowboys laughing at the tables
Cowboys whistling at the bar
Go whoopin' cowboy crazy
You know how cowboys are.

Jim Packard

GIT ALONG
LITTLE DOGIES

WHOOPEE-TI-YI-YO
GIT ALONG LITTLE DOGIES

As l walked out one morning for pleasure,
I spied a cow-puncher come all riding alone
His hat was throwed back and his spurs was a jingling,
As he approached me a-singin' this song,

Whoopee ti yi yo, git along little dogies,
It's your misfortune, and none of my own.
Whoopee ti yi yo, git along little dogies,
For you know Wyoming will be your new home.

Early in the spring we round up the dogies,
Mark and brand and bob off their tails;
Round up our horses, load up the chuck-wagon,
Then throw the dogies upon the trail.

It's whooping and yelling and driving the dogies;
Oh how l wish that you would go on;
It's whooping and punching and go on little dogies
For you know Wyoming will be your new home.

Some boys goes up the trail for pleasure,
But that's where you get it most awfully wrong;
For you haven't any idea the trouble they give us
While we go driving them along.

When the night comes on and we hold them on the bedground
These little dogies that roll on so slow;
Roll up the herd and cut out the strays,
And roll the little dogies that never rolled before.

Your mother she was raised way down in Texas,
Where the jimson weed and sand-burrs grow;
Now we'll fill you up on prickly pear and cholla
Till you are ready for the trail to ldaho.

Oh, you'll be beef for Uncle Sam's Injuns,
"lt's beef, heap beef," l hear them cry.
Git along, git along, git along little dogies,
You're going to be beef steers by and by.

traditional

COWBOY POETRY IN MOTION

Well, the mornin' starts at four am, the coosie rings the bell,
  Come-on, get up ya cowboys, comes a loud persistent yell!

Come-on, shake out the coffee's hot, don't lay their in yor soogans,
  Get'em up, roll'em tight, all bed rolls to the wagon!

Ya can smell the breakfast cookin', un that chill that's in the air,
  As ya gather round that chuck box, with un emotionless stare:

Ya grab biscuits drowned in gravy, un thank the God above,
  For givin' ya the piece of mind, to do the things ya love.

The cook calls out for seconds, better get it while it's hot,
  While the hoodie loads the bed rolls up, pulls the tarp, down ties the knots.

The jingler brings yer horses in, while the night hawk grabs some chuck,
  Und ya ponder bout the last few weeks, how ya'll got by on luck;

The mountains that ya trailed across, the rivers, streams, un swells,
  The thunderstorm's, the dust, un sweat, some days it felt like hell;

Und yer muscles, sore, un tender, from a colt that bucked ya down.
  Und knowin' today is the last day, und yu'll arrive in town.

Two hundred un ninety miles, wranglin' horses all the way.
  There's un emotion that can't be denied, when ya call positions for the day.

The team is almost harnessed up, the leaders start to paw,
  Make a circle boys, start'em slow, head'em up that draw!

In the East the stars they disappear, un blue gray takes its place,
  Un the pink cliffs now er standin' out where before there wuz no trace;

The herd busts, un thunders towards the draw, ears alert, un noses flared,
  Un cowboys racin' for the pass, with hard determined stares;

They glide through rock un timbers, with a ballerina's grace,
    Over logs, un brush, un ledges, like a royal steeplechase.

The dust it starts to foggin' up, ya smell leather, horse, un sweat,
    Un horses crashin' through the brush, but still there's no regret;

Manes un tails a flyin', spurs a ringin' out a tune,
    It's un illusion watchin' horse un man race towards a fadin' moon.

Down through the pines un cedars, where the scrub oak slaps yer chaps,
    Ya memorize this picture boys, for time has seemed to lapse.

With cowboys in position, the herd's now in control,
    Un ya watch the horses all line out as single file they go.

The sun it tops a ragged ridge, un the rays come bustin' through,
    Un ya watch the herd snake down the trail, in solemn overview.

It's a picture that can't be described by anybody's notion,
    'Cause pardner it's a feelin', "Cowboy Poetry in Motion."

Paul Bliss

HOME FROM THE WINTER RANGE

We gathered the winter range today,
and brought the cattle in.
The old cows still were fat as hogs,
but the two year olds were thin.
It's sixteen miles of downhill road,
and the cows all know the way.
They're tired of eating slough-grass,
and looking forward to some hay.

A cattle drive in January,
aint generally so nice.
But today the sun shone brightly,
on our world of snow and ice.
An easy day for horse and man,
because, as all cowboys know,
it aint too hard to chase a cow,
some place she wants to go!

Mike Puhallo

THE E. S. L. RANCH

Stranded, I was, in some cow town,
Out of work and down on my luck;
No way to pay for my next meal
With my finances at less than a buck

When a man drove up in a pickup truck,
Said he was looking for a worker to hire.
Hauled me off to the middle of nowhere;
Dumped me out next to a campfire.

I'd just settled in for a good night's sleep
To rest up for the coming day's work
When hell broke loose with a vengeance
And awakened me with a jerk.

Get up you waddy! some guy hollered,
Can't ya hear coosie a-callin'?
Haul yerself out of them sougans!
Roll up that hen-skin and paulin!

Put on a load of Mexican strawberries
An' some sinkers to line yer flue,
Then grab a kack and come on back
And I'll tell ya what you're to do.

Rattle yer hocks down to the cavvy
An' with a reata snag a cayuse,
Then light out into the brasada
And chouse any critters that's loose.

I stammered at the man, dumbfounded.
He said, *There ain't no time fer palaver!*
If ya wanna be a ranahan
Get forked and get out on the gather!

Well, I resigned my position on the spot,
Mind reeling and spirit broken—
Starving's easier than working a job
Where English isn't spoken.

Rod Miller

Glossary:

waddy (or waddie): a working cowboy
coosie: the cook, from the Spanish "cocinero"
sougans (or soogans): bedroll
hen-skin: blanket or quilt (often stuffed
    with feathers)
paulin: bedroll cover, a tarpaulin
put on a load: eat
Mexican strawberries: beans
sinkers: biscuits
line yer flue: fill your stomach
kack: saddle
rattle yer hocks: hurry, move quickly
cavvy: horse herd
reata: rawhide catch rope, for the Spanish
    "la riata" which also became *lariat*

snag: catch
cayuse: horse
light out: go, ride away
brasada: brush
chouse: chase, drive quickly
critters: cattle, in this case
palaver: talk, discussion
ranahan: good cowboy, top hand
get forked: get mounted, get horseback
the gather: a roundup
E.S.L.: highfalutin education jargon, English
    as a Second Language

REEL vs. REAL COWBOYS

To conjure a vision of 'Cowboy'
    could carry your mind two ways;
most common's the Hollywood version;
    'gun fights 'un adventure filled days'.

Tall, lean, and disgustingly handsome.
    Tailor-made shirt on his back.
Sittin' a'straddle, a near silver saddle,
    just matchin' the rest of his tack.

His hat is a Johnny B. Stetson,
    pure white and at least 30 X.
Engraved in the band, his initials and brand,
    and would you believe that it's "Tex" ?

The horse is a story worth tellin',
    A high steppin', single foot bay.
That baby will run, 'till the villain is done—
    not one drop'a sweat from the fray!

His shootin' goes way beyond braggin',
    usually *one shot* and they're done,
Then twirlin' the pistol, gives 'em a fistful,
    while smilin' as though it were fun.

Can swaller a glass of bar whiskey
    without ever makin' a "face."
Walks with a swagger, never does stagger.
    At poker he draws every ace.

Seldom needs sleep or good victuals.
    Knows all'a them cowboy clichés,
and if he gets shot, it's in a good spot!
    Back ridin' in just a few days.

When leavin', swings into his saddle,
    not usin' the stirrups, of course!
The last look ya gets, is as the sun sets,
    he's singin' a song to his horse.

Some swaller this bogus description,
    though most view the picture as strange.
Let's look at another, cow punchin' brother,
    and follow his day on the range.

Now—picture this work-a-day feller;
    five-eight, and he's built sort'a slight.
Boots decorated with cow-salve,
    and clothes that ain't fittin' just right.

His face might'a wore out two bodies.
    Hair brings ta mind moldy hay.
a big easy smile, breaks out'a that pile,
    "Disguise keeps the gu-rills a-way."

The coat he's a wearin's a "wonder,"
    you "wonder" the source of the thing.
But now you know who, might'a skinned that old ewe,
    that died of consumption last spring.

Its sleeves are too long, so he cuffs 'em,
    a tear has been patched with some twine.
Out front is a juttin', a stick fer the button.
    But keeps out the weather just fine.

His horse ain't a whole lot to look at,
    sure-footed and smart as an ass.
Turns on a dime, but stops every time,
    it comes to a stand of good grass.

The saddle he's sittin' is weathered,
    but still sports a good solid tree.
Some stitchin' still loose, from when his cayuse,
    hit oaks on account of a bee.

His gun is a rusty old carbine,
    scarred stock juttin' out'a the boot.
It's rode a long ways, and seen better days,
    with a good chance it won't even shoot.

Says; "Gamblin' don't treat him too kindly,
    in fact, nearly caused him a wreck;
Last time he played poker, was caught with a joker,
    that weren't s'posed to be in the deck."

Quit drinkin' "hard likker" fer reason,
    says; "Beer better matches his wage,
and sometimes that whiskey, would make him so frisky,
    they'd keep him in town in a cage!"

Been known to climb into his saddle—
    (if no one's behind him ta gawk)
by leadin' his bay, up the trail a way,
    then crowdin' in close to a rock.

The last look ya gets at this cowboy;
    He's standin' there scratchin' his—chin,
a wonderin' how, to clear that ol' cow,
    that's in the barbed wire again!

S. A. Jackson

THE GUIDE

I've rounded 'em up in Dubois in the spring
    and shipped from Nevada in the fall.
I've summered the sheep and strung the barbed wire,
    hell I reckon I've damned near did it all.
But I live to throw the diamond loop on the lost Decker trails
    in the Clearwater, the Selway and the Bob.
Down the Absaroka and across the Grand Mesa
    and on the Kaibab is where I found my job.

From the mighty Peace river, the Bull and the Snake
    the Colorado and the Platte.
There's memories of 10,000 horses and trails
    stored under this old dirty hat.
I'm Apache and Crow, I'm Irish and Scot,
    I'm white and Mexican and red.
And my voice echoes with the sounds of old Decker men
    who are long since dead.

I can stitch 'em together like your granny's best quilt,
    20 head tied nose to tail.
Just to watch 'em blow up like an engineer's nightmare
    when old "silvertip" crosses the trail.
I've stood in the airport patiently waiting
    while you royally stepped off of the plane,
And I shook your hand and we said our howdies,
    but you've long since forgotten my name.

Hell, I sighted in your rifle, looked at pictures of your kids,
    I even know why you left your third wife.
I was there when you teared up over the first six point bull
    and I watched as you learned about life.
I've stood in the frost and saddled your horses
    while the sleep tent was quiet and still,
Then talked you through a long shot up in the Book Cliffs
    and you tipped me a ten dollar bill.
I've been your preacher, your wrangler, your bartender, your friend
    your carpenter, your judge and your cook.

Then I taught you things about mountains and men
    that ain't wrote down in nobody's book.
I took away your bottle when you had to much to drink,
    and shared mine when you hadn't enough.
And enjoyed breaking the spirit of both horses and men
    that spent too much time acting tough.
I walked off the San Juans in belt buckle deep snow
    with your lion hide hung 'round my neck,
Just to have the boss tell me my roll would be short
    'cause you called and stopped pay on the check.
My name is Chuck and Mark, Pedro and Wade,
    it's Wilf and Jake and old Clyde.
and God knows you've called me a hell of a lot worse,
    but mostly, you just called me "The Guide."

Michael Henley

FACSIMILE COWBOY

I was lookin' for a job, and they told me in town,
To head out to the J-Bar None.
The foreman said he only hired experienced hands,
Asked "Are you a cowboy, son?"

Said now, I can rope and brand a cow
And I can rope and doctor sheep.
I can earmark a cow or a hog
And I can work without any sleep.

I can build fence, dig post hole,
Fix a windmill pump,
Cut firewood, break new ground,
Dynamite a stump.

I can cook over a campfire, make good coffee,
Tell stories that will make people laugh.
Repair a saddle, put up hay,
Shoe a horse or pull a calf.

I can feed the chickens, gather eggs,
Mend a hole in a pair of socks,
Bake biscuits, milk a cow,
Churn up the butter in a crock.

I've rode rank horses, broke a few green 'uns,
I can harness and work a mule,
Been kicked by horses, bit by a few,
It's made me more careful, as a rule.

I'm lookin' to hire on as a cowhand,
Got my own horse and gear.
Now, I may not be a cowboy,
But I can take one's place 'till he gets here.

J. A. (Jake) White

STAMPEDE

Hollywood's "west" is glamorous indeed.
Western paperback novels are fun to read.
Cowboys get hurt, but barely bleed,
all in the excitement of a stampede.

Well, they did have the excitement right.
Chasing a herd of cows in the dead of night
sure will start your blood to pumping,
and prairie dog holes get your heart thumping.

Should your horse stumble, putting you down,
as you lie there on that shaking ground
knowing each minute might be your last,
as wild-eyed cattle go streaming past.

Nobody knows what sets cattle off.
The flare of a match or a "Nighthawk's" cough,
the creak of a saddle or a lightning flash,
a clap of thunder can start the mad dash.

Then it's ride like the devil is hot on your heels,
try to turn the leaders into a mill.
Settle and hold them 'til morning comes 'round.
Survey the damage—how many head went down?

Spend the day gathering them once more—
sleepy, tired, hungry, aching and sore.
Knowing that they might run again
before the sun rises and the long night ends.

Ask any cowboy who has ridden through one,
how glamorous it was when finally done.
All he needs to know is he gave his best,
some biscuits and beef and catch up on his rest.

Sometime later, passin' the time of day,
and yarns being spun, you might hear him say
something 'bout a stampede he once was in,
and how easy life was, as he hides his grin.

Sherrod L. Fielden

JUST ANOTHER CALF

"Not another calf?" I heard another rider say,
and then add, stoppin' next to me "why us, and why today?"
We'd had a day's hard ridin', and it wasn't over yet, not by a mile.

Lookin' down the bluff, most anyone would see, right off
this wouldn't be an easy one. This gulch was like a trough.
How he got there, who could say? But we both knew that this'd take a while.

There was nothin' but to do it, and we both knew what to do.
The storm was only gettin' closer and the dark was comin' too.
Lariats looped on saddle horns, he took the horses' reins. I took the walk.

He was standin' up there, starin' at those thunderheads off north.
I was slidin' downhill on my heels on soft, red, crumblin' earth.
The stray was bawlin' "mama"... an' as I climbed I prayed he wouldn't balk.

The calf took off when I hit bottom, and with him went those hopes.
I blessed Grandad for sayin' "Son, you always take two ropes!"
The spare was off my shoulder and it didn't take me long to make my toss.

I caught him with the first one and I played him like a bass,
A'mutterin all the while "C'mon, you stubborn little ass!
You keep me here an fightin' you much longer and we're both a total loss!"

The way he fought the rope I knew he'd never try the climb.
A rumble up the canyon said I didn't have much time.
So I tossed and tied him, thought a sec, then wrapped him in a sling rigged
      from my chaps.

I hitched him on and hollered "Let's go, now!" with all my breath,
then looked up and I saw a thing that scared me half to death.
The wall of water thunderin' at us made this gulch the deadliest of traps.

I threw myself down on that calf, and breathed a quiet prayer
that this new feller wasn't takin' his sweet time, up there,
then I heard him shout, and heard a slap, and we were slidin' up the wall.

The water hit me hard right at my gun-belt at the crest:
I may have some luck still comin'...but it's not a thing I'd test.
My unknown partner handed me my reins and softly sighed, and
       said "close call."

The foreman had a worried frown when we came ridin' in.
He poured two cups o' Joe and said, "Just where the hell you been?
We was thinkin' you was lost, or maybe you'd got caught in that flash-flood!"

He wouldn't have believed it, if we told him how it'd been.
I glanced at my new buddy and he flashed a little grin,
and said, "Just another calf. He'd wandered off and got hisself stuck in the mud."

Well, that ends the story, and also pretty much this song.
The other guy I mentioned? Yeah, he'll do to take along.
I told him, while we got our chow, "sure glad you were around to lend a hand."

He sorta smiled at that, bobbed his head and said "Me, too,
But as long as I was there, an' didn't have much else to do."
He took a bite and chewed, then said, "It's just a part of ridin' for the brand."

eric lee

STAMPEDE

Rusty spurs a' squeakin'
and saddle leather creakin'
in the faded, angry glow of the settin' sun

Restless long-horns bawlin'
overwhelm the night-birds callin'
Now the day is through, but the cowboy's work is far from done

Thunder clouds abrewin'
have got the foreman chewin'
on the corners of his handle-bar mustache

"Boys, we're doublin' up the guard
Best be ready to ride 'em hard
when the lightning strikes and the thunder starts to crash"

No sooner had he spoken
than the tension, it was broken
and the sky was filled with jagged bolts of blue

and the peace of night was shattered
as the cattle quickly scattered
and the cowboys to their haggard ponies flew

and the ramrod called above the din
"Go to 'em boys and bring 'em in
God grant us luck upon this fearsome night!"

There was no time to talk
as we charged out on our stock
our leaden hearts jammed in our craws from fright

So began the race all cowboys dread
'cuz someone always ends up dead
with naught to send back home except a name

Yet any cowboy worth his sand
who claims he's ridin' for the brand
would rather chase that devil's herd than die in shame

So we raced into that thundering night
with the static 'twixt their horns for light
and sent our ponies surging for the lead

then amidst the lightning and the rain
three thousand head were split in twain
and two separate herds were running in full speed

O'er the rock and sage we bounded
and I found myself surrounded
by a sea of surging horns where blue light danced

No man has ever stopped the ocean
from goin' where it takes a notion
and no man amidst a stampede has a chance

Yet, I drew my six-gun and it spoke
with a flash of fire and smoke
and the steer beside me nosed into the dirt

and a second bullet behind the ear
dropped another insane steer
and I edged my pony closer to the skirt

Then in the flash of light ahead
I saw another rider sped
and I watched in horror as his pony fell

No sooner had his steed stumbled
than Charlie, from the saddle tumbled
and disappeared...beneath the cloven hooves of hell

So I raced on, amidst this bovine flood
their horns tearin' gashes and drawin' blood
and neither my steed nor I dared slow our stride

Then of a sudden we were free!
of that ring-tailed, wild-eyed sea
and found ourselves abreast of the lowing tide

So we resumed again, our chore
which was to race up to the fore
and turn the steers whose pace the rest had held

and as the leaders were nearly expired
only a few shots needed fired
to turn the steers and set them wheeling upon themselves

Myself and five good cronies
sat upon our winded ponies
as the thousand head we'd captured slowly milled

How many cowboys would be missin'
when the sun had fully risen
How many men had this night's foray killed?

For tattered rags alone remain
of those men who rode in vain
to stop the maddened rush of the devil's breed

and sometimes, still, I wake a'screamin'
from a fitful night of dreamin'
that again I ride...amidst that wild stampede

Rusty spurs a squeakin'
and saddle leather creakin'
in the frosted, yellow light of the rising sun

Restless long-horns bawlin'
overwhelm the night-birds callin'
now the night is through...but the cowboy's work...is far from done.

Shad Pease

CURSE THE WINTER RIDE

For a man or beast to face the cold
Boy, it should be a sin,
To have to find and try to drive
Strayed cattle against this cold bitter wind.

Curse the job that put me here
On this freezing mountain side,
And curse the cattle that had to stray,
Making it necessary for this ride.

I stopped to make a small camp fire,
Haunched against the cold,
Cursing everything within a distance
Of this nearly frozen soul.

Curse the wind that chills my bones,
And keeps tryin' to put out my fire,
But a meal's a must in spite of the winds that gust,
Even for a man for hire.

My horse, he snorts and stamps an impatient foot,
And shakes himself to help ward off the cold.
He probably curses a foolish man squatted by the fire,
That brought him from his warm stall out into the cold.

But the fire she finally blazed,
And the meal warmed me inside.
Then I put it out and mounted again
To continue the searching ride.

There's places it seems that cattle dream
To challenge a man's integrity—
At least it seemed that way all day today
As the cold whipped around both horse and me.

The afternoon wore on with the whistling wind,
And temperatures that dropped while I searched out the cattle.
And by the time I'd found the last in late afternoon,
I felt like I was frozen to the saddle.

My hands felt painfully cold even through I'd worn my gloves,
That cold still cut through me clear down to the bone.
Chilled in spite of the extra clothes I'd worn...I couldn't wait,
Although by now it was late, to get those cattle home.

We found a few frozen to the ground,
We'd count them in the tally of the loss.
And with the cattle in I cursed again
At the luck that put me down as boss.

Janice N. Chapman

A REAL COWBOY!

They say I ain't much of a cowboy
And I reckon they could be right.
I'm really not a horseman
And I don't like to camp out at night.

I can't rope a cow or wrestle a steer.
I've never drank Redeye.
I hate warm beer,
But a soft bed at night, now that I hold dear.

I've never been bit by a rattlesnake
And I don't like to gnaw on a bloody, red steak.
Beans flavored with dust and soot from a fire
Just can't make my spirit soar higher.

Yeah, they say I ain't really a cowboy
And they're probably real close to right.
Cause my boots aren't always comfortable
And I can't wear my Levi's real tight.

I don't hang out with dance hall girls.
Stud poker was never my game.
I can't play the guitar or yodel
And "Slim" clearly ain't my nickname.

Herdin' cattle in blizzards don't sound like much fun
And I 'spect I'd just hurt myself with a gun.
I clearly ain't the strong, tall, silent type
That made sure the West was won.

But, I went to the Saturday movies
When I was just a boy
And I learned all the stuff that really counts
From Hoppy and Gene and Roy.

You've got to stand up
For the things that are right
And a cowboy don't let bad guys
Win without a fight.

You help out widows and orphans
Take care of the weak and the old.
A man never cheats in his dealin's
And his word must be good as gold.

You see, it ain't ropin' or ridin'
That makes a cowboy a man.
It's doin' the things that you know are right
And bein' the best you can.

So, they're wrong, I am a real cowboy.
I know that deep inside
And you can be a cowboy too
Although you don't rope or ride.

Just help out folks that need it.
Take troubles in your stride.
Bow your head in prayer to your maker.
Don't ever swell up with pride.

Live every day to its fullest.
Don't pretend that bad is good,
And even though you don't shoot or sing
You'll live like a cowboy should.

James H. "Jim" John

THE COWBOY'S LAMENT

I always thought a cowboy's life was happy and carefree,
    So full of pure adventure and devoid of misery,
Yeah, I imagined roundups and them long trail drives and such,
    And all the fights for water rights and how that meant so much,

Shucks, I could be a cowboy and I think I'd do just fine,
    Ridin' and aropin'; and adrinkin' cactus wine,
The sky would by my ceilin' and the dirt would be my floor,
    I'd sleep all night in pure starlight and wake up wantin' more,

Course, no one ever told me 'bout a three month cattle drive,
    An how in britches wore twelve weeks them ticks and chiggers thrive,
An no one ever mentioned how bad cold beans taste at dawn,
    Or gritty sounds from coffee grounds that yore a chompin' on,

Heck, cowboys never talk about them 20 hour days,
    Or carin' for that pony or them cattle's stubborn ways,
An ain't nobody brought up 'bout that hot September sun,
    Or coffee breaks or rattlesnakes or never havin' fun,

Shoot pard, I guess I'm gonna pass on all that cowboy stuff,
    Just thinkin' bout that lonely trail has made me tired enough,
I'll prob'bly find another line of work that ain't so strange,
    An warble "Home Sweet Home" while others sing "Home On The Range."

Tom Pollard

COWBOYS AND COUNTRY BOYS

I have never seen the Pecos, never crossed the Rio Grande,
Never ridden dry and dusty 'cross our desert western land.
But I feel a kind of kinship with the boys whose life that's been,
And I hope that they have happy trails to ride on now and then.
No, I've never roped a dogie, never set a burning brand
To a struggling yearling heifer, never drove a four-in-hand,
But I've spent a lot of hours with the cattle and the soil,
And I understand the challenge and have experienced the toil.
I've mown the grass and baled it up and hauled and stacked the crop
And, weary to the bone, have thanked the Lord when we could stop.
I've known the ax, the hoe, the saw, the hammer, and the plow,
And many times, day after day, have cared for calf and cow.
I've helped the mothers birthing and stood back to watch and laugh
As the cows made soft, excited sounds and nudged their new-born calf.
And when no one was watching, I've hugged and kissed them, too,
And I've wept when they lay down and died, and there was nothing I could do.
I've milked the critters daily, twice a day, year after year
And mostly stayed on one small farm. It's all been done right here.
I might have been a cowboy, too, but Great-Grandpa stopped here
Although he had some friends and kin that wandered on out there
And became a part of ranching with spaces broad and wide
Where junipers dot the ridges and cactus the countryside.
And Grandpa, coming after, liked clear running creeks and hills
And on a summer evening, the call of whippoorwills.
And so we settled here and stayed, but some wound up out west,
And we'll not argue or complain about which or where is best.
Let's just agree that here and there there's work to do that's good,
And that we're honored to help out providing folks their food.
I might have been a cowboy, but a country boy's not bad,
And there are things we both can see that the other never had.
There are marvels there and marvels here that make a wondrous sight,
And if we bloom where planted, I guess we'll be all right.
No, I've never seen the Pecos, never crossed the Rio Grande,
Never ridden dry and dusty 'cross our desert western land,
But the kinship's there, old cowpoke, so let's ask God on our knee
To send more happy trails for us to travel, you and me.

Lee Neill

MOVIN' ON

That cowboy was real good lookin', great smile and blue eyes.
I sure never dreamed that I would win such a prize.
Folks said he was restless, wouldn't stay with me long.
Now, after all these years, I guess he's proved 'em all wrong.

I've spent years cookin' and cleanin' and feedin' the crew
Sortin' and brandin', even pulled a calf or two.
He knew he could count on me to always be there
Livin' and lovin' this good life we've gotten to share.

It seemed we moved around a lot in the early years.
Leavin' family and friends, I cried a few tears.
Some places weren't much better than sleepin' outside
But I was always glad I was along for the ride.

What a way to raise our kids, who've grown and moved away,
But they always laugh when they remember those days
When they had chores to do before goin' to school.
Those responsibilities taught them life has some rules.

Now ya know most cowboys work at the whim of the boss
But sometimes they move on 'cause there's rivers to cross.
We'd been livin' here longer than we'd lived anywhere
And I hoped we might stay, since there was gray in our hair.

But he says it's time to move on, it'll all be fine.
That's life with a cowboy—just one day at a time.
That look in his eyes says he is ready to go
And so I'll be ready, too, if I don't pack too slow.

One more garden will be left for the new hired man's wife.
I hope it will ease some of the stress in *her* life.
There'll be some memories in this place that I'll leave
But it's just not in my nature to sit down and grieve.

The two of us together is the way it should be.
Staying anywhere without him don't appeal to me.
So I'm packin' our things with a smile on my face.
The sadness I'll hide, and look forward to a new place.

They sang "Whither Thou Goest" at our weddin', but see
I had no idea what that would mean for me.
Now I know it means I'll go wherever he goes
And where we're gonna end up, well the Lord only knows.

This move could bring us closer to a place of our own.
Yes, I married that cowboy, and I've always known
There'll be new and greener pastures somewhere to ride
And, Lord willin', we'll ride them together, side by side.

Diane Thompson

AND THE SKY IS
NOT CLOUDY ALL DAY

⟳ THE WESTERN HOME ⟳

Oh, give me a home
Where the buffalo roam
Where the deer and the antelope play,
Where seldom is heard
A discouraging word,
And the sky is not cloudy all day.

A home, a home
Where the deer and the antelope play,
Where never is heard a discouraging word
And the sky is not cloudy all day.
Oh, give me land the land
Where the bright diamond sand
Throws its light on the glittering stream
Where glideth along
The graceful white swan
Like a maid in her heavenly dream.

Oh, give me the gale
Of the Solomon vale
Where the life stream of buoyancy flows
On the banks of the Beaver
Where seldom, if ever
Any poisonous herbage doth grow.

I love the wild flowers
In this bright land of ours,
I love, too, the wild curlew's scream
The bluffs and white rocks
And antelope flocks,
That graze on the mountain so green.

A home, a home
Where the deer and the antelope play,
Where never is heard
A discouraging word,
And the sky is not cloudy all day.

How often at night
When the heavens were bright
By the light of the twinkling stars,
Have I stood here amazed
And asked as I gazed
If their glory exceeds that of ours.

The air is so clear,
The breeze so pure,
The zephyr so balmy and light;
I would not exchange
My home here on range
Forever in azure so bright.

A home, a home
Where the deer and the antelope play;
Where never is heard
A discouraging word
And the sky is not cloudy all day.

Brewster Higley et al. 1873

☞ A COWBOY SEASON ☜

PART I
(Spring—in the Pastures)

In March, when the calves started comin'
the ground was still covered in snow.
That night twenty gave birth the temperature hovered
somewhere around three below.

By mornin' six calves were near frozen
and ten never lurched to their feet.
They lay stiff in their membranes of ice and placenta,
and the live ones were tremblin' and weak.

Then when the sun broke over the mountain,
After that night when so many were lost,
The snow hollows crusted, the ground turned to ooze
and you started to long for the frost.

But when the mist rose off from the pasture
clouds gathered, and then the rains come.
And a deep chillin' drizzle damped the back of your neck,
and your hands were so cold they turned numb.

Then the calvin' became a true nightmare,
what with heifers just plain built too small,
calves comin' backwards, that had to be pulled,
and you wondered if it was worth it at all.

You were gruntin' and gaspin' and covered in sweat,
cussin' to drown out the pain,
Neck deep in muck and cursin' the sky,
though you knew in July you'd need rain.

Then a little feller you'd thought was left dogie
answered the bawl of his ma,
and thrustin' his head 'gainst that cow's achin' udders
he sucked life from that muddy spring thaw.

And awareness come hard, like the thunder,
with that power that deep knowin' has.
There was no other place you would rather be
than right here, in the spring, birthin' calves.

PART II
(Summer—West Desert Range)

In July, the muck turns to powder.
Waterin' holes crackle like shards
of ceramic, the grass shrivels up,
and livin' just downright gets hard.

You're haulin' water sometimes sixty miles,
buyin' feed when the prices are high,
cursin' the heat and chewin' on devils
spinnin' dust 'cross a cobalt blue sky.

But at night your world fills with shadows,
and the splendor of moonlight and wind.
And evenin's coyotes pass you like ghosts,
and when they hear you singin', join in.

And together your voices will chorus,
low and mournful into that night sky,
like a dirge, or an anthem, with memories entwined
of the words to a child's lullaby.

And it's there, with the starlight and music,
and the clean smell of sage on the wind,
You remember, again, just who you are.
And you know there's no way you'd cash in.

PART III
(October— The Pasture Corrals)

In late autumn gnarled branches remember
their youth, and know they must die,
and at night they moan, and creak and cry out,
and bare tremblin' limbs to the sky.

And in those lost hours 'til the dawnin'
hoot owls hunt, and predators roam,
and out riding nighthawk you look over your shoulder,
feelin' fearful, and longin' for home.

But a coyote's been doggin' your late season calves,
and near the tank a bear print was found,
and the fences need mending, better get to that soon,
'fore your cattle stray off of your ground.

The wind stirs dry leaves in the shadows.
Is that a bruin, a hidin' in there?
Or could be a cougar, warily watchin'—
Or nothin' but restless night air.

"Aw, Come on," you mutter, and shake at your shoulders.
"Grab hold, man. This ain't no big deal."
It's just that October's got you feelin' spooked,
and out here the demons are real.

PART IV
(Winter—High Country Line Camp)

In those long hollow days of late autumn
when the cold is gathering strength
like a lariat coiled 'round the horn of a saddle
suppressing the power of its length,

Then you pull down your hat 'gainst the chillin',
hunch your shoulders to ward off the wind
and wrap up in lonesome, 'cause you'll face this alone,
and lock up your dreams, burrow in,

to wait out the long cold winter.
You'll tell time by the length of the day,
the duration needed for a piñon elbow
to burn to a powdery gray.

And you'll store up the things that you'll ponder,
sift the chaff and tune your heart strings,
sort out the worthy, discard the waste,
and make room for significant things

To hold on to, mull over, sustain you,
give repose through the long winter day,
A core to come home to, an essence to trust
when you're lonely, and long miles away

From the peg where your hat finds a welcome,
the hearth where your boots long to stand,
That place you will go when the winter and snow
have drawn back from this high country land.

Jo Lynne Kirkwood

∞ THE END OF THE DROUGHT ∞

We cowboys talk of starvin' stock
through lips all parched and dry.
For rain we lust, as clouds of dust
conceal an orange sky.
We reminisce, in wishful bliss,
beneath the moonlit haze,
and wonder how the drought persists
through months of summer days.

The worst we fear, yet, slickers near,
we say our prayers over,
and dream of weather blackening leather,
greenin' up the clover.
It's been three months, and more than once,
the sky's turned dark and cold,
and lightning's struck, but drops got stuck,
as storm clouds churned and rolled.

...Just one more time the sky was prime
to drench the thirsty dirt.
For what it's worth, ol' Mother Earth's
a brazen, teasin' flirt.
So life goes on from dawn to dawn,
with glimpses of her smile—
a dreary range, without a change,
for endless, grueling mile.

Yet, ridin' here, 'twixt cow and steer,
I feel one little drop.
That gal starts dishin' what I'm wishin'
and she doesn't stop.
The land's all soaked and clover-cloaked;
I'm wet, right to the core.
It's like the bliss of my first kiss,
to feel the rain once more.

Michael Sorbonne Robinson

HAYIN' IN THE CARIBOO

70 Mile they say has two seasons every year,
one is winter and the other is August, I fear.
This makes it difficult to try and fill the barn with hay
and we need lots to feed the critters through till May.

Now we try to make our hay on a swamp meadow,
A wet year seems I get stuck bout every second row.
A dry year's different, things can go along quite well
only bogged a couple of times, hardly a story to tell.

That's usually when you hear a big ugly bang,
you see a strip behind being missed, gosh dang.
Or maybe some other words from your mouth do spout,
but it takes some fixin' before you really start to shout.

Layin' under a haybind, well it's not my favorite spot,
Specially when the wife goes by, on her horse, at a trot.
She's taking out guests for a ride, to get a little pay,
So I can afford to fix the machine, and keep making hay.

Well hayin's ok I guess, but it gets kind of boring
goin round and round, listening to the engine roaring.
Seems you can go forever in a circle with a haybind in tow,
watching the grass fall behind row, after row, after row.

You have to think bout the winter months ahead,
and picture all the critters happy as they're fed.
Just think, you get it all made and bring it all in,
a few months, and you roll it all out where it was to begin.

Mark McMillan

∽ THE ODYSSEY ∽

Back in time many years ago, when Buck was just a boy
His Gran Pap gave him a maverick calf, which filled the lad with joy
This little cow was not a gift, old Gran Pap had a plan
The problems he'd have to face, would help him grow into a man

Buck gave him food and water, and brushed his coat to shine
Until a warm springlike day, when Gran Pap said, it's time
Get a rope and tie him down, the fire's hot, let's start,
He had a special branding iron, for burning in a mark

Buck finally grabbed the iron, knowing what must be done
He'd seen it happen many times, but this time he was the one
The smell of burnt hair hovered, the calf bellered and kicked a bit
Untied his feet and let him up, off he went, a Rockin' B on his hip

Buck's stomach was all in knots, but his heart was filled with pride
He'd passed his first big test, with his Gran Pap by his side
His second test was underway, the calf was now free to run
What kinds of lessons could be learned, to make a man of this Grandson

Buck often rode out with his Dad, to check up on the herd
He searched and searched everywhere, his Dad said not a word
The calf was Buck's responsibility, the sagebrush was dense,
A cow won't come when it's called, was there a hole in the fence?

Maybe a coyote took down its meal, if the youngster ran off to play
The herd would take care of its own, but not if he'd wandered away
That's part of the lesson for Buck, be careful in what you do
Things have both a time and place, otherwise, trouble will surely find you

Pretty soon Buck spied the calf, kinda playing hide and seek
He and two others of his kind, drinking down at the creek
Well Buck cut them back to the herd, his Dad smiled and shook his hand
Then showed him some animal tracks, outlined there in the sand

A great big mountain lion, lives somewhere near by
Up in the hills, where the rocks meet the sky
He'd come down to water, so the danger was real
A small calf like his, would make an easy meal

Over the summer they grew a lot, both the boy and his calf
Trying to keep the maverick clean, caused old Gran Pap to laugh
It won't be long until it's fall, a chill was in the air
Buck's calf would try and win, the blue ribbon at the fair

The calf would not cooperate, had a mind of his own
He didn't like the halter, or all the curry comb
But Buck had it in his mind, the calf would win the show
He kept him in the barn at night, bawling 'neath a lantern glow

The calf wanted out of there, to join the others like he
Grazing on the hillside, a life of being free
Buck himself was feeling low, he'd been working long and hard
He spent his time training, the calf to parade the yard.

Gran Pap took the boy aside, to explain the task at hand
Many jobs that need doin', would help him grow into a man
A rancher's life ain't easy, but some good times can be had
It might be hard to see the joy, through the eyes of just a lad

Buck he said, you're doing fine, and the calf might not even win
The fact that you gave your all, is what we're interested in
I gave your Dad the same test, when he was as young as you
He didn't like the halter either, but look at the man I grew

I have no doubt you'll be the same, when you're growed up and tall
The same as that calf of yours, that's penned up in his stall
Once he grows into a bull, and you set him free to roam
He'll wander back remembering, lessons learned at home

Summer passed into fall, a winter smell was in the air
Everything was ready, for the Carbon County fair
The calf had surely grown a lot, and the same for young Buck
One hundred pounds of calf, wasn't gonna get in the truck

With Buck at the halter, his Dad pushing from behind
Not til Gran Pap twisted his tail, did they get the calf to mind
Two youngsters rode in the back, Buck was having a ball
The calf stood there bug eyed, he wanted back in his stall

They arrived at the fair grounds, people were milling all around
The calf suddenly liked the truck, he didn't want to get down
Buck lead him to the barn, and found an empty stall
The calf had already decided, he didn't like the place at all

The calf took off on a run, dragging the boy behind
Buck's mother hollered, let him go, but the boy made up his mind
They finally came to a stop, Buck was red faced and mad
How could this have happened, in front of Gran Pap and his Dad

Well Buck led him back in the stall, brushed off the dust and dirt
His Mom was just a little mad, because of a tear in his new shirt
He got the calf cleaned up, then led him to the parade
His heart was beating loudly, as the judges choices were made

He didn't win the red ribbon, not even the blue or yellow one
His Mom gave the boy a hug, thinking that he hadn't won
Then the judges all walked up, and Gran Pap started to laugh
They handed Buck a gold ribbon, awarded to the boy and his calf

Best of his class it said, Buck's stomach felt nervous inside
He had gotten the highest award, Gran Pap's chest swelled with pride
His father had yet to speak, words don't always come easy to a Dad
A lump grows in your throat, to see a son do better than he had

His Dad finally shook his hand, then hugged him for all his might
They took a lot of pictures, of every thing in sight
A day to always remember, long after others are gone
The boy had taken another step, another test had been won

The years passed by quickly, Buck's testing was over
The calf retired as a range bull, feeding on sweet clover
Buck did become the man, big and strong like his dad
When his Gran Pap passed away, Buck felt really sad

The hardest test finally came, one cold September morning
It hit him hard, without having any warning
The bull had came into the barn, laid down in the hay
Buck was kneeling there, when the old bull passed away

Like his Gran Pap had said, the bull would recall
All the love Buck gave him, inside the stall
The bull must have known, the end was very near
The trust between calf and boy, abundantly clear

Buck had him buried in the meadow, brushed a tear away
His final test of manhood, he knew Gran Pap would say
It took over twenty years, for this odyssey to end
Boy to calf, man to bull, life, death; they won the gold ribbon.

Pete Evanson

∽ SEASONS ∽

A rancher rides a lonely trail
Packing salt, mending fence, feeding cows.
Each day brings some new travail
Some days with nothing but bills in the mail.

Up before the sun each day
Summer days start early.
Coffee, bacon, and flapjacks for pay,
The dawn is young when he rides away.

As the day turns old, he heads for home,
Fences mended and cattle moved.
The sun is set in the western dome,
Times like this he lets his spirit roam.

In fall when the hay's cut and cattle brought in
It's time to think of winter.
A farmer's been by to fill the grain bin
To last through cold times that are coming again.

On freezing cold mornings the winter sun's bright
The day starts later each morning.
It's hard to get all the chores done by night
If a blizzard hits late, feed's going to be tight.

Spring can't come soon enough to warm up the land
It's time for new calves to be born.
Up half the night giving a heifer a hand
His reward comes when the calf finally stands.

Now he's not alone by any rate
A woman stands beside him.
A daughter and son peek through a gate
Hushed by the miracle on this night so late.

On those early mornings when he must rise
She's been up before him.
The breakfast ready and it's no surprise
When she packs his lunch before sunrise.

She goes with him whenever she can
When her chores are through.
Gathers up the children, leaves her pots and pans
Wire cut colts and calving heifers know her gentle hand.

Not all the time are things real hard
There's things that make it all worthwhile.
Kids bottle feeding calves in the yard
With laughter so bright and a new pup on guard.

A wide blue sky, not a cloud in sight
Green grass, good cover and water.
More stars than they can count at night
A bond with the land that feels so right.

Though seasons range from drought to snow
They'd not have it another way.
For surely God would not bestow
This life on folks who cannot grow.

The work is hard, the rewards are great
When things get tough, folks draw close.
There's always a good hot meal on the plate
And a welcome sign hangs over the gate.

The little family is sure each day
To give thanks to their Creator.
For little things like a good crop of hay
To big things like a child's birthday.

A good cow horse, real close friends
Four generations in one place.
And no matter what the worldly trends
A faith in God that never ends.

Sherri Ross

SANDHILLS SEASONS

I don't have to wear a watch
To know the time of day
Or have a calendar at hand
To guide me on my way.

Here in cattle country
If you learn to read the signs
Everything has its own way
And gets done in its own time.

Early in the year
Before the grass is green
The cows know when it's time for them
And the calves show you it's Spring.

About the time things settle down
Branding rolls around
Get the irons heated up
The last pair has been found.

Then it's practice, practice, practice
For the rodeo's in town
And don't forget the hay crews
Working sunup to sundown.

Weaning time comes after that
Just hear those cattle bawl
It's payday for the ranchers
And that's how you know it's Fall.

The pace slows down, the bills get paid
The ranchers check their debt
Another year is winding down
Winter's nearly here and yet—

Here in the sandhills of Nebraska
We have learned to know the reasons
That work gets done when it gets done
With the changing of the seasons.

Mickee Cheek

DON'T FENCE HER IN

≈ THE COW-GIRL ≈

Out on the wild range, riding
    To the music of drifting feet;
As we lope o'er the sunburned prairie,
    I and the cow-girl meet.
The sun in the West is setting
    And shoots out its golden beams;
One falls on the face of the rider,
    The cow-girl of my dreams.

She's as lithe as the supple willows
    That grow by the bed of the streams;
Her hair like the golden sunbeam
    That falls on the girl of my dreams.
Her eyes are as dark as the shadows
    That creep down the canyon wide;
With a look like a half-broke broncho,
    Half fearful, yet trusting beside.

Her face like the roses in summer
    That grow in the coulees deep;
Her lips like the scarlet sand-flower
    That blossoms in cut-banks steep.
She's as fair as a summer morning;
    As pure as the prairie air;
She's as wild as the silver sage brush
    That grows by the grey wolf's lair.

The sky in the West has darkened
    As home to the camp we ride,
As I lope o'er the shadowed prairie
    With the cow-girl by my side.
We laugh and we talk together,
    To the music of drifting feet.
As we lope o'er the sunburned prairie,
    Where I and the cow-girl meet.

Rhoda Sivell, 1912

85

MY COWGIRL LIFE

I was just a little cowgirl of maybe two or three
And tired of riding horses upon my Daddy's knee,
So I was given this old stick horse and for hours I would ride
Chasing imaginary dogies with my collie dog by my side.

I toddled out behind my Dad 'cause I thought I was a hand
Just a regular 'ole cowpuncher riding for his brand.
But Dad was awful excited, he had something for me to see,
There saddled up beside the barn was this good paint mare for me.

The saddle we had was way too big, for I was pretty small,
But Daddy told me not to fret, this was no problem a'tall.
He took two old worn stirrups and laced them to a girt,
Then tied them to the saddle horn and I sat there pretty pert.

He then tied the old split reins into a hard fast knot,
Just so I wouldn't lose them when we began to trot.
I began that day to tag along where ever Dad would go
I was finally a cowgirl and my heart was all a'glow.

Well I grew to fit that saddle and to rein without the knot,
I even got a faster horse, 'cause Paint would only trot.
We'd ride up in the mountains rounding up the goats and sheep
We'd ride all day from dawn to dusk, then unsaddle, feed and sleep.

And now I am much older and I still run the ranch
My Dad will come and help me out when he has the chance.
I gather the cows in a pickup truck, with modern pens at hand
And sometimes my love of ranching is hard to understand.

Then I gaze at my very first stirrups hanging on the living room wall
And they remind me of that time when I was very, very small.
The life of a cowgirl in Texas is what I chose to lead
And all cowgirls in Texas are of a very special breed.

We are everywhere in the state from the Red to Rio Grande.
So please, when ever you see us, come over and shake our hand.
You'll find a very tender lady underneath our skin of brown,
And on our heads a well worn hat that we wear just like a crown.

We are the real heart of Texas with a will you can't deny
Our hearts and souls belong to God until the day we die.
So when you speak of Texas do not leave this thought unsaid.
And remember all us cowgirls we're Texas born and bred.

Linda Kirkpatrick

➤ TOMBOY ➤

I was raised with seven brothers
    near a place called Concho Lake.
There was Jamie, Jeff, and Joseph,
    Sam and Seth and Sid and Jake.
So I grew up rough and tumble,
    and I made my share of noise,
Romped the dogs and roped the horses.
    I was rowdy as the boys!

Skinny tomboy, seven brothers,
    and assorted brothers' friends
On our little cattle ponies,
    raced to hell and back again.
We'd roar down the dry arroyas;
    then we'd all come tearing back,
There was Buzz and Paul and Donnie
    and that rascal Charlie Black.

But one Spring, as I grew older,
    Mama firmly told me, "No!"
And when the boys went out on roundup—
    Mama said I couldn't go.
Then she tried to teach me cooking,
    how to sew, and keep the place;
But my heart was roping yearlings,
    and I longed to barrel race.

Once she washed my hair in soap weed;
    while it still hung limp and damp,
She stuck that rusty curling iron
    down the chimney of the lamp.
"Sister," she said, holding up a gingham
    dress that she had sewed,
"Andy's comin'! Now you wear this,
    so's your legs won't look so bowed."

Andy was the new young foreman
    of the ranch off to our west,
And of all my brothers' cronies,
    Mama showed she liked him best.
O, she was proud that she had made me
    look like something of a girl,
Got me out of faded Levis,
    forced my stubborn hair to curl.

Well, it wasn't long thereafter
    every time that Andy'd call,
And the boys were pitching horseshoes,
    Andy'd linger in the hall.
So he came to be my suitor,
    brought me candy, flowers and such,
And the night he brought me perfume,
    Well, I didn't mind too much.

Andy'd come 'most every evening;
    he was courteous and kind,
And it wasn't any secret
    what the cowboy had in mind.
Every Friday we'd go dancing,
    laughing clear to town and back.
Andy made me feel a lady—
    so I married Charlie Black!

Dee Strickland Johnson ("Buckshot Dot")

WILD STICKHORSE REMUDA

Ponytails and blue jeans
Sat at Papaw's knee,
Watching as he whittled
On old branches from a tree
    And while he talked of cowboys
And big old Texas ranches,
He trimmed away the rough spots,
While I dreamed of pony dances.

    A wild stick horse remuda
Began to run and play,
With every loving stroke,
As he peeled the bark away.
    Using his "Old Timer"
And carving in my brand,
The best that he could find
And cut and shape with his own hand.

    Now, each one of them was special,
And I felt I was too,
As they kicked up dust behind
This cowgirl buckaroo.
    With reins of pink hair ribbon,
Shoe strings and baling twine,
There was "Buckin' Birch" and "Oakie,"
And "Ole Sticky" made of pine,

    "Sassafras," and "Blackjack,"
"Willow," "Blaze," and "Scat,"
I never did corral 'em—
I just left 'em where they sat.
    But next mornin', on the front porch,
'stead of roamin' wild and free,
They'd found their hitchin' rail,
'cause Papaw lined 'em up for me.

Along our trails together
There were many lessons learned,
Like bein' a cowboy through and through
Is something that you earn
    We'd partner up together,
And team up in cahoots,
Once he defied my Mama,
Bought me red cowboy boots.

And often, when I wondered
What to do on down the road,
He'd always tell me, "little girl,
When you get there you will know."
    Sometimes you have to let things go,
Sometimes you stand and fight,
And anything worth doin',
Is still worth doin' right.

With my wild stick horse remuda,
We rode the range for miles,
I knew I'd won my Papaw's heart
By the way he'd laugh and smile,
    I still have his sweat-stained Stetson,
His boots, and his old knife
Sometimes I take them out
Just to measure up my life.

And hold him closer to my heart,
And know I have to try,
To live up to the honor
Of the wonder-days gone by.
    On my stick horse remuda,
I learned the cowboy way,
I'd give up everything I own
To ride with him today.

My wild stick horse remuda
Was quite the varied band,
Born and bred with me in mind
And trained by his own hand.
　　I'm longing for the legends,
And the way we used to roam,
With my wild stick horse remuda,
And the man that we called "Home."

Debra Coppinger Hill

~ QUEEN OF THE WEST ~

Our favorite treat when we were kids was the Saturday matinee,
      In times that seemed so innocent, those days of yesterday,
Where our comic book heroes would come to life on that silver screen.
      There was Hopalong, Randolph Scott, the Lone Ranger, Roy, and Gene.

Being the oldest, Joyce and I helped Dad with all the chores.
      Milkin' cows, breakin' colts, stackin' hay 'til our arms were sore.
We did all the jobs that our ranchin' neighbors gave to their boys
      And rarely had time for tea parties, dolls, or other girlish toys.

We knew our lives were different from the rest of the girls at school,
      'Cause, in town, they all wore dresses while we broke their cardinal rules
By wearing jeans, long-sleeved shirts, and high heeled, cowboy boots.
      All their teasin' and finger pointing just made us more resolute.

'Cause, you see, we had our hero, too, up on that movie screen.
      In all those Saturday serials, she was the only Queen.
In fringed skirt and rhinestone shirt, on Buttermilk she'd ride,
      To do right by all with Roy Rogers by her side.

She was the voice of wisdom and showed us girls we had a right
      To fight wrong and injustice, to be fair, good, and forthright,
To find within ourselves the courage to always do our best.
      She became our hero, Dale Evans, the Queen of the West.

The world seemed a little colder, today, when I heard the news,
      That my hero, Dale, had headed for that heavenly rendezvous.
I can hear Buttermilk's nicker as he lopes up to Dale's side,
      And see Trigger prancing up in welcome with Roy's smile a mile wide.

Upon a ridge rears Silver, and the Lone Ranger waves his hat "hello."
      While Champion slides to a perfect stop as Gene Autry hollers, "Whoa."
Bullet's barkin' up a storm, while he weaves among the horses' feet.
      Seems like all of the legends have gathered here to honor and to greet.

Hollywood's much dimmer now, as in a blaze of glory Dale will ride
      Into the fading sunset, with those cowboy heroes at her side.
You know His campfire's waiting, beyond the rise and 'round the bend
      Happy Trails to you, Dale, until we meet again.

FOR DALE EVANS 1912-2001
Janice E. Mitich

SWEET LUCILLE
THE FIRST COWGIRL

There have been many before her and many aft'
But, Miss Lucille was most excellent at her craft
Much like her friend Will
She developed her ropin' and trick ridin' skills
Chasin' cattle for her Daddy in the Oklahoma hills

In 1900, Teddy Roosevelt saw young Lucille show her ropin' ability
Then he made a suggestion to Lucille's Daddy
"Why don't you start your own wild west show?"
And off around the country they did go
Entertainin' folks
Just by bein' cowpokes

With Colonel Zack Mulhall's Wild West Show, in the early years
Tom Mix and Will Rogers began their show biz careers
Workin' along side Lucille even Geronimo appeared
They could be seen in Madison's Garden Square
And in 1904, at the St. Louis World's Fair
Wish I could have been there

The world saw the passin' of the old cowboy days
They couldn't get enough of cowboy ways
Remington and Russell were recordin' it all in their art
And Miss Lucille Mulhall was doin' her part

When Daddy's wild west show closed
Lucille became a star in the rodeos
A sweet, educated, feminine thing
She was tough as steel in the rodeo ring
She twice broke the world's record ropin' in competition with men
What contests those must have been

Some say it came from Teddy
Some say it was Will
But, the fact remains still
Lucille was the first in this world
To be called "cowgirl"

Lucille didn't stop with rodeo
She found a new place to put on her show
The Oklahoma cowgirl in her new venture went far
MISS LUCILLE MULHALL SILENT WESTERN MOVIE STAR

FOR LUCILLE MULHALL 1885-1940
Paula Sisk

95

STRANGE THINGS DONE

THE CREMATION OF SAM MAGEE

There are strange things done in the midnight sun
By the men who moil for gold;
The Arctic trails have their secret tales
That would make your blood run cold;
The Northern Lights have seen queer sights,
But the queerest they ever did see
Was that night on the marge of Lake Lebarge
I cremated Sam McGee.

Now Sam McGee was from Tennessee, where the cotton blooms and blows.
Why he left his home in the South to roam 'round the Pole, God only knows.
He was always cold, but the land of gold seemed to hold him like a spell;
Though he'd often say in his homely way that he'd "sooner live in Hell."

On a Christmas Day we were mushing our way over the Dawson trail.
Talk of your cold! through the parka's fold it stabbed like a driven nail.
If our eyes we'd close, then the lashes froze till sometimes we couldn't see;
It wasn't much fun, but the only one to whimper was Sam McGee.

And that very night, as we lay packed tight in our robes beneath the snow,
And the dogs were fed, and the stars o'erhead were dancing heel and toe,
He turned to me, and "Cap," says he, "I'll cash in this trip, I guess;
And if I do, I'm asking that you won't refuse my last request."

Well, he seemed so low that I couldn't say no; then he says with a sort of moan,
"It's the cursed cold, and it's got right hold till I'm chilled clean through to the bone.
Yet 'tain't being dead—it's my awful dread of the icy grave that pains;
So I want you to swear that, foul or fair, you'll cremate my last remains."

A pal's last need is a thing to heed, so I swore I would not fail;
And we started on at the streak of dawn; but God! he looked ghastly pale.
He crouched on the sleigh, and he raved all day of his home in Tennessee;
And before nightfall a corpse was all that was left of Sam McGee.

There wasn't a breath in that land of death, and I hurried, horror-driven,
With a corpse half hid that I couldn't get rid, because of a promise given;
It was lashed to the sleigh, and it seemed to say: "You may tax your
    brawn and brains,
But you promised true, and it's up to you to cremate these last remains."

Now a promise made is a debt unpaid, and the trail has its own stern code.
In the days to come, though my lips were dumb, in my heart how I
    cursed that load!
In the long, long night, by the lone firelight, while the huskies, round
    in a ring,
Howled out their woes to the homeless snows—O God, how I loathed
    the thing!

And every day that quiet clay seemed to heavy and heavier grow;
And on I went, though the dogs were spent and the grub was getting low;
The trail was bad, and I felt half mad, but I swore I would not give in;
And I'd often sing to the hateful thing, and it hearkened with a grin.

Till I came to the marge of Lake Lebarge, and a derelict there lay;
It was jammed in the ice, but I saw in a trice it was called the *Alice May*.
And I looked at it, and I thought a bit, and I looked at my frozen chum;
Then "Here," said I, with a sudden cry, "is my cre-ma-tor-eum."

Some planks I tore from the cabin floor, and I lit the boiler fire;
Some coal I found that was lying around, and I heaped the fuel higher;
The flames just soared, and the furnace roared—such a blaze you seldom see;
And I burrowed a hole in the glowing coal, and I stuffed in Sam McGee.

Then I made a hike, for I didn't like to hear him sizzle so;
And the heavens scowled, and the huskies howled, and the wind began to blow.
It was icy cold, but the hot sweat rolled down my cheeks, and I don't know why;
And the greasy smoke in an inky cloak went streaking down the sky.

I do not know how long in the snow I wrestled with grisly fear;
But the stars came out and they danced about 'ere again I ventured near;
I was sick with dread, but I bravely said, "I'll just take a peep inside.
I guess he's cooked, and it's time I looked" then the door I opened wide.

And there sat Sam, looking cool and calm, in the heart of the furnace roar;
And he wore a smile you could see a mile, and he said: "Please close that door.
It's fine in here, but I greatly fear you'll let in the cold and storm—
Since I left Plumtree, down in Tennessee, it's the first time I've been warm."

There are strange things done in the midnight sun
By the men who moil for gold;
The Arctic trails have their secret tales
That would make your blood run cold;
The Northern Lights have seen queer sights,
But the queerest they ever did see
Was that night on the marge of Lake Lebarge
I cremated Sam McGee.

Robert Service, 1907

DESERT RAT

Way back in the eighteen hundreds men sought the yellow gold.
They burned in the desert heat and froze in the bitter cold.
Each man had his own reason for seeking the motherlode.
Gold fever pushed them on as they saddled up and rode.

A few got rich but most of them stayed poor.
They sought the gold and left it, worse off than before.
Long hard days of digging dirt and then to come up dry.
For some the dream of riches turned out to be a lie.

There was a breed of man who didn't care where the gold was at.
His love was in the quest for it, and he was called a desert rat.
Followed by a loaded jackass wherever he might go.
He roamed the mountain peaks and the valleys way down low.

With a pack mule and a shovel he sifted through the dirt.
Once in awhile, he'd find some gold but not enough to hurt.
A man alone on the prairie beneath a starlit sky.
In the company of a mule, and no one knows just why.

He sleeps out on the prairie with the coyotes and rattlesnakes,
And at the crack of dawn, he'll be cooking up sourdough cakes.
Some folks would say he's crazy and they'd be as right as rain.
Too long with the yellow fever can drive a man insane.

He bellers out "Oh Susanna" as he moves at his own slow pace,
And his mule is singing backup and braying out the bass.
The day did finally come when he found the motherlode,
But he covered it back up and across the prairie he rode.

He never left a marker, not one single way of going back.
All that gold in the ground and he covered his own track.
That Sourdough knew the secret of what this life is all about.
True security lies not in what you have but what you can do without.

Verlin Pitt

FRIENDS

The stagecoach out of Abilene
With mail stops on the way
Takes twenty-four long hours
Til you get to Santa Fe
There only were two passengers
This little gal and me
She wasn't much fer talkin'
She was sad as she could be

We rode along in solitude
Fer maybe fifty miles
And then she loosened up and spoke
With heavyhearted smiles
She told me 'bout a funeral
That she would soon attend
A lady that she'd known fer years
Her absolute best friend:

"We both grew up in Texas
    And, together, learned to ride
Eight years in that old schoolhouse
    Where we studied side by side

We both would go to parties
    Like young girls we'd be excited
But one would never go
    Unless the other was invited

Throughout the years, we'd meet in town
    We'd dine, then go out dancin'
That's when I found the cowboy
    That I soon began romancin'

I'll always miss my closest friend
    Although she done me wrong
She upped one day and ran away
    And took my man along

Forgiving her is difficult
   I'm tryin' to forget
In spite of what she did to me
   I know I'll miss her yet."

The stagecoach rumbled through the night.
She nodded and she sighed.
I wondered and I asked her,
Did you know when yer friend died?

   "I know exactly when and where
    It causes me great sorrow
      Our last goodbye?
      When did she die???
   I'd say, high noon...tomorrow!"

Omar West

DOG SWAMP STRANGER

I remember that chilly October midnight
When we rode side by side through the swamp
Through the low-hangin' fog and the evil moonlight
After visitin' town for a romp.

Our horses clip-clopped us a tap dancin' tune—
Like they's walkin' on coffins or tombs.
And occasional light from a peek-a-boo moon
Lit their nostrils' thick vaporous plumes.

I said to Ol' Earl with a whisperin', "Whoa,
I ain't never seen Dog Swamp so foggy."
And progress got painful an' terrible slow
'Cause the footin' got treacherous' boggy.

Now it happened to be that eventually
Me an' Earl found ourselves overlookin'
A poor man, we agreed, what's appearin' to be
Down a path that he shouldn'a tookin'.

That cowboy was sittin' there under his hat
And he'd made it to maybe mid-bog.
Then he sunk to his waist in a sneaky mud flat
No doubt hidden by darkness and fog.

We both told him, "Hey," and he said, "Howdy do."
And we offered to toss him a rope.
But to our great surprise he just sat in the goo.
He just sat there, then spit, then said: "Nope."

So we asks him, "Why not?" as he sunk to his chest,
"You're too young t' be fixin' t' die."
Then me and Earl sat, having made our behest,
And we waited to hear his reply.

"Now, I left me a wife back in St. Louie, Mo"
He explained with an unbalanced grin.
"And I left me another in Colorado"
Then he sunk in the mud to his chin.

"But to leave this poor filly jus' wouldn't be right,
No, not even if I had my druthers.
For she brung me this far without nary a fight,
N' that's more'n I can say for them others."

———————————————————

So we stared at the hat that still floated quagmired
As we passed it circuitously,
And we knew that the stranger we just seen expired
But for fortune was Ol' Earl and me.

French Camp Red

BAD PETE'S COMIN' TO TOWN

I 'uz in the town of Rattler's Gulch
In th' Cut an' Shoot Saloon
The borin'est place in the world to be
That Saturday afternoon

But me, I was curi'us I wanted to see
If this yahoo was really bad
So I didn' leave, but afore too long
I was shore wishin' I had

'Cause they come a blood curdlin' yell
You could hear fur an' wide
An' a big wild Brahma bull slid in
To a screechin' halt outside

Off jumped this feller 'bout 8 foot tall
With a cannon on his hip
Spurs as big as wagon wheels
A live rattlesnake fer a whip

A cougar leaped down to the ground
Yowlin', hissin', an' spittin'
He give it a look an' it laid down
An' purred jist like a kitten

He led that bull to the hitchin' post
An' after it was tied
He coiled up that rattlesnake
An' hung it on his side

He come stalkin' in the door
Big, an' mean, an' wide
Had a grizzly bear skin 'round his neck
An' the bear was still usin' the hide

His eyes they was like burnin' coals
They looked around so sharp
You knowed shore if you messed with him
You'd soon be playin' a harp

He bellied up to the bar 'n' said
"The best rye whiskey ya got
An' don't be givin' me no sass
I'm tired, thirsty, 'n' hot"

The bartender tried to pour him a drink
He grabbed it an' said, "aw heck!"
Broke off the top agin the end of the bar
'N' drunk it right from the neck

He wiped his mouth on that grizzly bear's fur
Grabbed another bottle of rye
Then he broke off the top of it
An' he drank that one dry

He got quiet fer a minit 'r two
We all set there real still
We figgered he'uz tryin to make up his mind
Which one of us he'uz gonna kill

The bartender said in a shaky voice
"Sir, would you like another round?"
He said, "I would, but I gotta git,
Bad Pete's comin' to town."

JK Reese

BAD PETE'S COMIN' TO TOWN

I 'uz in the town of Rattler's Gulch
In th' Cut an' Shoot Saloon
The borin'est place in the world to be
That Saturday afternoon

When this feller busted through the doors
Shoutin' an' jumpin' around
Said "Folks, we's in for a heap o' trouble,
Bad Pete is headin' for town"

Now none of us had ever seen Bad Pete
But if half we'd heard was true
They wasn't really many folks
That ever wanted to

But me, I was curi'us I wanted to see
If this yahoo was really bad
So I didn' leave, but afore too long
I was shore wishin' I had

'Cause they come a blood curdlin' yell
You could hear fur an' wide
An' a big wild Brahma bull slid in
To a screechin' halt outside

Off jumped this feller 'bout 8 foot tall
With a cannon on his hip
Spurs as big as wagon wheels
A live rattlesnake fer a whip

A cougar leaped down to the ground
Yowlin', hissin', an' spittin'
He give it a look an' it laid down
An' purred jist like a kitten

He led that bull to the hitchin' post
An' after it was tied
He coiled up that rattlesnake
An' hung it on his side

He come stalkin' in the door
Big, an' mean, an' wide
Had a grizzly bear skin 'round his neck
An' the bear was still usin' the hide

His eyes they was like burnin' coals
They looked around so sharp
You knowed shore if you messed with him
You'd soon be playin' a harp

He bellied up to the bar 'n' said
"The best rye whiskey ya got
An' don't be givin' me no sass
I'm tired, thirsty, 'n' hot"

The bartender tried to pour him a drink
He grabbed it an' said, "aw heck!"
Broke off the top agin the end of the bar
'N' drunk it right from the neck

He wiped his mouth on that grizzly bear's fur
Grabbed another bottle of rye
Then he broke off the top of it
An' he drank that one dry

He got quiet fer a minit 'r two
We all set there real still
We figgered he'uz tryin to make up his mind
Which one of us he'uz gonna kill

The bartender said in a shaky voice
"Sir, would you like another round?"
He said, "I would, but I gotta git,
Bad Pete's comin' to town."

JK Reese

THE RAT PACK MINE

Uncle Raymond had this tale to tell
Back in 1936
When they moved to Arizona
And lived out in the sticks.

It wasn't such a real great time
To be huntin' jobs and all,
The Depression had made its dent
And caused economy to fall.

So one of the older brothers
Packed up his gear and went
Out in the open desert
To find gold that could be spent.

One starry night a-sleepin'
Under the desert sky,
The moon it was a-peepin'
From her perch away up high.

Suddenly, some sounds were heard
Grunts, puffin', and a wheeze.
He opened up his eyes real wide
He scarcely dared to sneeze.

Cautiously, he looked around
And much to his surprise,
There sat an enormous pack rat,
Right before his eyes.

That pack rat was rollin' sumpin'
Across the desert floor
He tossed aside his bedroll
And went off to explore.

Takin' up the object
Back to his fire he scoot
In his hand a golden nugget
As big as passion fruit.

He stored it in his knapsack
But then he got to feelin' bad
For the pack rat's loss of treasure
And the hard work that he'd had.

So he got his flask of whiskey
And poured some in the cap.
That pack rat came right over
And started in to lap.

The pack rat looked right up at him
In his button eyes a twinkle.
He chittered at my Uncle
And gave its nose a wrinkle.

Then off it went into the night
My Uncle back to sleep
Then several hours later
He heard a kind of cheep.

Startled, he sat straight on up
And looked around real quick
There sat that crazy pack rat
With nuggets layin' thick.

That pack rat took his paw
And placed it on Unc's hand.
Then he pointed to the nuggets
Then to the whiskey can.

So my Uncle poured another shot
For that pack rat to imbibe
Pretty soon the trade got brisk
For that rat had brought his tribe!

So that was how that Burdic
Became a millionaire
By trading hootch with pack rats
For gold both pure and fair.

For those of you who wonder
About how the trend did start
To carry snake bite medicine
Into the desert's heart.

You needn't look farther than this.
Because this tale is true.
You never know when pack rats
Will need a shot or two.

Debbie Burdic

THE CROSS-EYED BULL

While I was going to college I ran a show string of the Angus breed
I've always been very competitive, I wanted blue ribbons, I showed my greed
I had a Senior Yearling Bull that stood above all others by a hand
In all his competition, Grand Champion he would stand

We won at Gray and Greenville, Newport was the next stop
He would surely win for his pedigree and stature were the top
Of all the competition that had gathered in Cooke County that day
If anyone would have said he would lose, I would have said, There ain't no way

When the judge said. "Walk-em boys." I was filled with confidence
Then the judge started laughing at my bull and I rushed to his defense
He said surely in selecting a show string, this animal you would cull
I can't judge for laughing at this cross-eyed bull

Well his eyes weren't crossed when I brought him there so I called a local vet
He said after examining my champion, "That's the funniest looking critter
      I've seen yet"
He then put a long glass tube in his rear after penning him in the head-gate
Then he blew and blew and blew until the bull's eyes were straight

He said. "That'll be fifty dollars." I figured that was way too high
But I could make it up in the winnings so I let the fee go by
We won again at Knoxville, but then at Nashville when we pulled in
When I walked him off the truck, his eyes were crossed again

I knew I had to correct this problem, or he would surely stand last in his class
I didn't want to spend another fifty dollars, so I found me a long tube made
      out of glass
I could straighten his eyes, in that I had no fear
So I put him in the head-gate and shoved the glass in his rear

Well I blew and blew and blew, but nothing happened
I tried twice more, but when I looked at the other end
His eyes were still crossed, he would surely stand last in his class
Then I looked down the barn aisle and noticed that the vet had just passed

I ran him down and said. "Hey Doc. I've got something you should see."
He could tell by the glass tube in the bull's rear, I was trying to save the fee
But he said. "For another fifty dollars, I'll again perform my miracle."
I figured that was better than showing a cross-eyed bull

Well he pulled the glass tube out of the bull's rear and turned it around
He inserted the other end and placed both feet firmly on the ground
He then blew and blew and blew until the bull's eyes were straight
He said. "That'll be fifty dollars," as he opened the head-gate.

I said. "I'll give you your fifty dollars, but I am curious.
I tried the same as you, I just must not have the touch.
But why did you take the glass tube out of the bull's rear and turn it north
    to south."
He said. "You didn't expect me to blow on the same end as you had in
    your mouth."

Leon Overbay

BEAR TALE

Me an' Jim quit camp at dawn,
Hunkered 'gin the cold.
Our ponies sniffed and spooked along,
Seekin' a firm foothold.

The snow had started three days past,
Forcin' us to stop.
We'd planned to cross the ridge real fast,
Campin' below the top

Where cabin, wood, an' lots a'chuck
Now lay beyond our reach,
Cause Mother Nature'd turned our luck
With sermons She would preach.

The need for meat pushed us along
Cravin' elk—or deer.
We'd gone without for far too long.
Hunger'd turned to fear.

It was early in a "mild" October,
Bears not yet denned,
Squirrels and rabbits, fat an' sober,
Waitin' fer fall to end

Which left some standin' unprotected,
Caught within our sights.
We bagged two rabbits unexpected,
There would be meat tonight!

But the taste for elk meat pushed us on
Past some columbine
Where we caught a glimpse of cinnamon—
Brown bear in a pine!

I questions Jim, "Would you eat bear?
Ít's hard to get a shot."
He says, "I"ll chop him out of there!"
His axe revealed the plot.

He clum' that pine til he was held
Right below the bruin,
You shoot him when he falls, he yelled,
"I"ll send him to his ruin!"

I was set to make a shot that counts
When ol' bear hit the snow.
But, he didn't hit—he sort of bounced,
He didn't stay below.

He flew up that tree a'gainin' speed,
A falcon on the wing!
His destination seemed to be
A cloud from which to cling.

An' Jim (who'd been lookin' up before,
Now found the bear astern)
Commenced to swingin' mighty blows,
His axe—a dasher in a churn!

An' me, tryin' to clear myself to shoot
At what? The devil take us!
To plug bear, or man, was almost moot,
I had to stop the fracas.

The gods were with me, thank the Lord!
I nailed the pesky beast.
Poor Jim, hard-pressed to say a word,
Was sure he was deceased.

The weather broke, we cooked some grub
(Grease of bear on hare),
We got to join the survivor's club,
An' beat it out of there.

Well, we got home, an' we got warm,
An concluded, then an' there,
We'd settle at the county farm
A'fore we tried more bear!

Lynn Harwell

MIDNIGHT COWBOY

We signed up for the cattle drive, my city friends and I
A week of herding cattle, under the big Montana sky.
They called us dudes behind our backs,
And snickered as they loaded the packs.
It's true we weren't real cowboys, and didn't even come near.
But we longed to see the place of antelope and deer.
For we had grown up with the cowboys on screen,
We longed for adventure, I think you know what I mean.
So we herded the cows, worked hard for long days.
And at night in sleeping bags, under the stars we lay.
One night I awoke before my time was due,
Across the fire sat a man, all dressed in shabby blue
"Who are you?" I asked, sounding a little afraid,
"It's all right, I'm Lou, here's some coffee I made."
He handed me a cup, with fingers that were bony,
They match his horse I thought, as I looked over at his pony.
"I've been here before," he said, "a long time ago
Something just told me, that you would want to know.
I looked at the stars, and gazed off to those hills."
As he spoke of their beauty, he gave me the chills.
He spoke of the war, and his drifting life.
How very sad he was, since he lost his wife.
How the world had changed and now he had no place.
As he spoke, I studied the sad lines of his tired face.
He finished his coffee and got up to leave
Why I didn't stop him, I cannot conceive.
I never spoke of my Midnight friend,
But the next day the trail took a northeast bend.
I noticed some rocks piled with a cross,
Something pulled me and I turned my horse.
There on the cross, held up with a stone,
Read "Here lies Lou Black, he died all alone."

Diane E. Harper

WHO'S THERE?

As I was layin' out one night,
The clouds shut out the moon's dim light.
My fire was all that helped me see;
But that was still ok by me.
The herd was still, all bedded down,
And breezes dancin' all aroun'
I spied this wrangler in the clear
And wondered, "What's he doin' here?"
So I thought I'd palaver make.
I offered him a seat to take.
"Say, Pard, I see you over there;
Come set a spell in this ev'nin' air
The coffee pot is on the heat,
'Cept I ain't got no grub to eat.
But come on over here and set;
I don't think we have ever met.
Now, by what handle do you go?
My handle's Jake if you want to know."
"Who?" was the word that I heard back.
I know that some folk's hearin' 's slack;
So I repeated "Jake" real loud;
But he was quiet as the passing cloud.
"Now look here pardner, can't you talk?
You come on o'er. Ain't fer to walk.
The foreman's comin' soon this way.
If you don't talk now, he'll have his say."
"Who?" was the question in the wind.
I saw him stretch and start to bend.
I felt my Colt, my forty five.
"Ol' Jim's the foreman of this drive.
And if you're here to trouble make,
He'll shoot you down, your life he'll take.
So, afore you risk bein' in the sod
Better say your name, or meet with God."
"Who?" —That got my goat at its worst!
He asked the question he asked at first!
I fired three rounds to make him skeered;

But he stood still, none more afeared.
Then I rushed forth to knock him down;
And this is what I up and found:
I banged my head as the owl flew free.
"Whoo, Whoo," he said. I had shot a tree.

Then, I had to climb that tree real fast
'Cause since my gun made such a blast,
Them cows thought, Well, it's time to go;
And they headed straight for me, don't you know.
I couldn't even see my horse;
He'd joined that herd of cows, of course.
So I just held on to that branch
And hoped I'd live to see the ranch.
When all the dust had settled down
And others brought the herd aroun'
Ol' Jim came ridin' up the road.
He sure was mad, and that I knowed.
'Cause he had put me there in charge
Of all that beef, both small and large;
And he said any blasted sound
Would start them hooves to stomping ground.
My face was messed up from the fray,
My clothes were torn, hat blown away,
I looked a sight; but that was good
'Cause he did what I thought he would.
"Where are you, Jake? How do you plead?
I'll have your hide for this stampede!"
Then, he seen me, "Jake, ain't that you?"
I quietly answered him back, "Who?"
"Jake!"—"Ah, nah, my name is Sam;
I'm not that Jake you think I am.
And, ah, the reason why that I am here,
Well, ah,—I was out here huntin' deer..."
He pulled the kerchief from my face.
"Even for a liar, you're a disgrace!
Why, I've a mind to string you up,
Or put some poison in your cup!

We lost ten head because of you!
And you got the nerve to ask me, 'who!'
So 'fore I lose my ev'ry wit,
You hit the road! You're fired! Now git!"
Didn't even ask him for my pay.
Just found my horse and rode away.
Now, if some day I meet with you
And ask your name, please don't say, "Who?"

Billy James

KICKIN' BACK

THE SIERRY PETES
(OR, TYING KNOTS IN THE DEVIL'S TAIL)

Away up high in the Sierry Petes,
Where the yeller pines grows tall,
Ole Sandy Bob an' Buster Jig,
Had a rodeer camp last fall.

Oh, they taken their hosses and runnin' irons
And maybe a dog or two,
An' they 'lowed they'd brand all the long-yered calves,
That come within their view.

And any old dogie that flapped long yeres,
An' didn't bush up by day,
Got his long yeres whittled an' his old hide scorched,
In a most artistic way.

Now one fine day ole Sandy Bob,
He throwed his seago down,
"I'm sick of the smell of burnin' hair,
And I 'lows I'm a-goin' to town."

So they saddles up an' hits 'em a lope,
Fer it warnt no sight of a ride,
And them was the days when a Buckeroo
Could ile up his inside.

Oh, they starts her in at the Kaintucky Bar,
At the head of Whiskey Row,
And they winds up down by the Depot House,
Some forty drinks below.

They then sets up and turns around,
And goes her the other way,
An' to tell you the Gawd-forsaken truth,
Them boys got stewed that day.

As they was a-ridin' back to camp,
A-packin' a pretty good load,
Who should they meet but the Devil himself,
A-prancin' down the road.

Sez he, "You ornery cowboy skunks,
You'd better hunt yer holes,
Fer I've come up from Hell's Rim Rock,
To gather in yer souls."

Sez Sandy Bob, "Old Devil be damned,
We boys is kinda tight,
But you ain't a-goin' to gather no cowboy souls,
'Thout you has some kind of a fight."

So Sandy Bob punched a hole in his rope,
And he swang her straight and true,
He lapped it on to the Devil's horns,
An' he taken his dallies too.

Now Buster Jig was a riata man,
With his gut-line coiled up neat,
So he shaken her out an' he built him a loop,
An' he lassed the Devil's hind feet.

Oh, they stretched him out an' they tailed him down,
While the irons was a-gettin hot,
They cropped and swaller-forked his yeres,
Then they branded him up a lot.

They pruned him up with a de-hornin' saw,
An' they knotted his tail fer a joke,
They then rid off and left him there,
Necked to a Black-Jack oak.

If you're ever up high in the Sierry Petes,
An' you hear one Hell of a wail,
You'll know it's that Devil a-bellerin' around,
About them knots in his tail.

Gail I. Gardner, 1917

⟿ WESTERN WEAR ⟻

The tourist looked at the cowboy, her eyes filled with curiosity.
She had never seen such a get-up, and she wondered how it came to be.
"Mr. Cowboy, can you tell me why your choice of clothing is so strange?
Is there some reason why you dress that way to work out on the range?"
The cowboy rolled his eyes and sighed, he'd been through this before,
Yet, he answered her politely and went through it all once more.
"Ma'am, this big sombrero that I'm wearin' is a pure necessity.
It shades me from the sun and keeps the rain and snow off me.
It will fan a campfire into flame, or carry water to dowse one out.
These bonnet strings anchor it in a storm, or when I'm ridin' flat-out!
The silk kerchief around my neck is also a very necessary thing.
It's a face wipe, dust mask, sling, tourniquet, or even a piggin' string!
A coat would just encumber my arms, but this snug vest fits the bill.
It won't catch on the saddle horn, and it wards off the morning chill.
These jeans are made with the seam outside, so the saddle don't rub me raw,
And, when I really need protection, I got the best chaps you ever saw.
Not the kind you see at a rodeo, or like they wear at a big parade,
But I can ride through brush and cactus and never have to be afraid.
Now, these tall boots are lifesavers. They protect my lower leg, you see,
'Cause my horse might brush against a fence or whack my leg against a tree.
See how the toes are kinda pointy? That helps me pick up my stirrup quick.
And the high heels won't let my foot go through the stirrup when it's slick.
I'm not wearin' my spurs, but when I do, I have a much better hoss.
I seldom use 'em, but their jingle-jangle reminds him who's the boss.
Now, Miss Tourist, I hope you don't think it's impertinent of me,
If I turn this quiz around to you, and have you explain just what I see.
You're wearing big sunglasses, the briefest shorts, the tiniest swimsuit top,
With white stuff painted on your nose, I guess, to make your sunburn stop.
Your feet are shod with funny clogs, made from someone's old used tires.
And you're askin' me why I look strange...I think somebody crossed your wires!"

Neal R. Torrey

⇢⊸ POETIC COMPETITION ⊷⇠
(COWBOY STYLE)

A colorful contender
for the Cowboy Poet crown,
attracted great attention
when he ambled into town.

He came across as vivid
with a multi-hued onslaught—
His cowboy hat was purple,
and his shirt gold polka-dot.

He wore a pair of yellow cuffs
with inserts done in plaid,
and boasted of a wardrobe
like no other poet had.

There was a red bandanna wrapped
around his scrawny neck,
and his moustache, combed and waxed
was long enough to cause a wreck.

His costly Tony Llamas
were a loud and glaring pink;
His wooly orange sheepskin chaps
would make your eyelids blink!

They called on him to do his thing
and when he took the stage,
his lip began to tremble,
then he flew into a rage!!
He calmed, and said
"I'm sorry folks—
I gotta go back home;
It took so long to git dressed up
I plumb forgot my poem!!"

Don Tidwell

⇒ LINE DANCE LESSON ⇐

I was walkin' up town past the hardware store,
I noticed a poster stuck on the door.

Out the corner of my eye, I gave it a glance,
Saw that it said, "Come On and Line Dance."

For an older cowgirl, I'm pretty light on my feet,
I can do pretty good by a good steady beat.

So later that evenin' when the chores got done,
I pulled on my best boots and headed out at a run.

I got to the hall—'bout the last to get in,
The first thing I noticed, there weren't many men.

Real cowboys don't line dance, I've heard some folks say
Real cowboys ride broncs, brand calves and buck hay.

I've seen 'em on tv in Stetson hats and fancy clothes,
Pants tucked in new boots with real pointy toes.

The gals are all wearin' short skirts or tight jeans,
Some lookin' real cute, some bustin' their seams.

Well, now we're all here, there's a dozen or so.
The teacher up front says, "We'll start out real slow."

She's sayin' some stuff 'bout stomps, heels and toes,
And how we'll look nice if we stay in our rows.

I know right quick this will be hard for me,
I'd forgot the first step when we got to step three.

The folks all around me are vinin' and turnin',
It's becomin' apparent, I'm pretty slow learnin'.

Now they're all at the end and I'm still at the start,
I reckon I missed the whole middle part.

She puts on some music, says "Now—let's do it faster."
Now it becomes a real bad disaster.

Dang! I can't remember my left from my right,
I'm startin' to sweat and I'm lookin' a sight.

A guy on one side gives me a stare,
Says "What'cha doin' here? Ya'll should be over there."

Now we all turn around and I'm thinkin', Oh! Brother!
They're all goin' one way, and I'm goin' another.

A gal on my right is lookin' real mad.
I'd stomped on her foot, guess it hurt pretty bad.

I tell her I'm sorry, guess I went wrong,
"By the way," I say sweetly, "How long's this dang song?"

Finally it's over and I'm headin' for the door,
The teacher is hollerin', "Don't go there's still more."

Well, I ain't goin' back. I ain't takin' a chance,
I ain't gettin' beat up just learnin' to dance.

Janice Gilbertson

⊷ AT THE AIRPORT ⊷

"He's got a bomb!" She yelled out loud.
"It's somewhere in his pants!"
Up against the wall she screams
"We cannot take a chance!"

She probed me with that wand up close
Went off just like a bell.
"It's jail for you and no way out,
You terrorist from hell!"

"It's just them steel shanks in my boots."
I pleaded for my life.
"Take 'em off and walk back through."
Her heart was cold as ice.

Stockin'd foot, a crowd around
I tried it one more time.
Them bells and whistles sang their song,
"My flight I'll miss real fine!"

"Up against the wall," She says
"You no good terrorist!
Get the cuffs, we'll lock him up,
Just slap 'em on his wrists."

I empty out my pockets now,
Coins and keys and such.
Weren't nothin' left I figured now
I never had that much.

That damn machine went off again!
The crowd began to build.
"It's him!" She yells, "Remove that shirt!
That Cowboy hat is filled!"

"There's dynamite or some such thing,
It must be in your pants!
Take 'em off!" She said to me,
"We cannot take the chance!"

The crowd's intense and lookin' on,
My buckle's on the floor.
No shirt, no boots, and now my pants,
Embarrassin' for sure.

I walk back through that cattle chute
My skivvies all I had.
This airport travel ain't much fun
In fact, it's pretty bad.

No bells or whistles screamed this time
Slipped through without no fuss.
I think by Gawd it's easier,
Just to take the bus.

Michael Schroll

THE ROUGH RIDE

She left the big city for a much-needed rest,
A vacation in Montana, the last frontier of the west.
She pictured herself sitting tall in the saddle,
Riding along in the sun, herding cattle.

Now, in a western look she had seen on T.V.,
She was dressed up in her best,
Black simulated, artificial leather pants,
And a bright pink leopard print vest.

From her stiletto heeled, pointy-toe boots,
And a belt in matching bright red,
To the velveteen, two inch brim cowboy hat,
Perched there on top of her head.

The horse sitting quiet as she climbs aboard,
She's sitting there thinking this isn't so hard.
Then the horse springs to action, a steady pace,
A nice even rhythm, there's a smile on her face.

Ever so slowly she starts from the saddle to slip,
She grabs for the mane, but she can't get a grip.
Panicked she tries to avert the impending wreck,
By throwing her arms around the bay's neck.

Faster and faster the horse speeds along,
But she's losing her frail hold.
There's one last chance; it's time for her move
An opportunity daring and bold.

With all of her might and all of her will,
She attempts to throw herself clear,
But her foot hangs up in the stirrup,
Her eyes wide with terror and fear.

Her hat falls off; her hair brushes the ground,
And the jolts are painful and sore.
In fear and terror she's hoping and praying
That she'll live to see one day more.

Well she is battered and moments away,
From being knocked into next week,
When Bill the Wal-Mart greeter sees her,
Reaches out and unplugs her runaway steed.

Bruce South

THE AUTOMATIC ROPE

Curley was a genius, though most thought he was a dope,
He brainstormed up the idee one day for an automatic rope,
Throw a switch up on the saddle, the rope would then take flight,
Equipped with Doppler radar, 'round the horns it would alight,
Ballistic models would calculate its pathway through the air,
Computing for the cowboy just when to launch—and where,
Computer driven logic would cause the rope to loop,
It'd do its own tricks, tie its knots, do everything but "Whooop!"

So Curley got to work that night, a'hammerin' in his shack,
Building up a prototype he could launch and then call back,
The mainframe logic center had a hunnert' kilobytes,
He installed it in a wagon 'cause it was anything but light,
The infrared optics had to be refrigerated,
So he put a cooler in there too, it was starting to get weighted.
Then he built in a joystick—and a full, heads-up display,
Had to add another mainframe, but he did it anyway.

He'd put a batt'ry in it later, an extension cord would do,
To run Curley's proto-typical computerized lass-oo,
And as the dawn was breaking, Curley rolled out his creation,
Hadn't had a wink of sleep, but he was full of inspiration,
He saddled up Old Daisy, hitched the wagon on behind,
Draggin' two miles of 'lectric cord, they rode the range to find,
A vick-tim for the first test, to see if he was right,
And the rope would work, unerring aim in true and stable flight.

They found Bessie munching breakfast, a juicy patch of grass,
Up on a rise and all alone, so Curley could harass,
That cow without disturbing any others standing near,
He switched on the weapons system and booted up the gear,
He checked on all the systems, selected targeting for "HORNS,"
He launched his lariat, his radar showed some strange returns,
That rope sailed high o'er Bessie, it went beyond the rise,
It kept on going. Curley'd missed. Then came a big surprise.
The system showed a target lock, and then it showed "ENGAGE,"
And as that looping lariat sailed o'er cow and rise and sage,

The computer showed a target hit, and Curley was astounded,
But it was coming. "Must be big..." Dust flew as hooves a'pounded,
That cow let loose a bellow, she ran 'cause she was loose,
And o'er that leetle bitty rise came a two-ton bull moose,
With antlers big as Daisy, entwining 40 feet or so,
Of Curley's proto-typical computerized lasso.

Snortin' like a freight train and with eyes a'blazing red,
Rompin' and a'stompin'! 'Course, Curley knew he'as dead,
Old Daisy took to screaming, she tried to spin and bolt,
Her iron shoes skipped. The wagon tipped. She tumbled with a jolt,
Curley rode her to the ground, got tangled in his saddle,
The situation grew intense with no way to do battle,
Then the wagon started smoking and the sparks began to soar,
The moose turned and put his head down, hit that wagon with a roar.

The shock was catastrophic, that blast would kill the average bull,
Dropped the moose with Curley's lasso noose, stunned him hard and full,
Daisy got her wind back, and Curley dropped the buckboard,
Cut loose the moose's lasso noose and untangled the 'lectric cord,
Well, Curley canned the project, left the automatic rope,
Out there, on the lone prairie with the deer and antelope,
As Daisy carried Curley home, that moose came to, complete,
But the scare had sparked a new idee,
"Rocket shoes for horses feet!"

Ed Parrish

RUNNIN' FER 'IS LIFE

One time out thar on tha rockin' W Ranch sticks
We had us a pit fer dippin' them cows fer ticks.
We 'as a way out thar on tha ol' back forty
A havin' us a big ol' tick dippin' party.
Of a sudden we peered crost tha prairie brush
'N' saw a commin' fast a big cloud o' dust.
It come nearer 'n we could see fer goodness sakes
'Twas a cowboy on a big barr a whuppin' 'im with snakes.
He rode up, alit, kicked tha griz 'n tied 'is head
With them two rattlers 'n, they wuzzent dead.
He said. "QUICK! I shore does needs sumthin' ta drank."
We 'uz plum outta warter, 'cept in tha dippin' tank.
He asked, "Whuts that thar in them gallin jugs?"
"Tick dip," I said, he tarned wun up, GLUG, GLUG, GLUG,
Then started untyin' the barr, made 'im kneel 'n got back on,
Lashed 'im good with them two snakes 'n in a flash wuz gone.
I hollered atter 'im, "Hey! whut makes yew in sich a hurry?"
We heared 'is voice commin' back outta tha dust so blurry,
"Ain't got no time ta stop 'n chat with yew fellers today,
Thar's a mean hombre atter me 'n 'e's a commin' this way!"

Wild Bill Halbert

135

⊶ SWEET THING ⊷

Looking through the Caller Times,
Ole Jim Bob by chance read.
The advice page by "Dear Abby,"
Absorbed every word she said.

She spoke of the perfect match,
Between man and his mate.
Common interest she did stress,
For the perfect syndicate.

Now, Jim Bob, had one interest,
His love of roping steers,
Had to find a gal who roped,
For marriage to persevere.

It wasn't long before he met
His perfect little gal.
She threw a real good heel loop
Became his trusted pal.

In time they marched down the aisle,
Became they man and wife.
He didn't know the role she'd play,
This implant on his life.

But soon the honeymoon shut down,
And Jim Bob had the urge,
To pen his roping steers and rope,
When Sweet Thing did emerge.

"I think I'm going to rope with you,
So don't call Rick to heel.
The way he's been missing
He would only cost us bills."

"And anyway he always brings,
His case of Miller Lite.
That stuff will rot your liver,
I'll ice you down a Sprite."

"Put your snuff can on the post,
You sure don't need a dip.
I don't like the spray I get,
While riding at your hip."

"I don't load steers in the chute,
I sure don't strip no horns.
Daddy did all this for me,
From time that I was born."

The first steer she heeled him,
She cold trailed half the night.
Jim Bob kept yelling "now rope."
She'd yell back, "things ain't just right."

She wouldn't rope ole number five,
He did not pull real straight.
Came out ahead of number ten,
Turned him back at the gate.

"You didn't handle that steer right"
Was often her complaint.
"If you think I'm Camarillo,
Then think again I ain't."

Jim Bob went through years of life,
Of husband, wife, team work.
Never lost his cool one time,
He never went berserk.

But often wished for times that were,
When Rick would heel his steers.
To dip his snuff when ere he pleased,
To drink just one cold beer.

He quietly got a plan in mind,
That would cause no remorse.
He went to a barrel futurity,
Bought a winning barrel horse.

Now Sweet Thing runs her barrel race,
And Jim Bob ropes his steers.
Their life a perfect marriage;
Has endured twenty years.

Jimmi Naylor

RUDY'S HANDLEBAR MOUSTACHE

How long did it take you to grow that moustache?
What do you put on it to keep it in place?
Does it stand out on it's own when you greet the dawn,
or does it hang down in utter disgrace?

Seems I'm always plagued by these questions,
can I touch it, and is it for real?
Is it greasy or slippery perhaps?
How does it stand out like it's made of steel?

Well I answer these questions politely,
I been sport'n this growth thirty years.
I grew it back when...I guess I was ten,
an' to part with it might bring me to tears.

I've never put anything on it,
such a sin might cause me to fall.
It stands out so fine cause whenever I dine,
I don't use a napkin at all.

Amidst all this hair there's biscuits n' gravy in there,
an' some juice from old rabbit stew.
There's of course bacon grease when I cooked me some geese,
an' something weird I ate colored blue.

Oh I use to keep it much longer,
why it once stuck clear out to here.
But while running my horse into the wind's mighty force,
it got to snap'n and near took off my ear.

Why you'll be forced to give up romance,
'n kisses you can forget about those.
'Cause it's hard for a lady to kiss you,
with your moustache stuck in her nose.

It can sometimes be quite a bother,
like when shoeing some high spirited mare.
When it's all you can do just to tack on a shoe,
then you tickle her with that long moustache hair.

Why does a cowboy grow such a moustache?
Is being different how he gets by?
You can't even dance close with the one you love most,
without poking her right in the eye.

So why do we sport such a nuisance?
Well the answer is worth more than cash.
It's all worth it that day when someone walks up to say...
HEY THERE...I SURE LIKE YOUR TASH!"

Rudy Gonzales

⤳ A COWBOY'S COMPUTER ⤝

A long time ago I had a job at a store
Computers were all that we sold
One day thru the door came a cowboy named "Mike,"
And this is the tale that he told—

I'm interested in them thar contraptions
He said pointing to a Gateway PC
But this computer talk has got me befuddled—
Can you explain them all to me?

I thought about my sales approach,
and then I said that I could.
I started right in to explain
And thought I covered them all real good!

And when I had finished
He still looked like he didn't believe
These terms, ma'am, they don't seem to add up
Listen, now! I'll say what I mean.

To me windows is what we shut when it's cold
The screen is shut during mosquito season,
A byte is what we get if we don't
So it's shut for a very good reason.

A keyboard hangs next to the door for my keys
To my truck that takes me on the hard drive
Through Wyoming snows to get me some wood
That then I hafta download so's we can survive.

I log on when I want my fire hotter
And log off when it's plenty hot
Prompt is what the mail ain't in the winter
When it snows and it blows a whole lot.

Our huge R-A-M lives in the P-E-N—
It keeps him away from the ewes.
And he'll have to stay there, until he learns
about minding his p's and his q's!

And the mouse in my house lives not on the desk
His mouse pad's a hole in the wall
He's been with us for years. He's happy.
He lives with no cares at all.

He does what he pleases
That mouse causes trouble non-stop
Because my lazy black cat refuses
To give up his seat on my lap top.

And to me those chips you talk about is leavings from the cows
Microchips is leavings from the calves, Mike said
Now don't I make some sense? he asked.
And from a cowboy's point of view, he had.

After that speech I gave up on that sale
And waited for him to bolt for the door
I was shocked when he reached for his wallet
And said "What the hell! Wrap 'em up! I'll take four!!"

Diana N. Wray

⊶ GRADUATE ⊶

On a stage bound for Reno sat a Harvard graduate, beside him a cowboy
    of bronco riding fame.
Said the graduate to the cowboy as he offered this little game.
"If you ask me a question and I git the answer wrong.
I pay you a dollar bill and we do this all night long.

"But if I ask you a question and you don't answer right.
You just pay me fifty cents and we do this through the night."
Well odds of two to one were better than the bronco riding biz.
If all he had to do was sit here and face this Harvard graduate's quiz.

The graduate sat there cocky like, the cowboy all alert.
The graduate felt his education would protect his fancy shirt.
Sez the cowboy, "What has feathers 'n horns, can't be rode or fenced 'n
    crowhops just for thrills?"
"Feathers 'n horns?" the graduate scratched his head, said he didn't know,
    "Here's your dollar bill."

T'was the graduate's turn to question as he said, "Oh by the way."
The cowboys eyes were twinkling, he knew exactly what to say.
"What critter you describing with feathers 'n horns that can't be ridden
    or fenced?"
The cowboy said, "Dammed if I know, here's your fifty cents."

R. L. Ron Brinegar

⇒ EACH LINE ⇐

Each line on this cowboy's face told of years and years of toil.
One by one, I was sure, well-earned by working this earth's soil.
Every wrinkle looked like it was placed there by a loving hand.
I read in his face his love of his country and his land.
His horse was brushed and fed and ready for the night.
This would be the first face he would see in the morning light.
His saddle was his pillow, a thin blanket to keep warm.
His trusty dog lay by his side keeping him from harm.
As I sat across the campfire from him and looked into his eyes,
I saw a weary, lonely man that brought a tear to mine.
The hands that held that old guitar were roughened by the sun.
His legs were bowed, he had a limp, that rodeo had surely done.
I couldn't help but tell him how he had touched me so.
The stories he must have locked inside were ones I yearned to know.
I begged him to share his life with me, one line at a time.
He looked at me like I was nuts and said, "I'm only 29!"

Diane Durrill

GOPHER HOLES

When my southern cousin came to visit,
Charlie dogged me way too long.
Then we had that argument,
found family ties ain't that strong.

One day we went a ridin'
I rode Commanche, my black steed.
I set him astride slow Nellie,
cause she wasn't much for speed.

We set across the meadow
the horses sneakin' a bite and chewin'
Old Nellie kicked up a nest of bees
and the bickerin' started brewin'.

Old Nellie started crowhoppin'
any horse would, even one that's mild.
But cousin Charlie started yellin',
"You gave me a horse that's wild."

I watched Nellie racin' thro the daisies;
Ole Charlie bouncin' up and down.
Then old Nellie stumbled,
pitchin' Charlie to the ground.

I rode to Charlie's rescue;
nothin' hurt but his pride, of course.
But Charlie started yellin',
"I ain't gettin' back on that horse."

"Nellie ain't a wild one," I said
as I listened to Charlie squawk,
"And if you don't want to ride her,
I guess you'll have to walk."

Ole Charlie started slappin' dust
the way bucked-off rodeo cowboys do.
He looked at me with fire in his eye,
and said, "I'll hitch a ride with you."

I don't believe in ridin' double;
prefer not to burden a horse like that
and if'n I'd knowed the trouble he'd cause,
I'd left Charlie where he was at.

I yanked ole Charlie up behind
and grabbed Nellie by the rein.
I shoulda let Charlie walk off his steam
rather than listenin' to him complain.

I tried speakin' in my purtiest voice,
"Why Nellie's the gentlest horse around,
she hit a nest of bees and a gopher hole's
what throwed you to the ground.

I'll come back and set some traps,
those gophers won't be missed."
Ole Charlie gasped, "You can't do that,
they's on the endangered list."

"Since when's there a shortage of gophers?"
I yelled back at the guy astraddle.
I may not be the smartest cowboy,
but Charlie's reins don't quite reach his saddle.

"We used to trap gophers," said Charlie,
"weren't no better gopher skinner than Pa,
and oh, those gophers were mighty fine,
but now it's agin the law."

"I'm gonna set them gopher traps,
just gotta go home and fetch 'em."
Charlie leaned up and said, "If you must,
but we all used wash tubs to catch 'em."

Charlie thinks gophers are mighty fine?
He must be some kind of dope.
Wash tubs to catch em? I shore do spect,
Charlie ain't got no knot in his rope.

When you're dealin' with a crazy man,
you have to handle 'em lightly.
"Whatta ya do when the wash tub's full?"
I said, tongue-in-cheek, so spritely.

"Why we fry 'em or make dumplin's'"
Charlie said with his southern drawl.
The thought of eatin' them gophers
started makin' my insides crawl.

By now I was sure Ole Charlie
couldn't be playin' with a winnin' deck.
And I knew this southern madman
was makin' me a nervous wreck.

Then I KNEW what I had to do,
reared Commanche, afore Charlie could open his mouth.
Charlie slid off, and I ain't seen him since,
I'm just hopin' he headed back south!

Kay Holmes Gibson

(Alabama "gophers" are huge inland turtles)

⇒ I SEEN JOHN WAYNE ⇐

I seen John Wayne
Working in the rain
Having a battle
Trying to rope cattle

I grabbed a rope
From off the post
To help John Wayne
Working in the rain

Roping the cattle
Is a very hard battle

Jesus Cervantes

⋯⊷ NADACOWBOY ⊷⋯

I am not a cowboy, though I wear a cowboy hat
and the boots I wear have pointed toes and heels that ain't near flat.
I want to be a cowboy, but I'm stopped by one condition
I just can't get a handle on those cowboy definitions.

When you say Chaps, I think cologne, and that's not all, there's more
a Quarter Horse is what kids ride outside the Kmart store
A Bull is the just first part of an expletive deleted
and Pony's just a little keg of beer, too soon depleted.
I'm not sure what a Cayuse is, but, it's my recollection
that the Spurs play basketball and Red Eye's an infection.

No, I am not a cowboy, and I guess that's clear to you
but, I read books by Cowboy Poets to find out what to do.
How I should walk, how I should talk, and even how to spit.
When to drink and when to eat and when to take a sit-
down with some pardners, play some cards and chew the fat
about the Dallas Cowboys and topics such as that.

A fella told me "get a horse," that's the thing that I should do.
So, I got a little Pinto, but the body rusted through.
I used to have Colt 45's. I'd drink some every day
now, the Saddlebags it gave me just won't go away.
Roundup kills weeds, I know because I use it now and then.
When you say stirrups, all I think is O-B-G-Y-N.

Yeah, I want to be a cowboy, wearin' jeans and denim shirts
and dance that Texas Two Step till my old doggies hurt.
I'll eat my Texas Chili hot, washed down with Lone Star Beer.
I'll vacation at a Dude Ranch and maybe milk myself a steer.
No, I am not a cowboy, but I think that I could be
once I get a handle on the terminology.

Jeff Hildebrandt

BRONC BUSTIN'

THE STRAWBERRY ROAN

I was laying round town just spending my time
Out of a job and not makin' a dime
When up steps a feller and he says, "I suppose
That you're a bronc rider by the looks of your clothes?"

He guesses me right. "And a good one I'll claim
Do you happen to have any bad ones to tame?"
He says he's got one that's a good one to buck
And at throwing good riders he's had lots of luck.

He says this old pony has never been rode
And the man that gets on him is bound to be throwed
I gets all excited and I ask what he pays
To ride this old pony a couple of days.

He says, "Ten dollars." I says, "I'm your man
The bronc never lived that I cannot fan
The bronc never tried nor never drew breath
That I cannot ride till he starves plumb to death."

He says, "Get your saddle. I'll give you a chance."
We got in the buggy and went to the ranch
We waited till morning, right after chuck
I went out to see if that outlaw could buck.

Down in the corral, a-standin' alone
Was this little old caballo, a strawberry roan
He had little pin ears that touched at the tip
And a big forty-four brand was on his left hip.

He was spavined all round and he had pidgeon toes
Little pig eyes and a big Roman nose
He was U-necked and old with a long lower jaw
You could tell at a glance he was a regular outlaw.

I buckled on my spurs, I was feeling plumb fine
I pulled down my hat and I curls up my twine
I threw the loop at him, right well I knew then
Before I had rode him I'd sure earn my ten.

I got the blind on him with a terrible fight
Cinched on the saddle and girdled it tight
Then I steps up on him and pulled down the blind
And sat there in the saddle to see him unwind.

He bowed his old neck and I'll say he unwound
He seemed to quit living down there on the ground
He went up to the east and came down to the west
With me in the saddle, a-doing my best.

He sure was frog-walkin', I heaved a big sigh
He only lacked wings for to be on the fly
He turned his old belly right up to the sun
For he was a sun-fishin' son of a gun.

He was the worst bronco I've seen on the range
He could turn on a nickel and leave you some change
While he was buckin' he squalled like a shoat
I tell you that outlaw, he sure got my goat.

I tell all the people that pony could step
And I was still on him a-buildin' a rep
He came down on all fours and turned up on his side
I don't see how he kept from losing his hide.

I lost my stirrups, I lost my hat,
I was pullin' at leather as blind as a bat
With a phenomenal jump he made a high dive
And set me a-winding up there through the sky.

I turned forty flips and came down to the earth
And sit there a-cussing the day of his birth

I know there's some ponies that I cannot ride
Some of them living, they haven't all died.
But I bet all money there's no man alive
That can ride Old Strawberry when he makes that high dive.

Curley Fletcher, 1915

MY OLD AMIGO LUM

He ain't much on conversation
His old mind, it wanders some
But a better compadre ain't lived or breathed
Than my ole' amigo Lum

Now Lum, he's plenty punchy
Ya won't find a tougher old coot
But down right, plain old common sense
Ain't one of his stronger suits

You won't find a better feller
To have round ya in a pinch
His head's as hard as granite rock
And he won't give an inch

We were cowboyin' up in the Keechi hills
It was one of our lighter days
But we'd 'bout had our bellies full
Of cuttin' those cedar stays

The weekend, now was comin' up
Time for the big rodeo in town
Been quite a spell since we'd been in
Lum and me would ride on down

Now Lum ain't no spring chicken
But he acts just like a kid
When the bullriders finally mount the beasts
Used to twist 'em himself, he did

The crowd gathered 'round the buckin' chutes
They were thick as bitin' fleas
And Lum, his stature's lackin' some
Makin' it tough for him to see

Ole' Lum sure ain't no genius
But what next he did made sense
He climbed up near the buckin' chutes
And sat upon the fence

The fence sure ain't as comfy
As his recliner back at the shack
And the cable through the cross-tie posts
Seemed to be a little slack

Now ole' Lum, he's kinda portly
Of a diet he ain't thought
So the cable strand he sat upon
Down the line had been drawn taught

The announcer's voice boomed loudly
Of the high horned brindle beast
Two thousand pounds of ragin' hell
Was soon to be released

On Widowmaker, they kicked the latch
He followed the gate around
Then planted his feet and sucked back left
And slammed that cowboy down

He gave the clown a hookin'
Made a lap around the pen
But there ain't a fence for a hundred miles
That could hold this brindle in

The Widowmaker, he sized it up
Then made a fitful run
He was intent on clearin' that fence
Just four posts down from Lum

He quit the earth in one great leap
Now comes the change of events
A solid ton of snortin' beef
Hit smack on top of that fence

Ole' Lum, he's cool, just sat there calm
With both hands in his pockets
But a ton of bull on that cable strand
Shot Lum off like a rocket

Now Lum survived the launchin'
And annihilation merely by chance
But he didn't make re-entry
'Till halfway through the dance

Lum told me it wasn't the launch
Nor the fallin', nor the drop
The thing that hurt his ole' body so
Was that mighty sudden stop

Lum believes the moral here
Needs tellin' to all you fans
It's best to watch the rodeo
From somewhere in the stands

Jay Snider

TY MURRAY—EAT YOUR HEART OUT

You've seen 'em in the big shows from Cheyenne to San Antone,
Sittin' straight and spurrin' bulls or broncs atop the leather throne.
Jim Shoulders, Casey Tibbs and Larry Mahan ran the race;
Now a youngster named Ty Murray sets the rough-stock riders' pace.

They wear them shiny rainbow shirts and leggins bright and bold,
With fringe and stars and dollar signs of silver, green and gold,
And they rock in perfect rhythm, scratchin' Hell to thunderation,
But I'd like to offer my opinion, as a declaration.

B-O-R-I-N-G

There's an art to entertainin', fellers, take it from a pro.
If you wanna leave 'em talkin, boys, you've gotta make a show
And keep the tourists guessin' what your next move's gonna be.
Listen up, you'll get your money's worth, 'cause this advice is free.

When Ol' Black John, the wagon boss, tells me to fork a nag,
He knows I'm gonna screw down tight to fortify my brag.
At breakfast time the boys make bets, at supper they're delighted
As they pow-wow 'bout my hang-time and if I've yet alighted.

'Cause I've built my reputation on the bosom of my pants.
Hell, I know that I can't ride the brutes, but they all get the chance
To slam me in a waterhole or toss me off a cliff,
For hope still beats within my chest, that maybe, someday, if...

If I can fit a ride upon the rankest brute that walked,
I could hold my head up high and justify the talk I've talked.
Then one day I found my prospect, meaner than an alligator
With the scours and a tooth-ache, and they called him Terminator.

Fast Floyd, the local gent who deals in horses, hides and glue,
And who knew my aspirations, said "I've got a bronc for you.
Look yonder in the waterlot." My hackles caught on fire
At a lone cayuse a-grazin' there on gravel, snakes and wire.

Seedy-toed, with quarter-cracks on hooves the size of platters,
Made me choke and wonder just how many men he'd thrown and splattered.
A backbone like a razor-blade from withers to his hips
Had me sore just lookin' at it, and that loose and danglin' lip

Curled back from shiny tiger's teeth. I thought to myself, "Dennis,
You'd probably be safer lobbin' hand-grenades for tennis."
But, cowboy-like, I bragged to Floyd, "I'll beat your ace's trump,
If you'll tell me what's them twenty X's burned acrost his rump?"

His snake-eyes glowed. "They mark the punchers Terminator's killed."
"Twenty men?" I squeaked through tremblin' lips before my voice was stilled.
"I don't think you understand," he hissed. "You're just one cowboy more;
Each X marks a dozen at the undertaker's door."

Something snapped! My cowboy pride had rudely been insulted,
And I take the blame and guilt for all the carnage that resulted.
"Tomorrow, then, at dawn," I vowed, "a duel like none before."
Midnight oil was burned in preparation for the war.

Word spread through the grapevine, folks showed up from miles around.
The schools were closed and convicts tunneled up from underground.
Charter buses clogged the roads and choppers filled the skies.
Saddam Hussein showed up in drag and Gorbachev sent spies!

Giraffes were brought from local zoos; folks perched upon their necks.
Government shut down for lack of people wantin' checks!
Bets were placed in Vegas; civil war inflamed the band
Of folks who yelp for critters' rights and them that work the land.

Amidst the roil and ruckus, standin' proud and brave and free
Was the center of attention, folks; that's right, you guessed it...me!
The Terminator's fire was stoked: it took a dozen men
With ropes tied hard to saddle-horns to choke him down, and then
To wild applause, I swaggered with my 'Sociation kack
And laced it in the middle of that humpy camel's back.
The cinches, pads and blankets I'd filled up with cockleburrs,
And blue flames lit the mornin' where I'd 'lectrified my spurs.

A double six-gun holster complemented my attire
With 50,000 volts of Franklin's motivatin' fire.
A bob-wire bit in Terminator's jaws he gnawed like hay.
With hat pulled tight and hunkered deep, I whispered "Make my day."

Lightning crashed and thunder rolled across the cloudless skies.
I reached with spurs and marked that Devil-spawn between the eyes,
Then polarized that pony with a jolt beneath the tail.
Experts claim the blast was measured on the Richter scale!

Terminator climbed the ladder, kickin' out the rungs.
The crowd commenced to waller 'round and speak in furrin tongues.
Scratched a hell-stick on my whiskers, lit the makin's of a smoke;
As regards the fabled killer, boys, I claimed him for a joke.

The cock-eyed world sat hypnotized on satellite TV.
A hundred million women named their first-borns after me!
The Terminator lost his mind; I matched him stroke for kick.
Them Energizer batteries just never missed a lick.

For that fleeting, famous instant then, I'd not have traded places
With a sultan for his harem, or a poker hand of aces.
With an eye for reputation, I waved off the pick-up man.
I shudder to recall it, but the horse-turd hit the fan!

The saddle-horn collided with the buckle of my pants.
Though I hadn't chewed my breakfast well, I got a second chance.
I kept a constant cadence as my noggin slapped his rear,
And punished him severely when my chin bounced off his ears.

He launched me like a missile, not a Patriot, a Scud.
No tellin' where I'd land or if I'd blow or be a dud.
I lit atop the saddle-horn; it made an awful thud,
And with surgical precision made a geldin' from a stud.

I melted in the saddle-seat and slipped into a coma.
I thought I'd died and gone to Hell or maybe Oklahoma.
That saddle-horn had fingers! Lord, I swear it came alive
And grabbed my off-suspender when the Terminator dived.

There's certain laws of physics, folks, that cannot be denied,
And action breeds retraction when elastic fouls the ride.
At the zenith of my orbit I was dodgin' asteroids;
Half a heart-beat later I was countin' hemorrhoids.

The saddle slipped to left and right, then underneath the brute.
The sun was burnin' blisters on the bottoms of my boots.
He bucked right through the riggins, shucked the saddle off his head;
My oratory blasphemies are better left unsaid.

My feet was in the stirrups and my buns was in the seat;
With a death-grip on the bridle-reins, I'd not concede defeat.
Rockin' like a metronome, he slapped me back and forth,
North, then South, then North, then South, then North, then
    South, then North.

Centrifugal convulsions caught the early mornin' light.
Seven hundred tourists died from nothin' more than fright.
The Terminator's afterburners fortified his motor;
I was sailin' like a monkey on a helicopter rotor!

I wound up in a stock tank 'midst the mud and tulie plants.
It shorted out the batteries and wirin' in my pants.
I cursed the day of bornin' of that Terminator critter,
While I lay there in the slime and muck, fryin' like a fritter.

Doctors fixed the parts they could, but others they just can't.
They told me what I needed was a total brain transplant.
But this story happened just the way I've told it here to you.
Why, the *National Enquirer* turned me down because it's true.

So, Ty Murray, eat your heart out; I'm the top dog of the breed,
And history will long record the glory of my deed.
But there's one consolation, and I'll tip my hat to you.
Congratulations, pardner, you are the very best at what you do.

Dennis Gaines

THE MOUTHPIECE

The old man perched on the bucking chute
Watching the young guys ride
He cocked a weathered brow at me
As I sat down by his side

His clothes were old and faded
And his thinning hair was white
But when he turned to talk to me
His eyes were full of life

He said "Now look at these young peacocks
With padded vests and fancy chaps
Back when I was young and riding bulls
Weren't none dared look like that

Our gear was stained and dirty
With here and there a tear
And our smiles would usually have some gaps
Because no mouthpieces did we wear

Now, after biting my tongue a time or two
And getting yanked down on some horns
I got to figuring by age twenty-some
I'd be smooth-mouthed as a baby born

So I bought a big tobacco plug
And I crammed up both cheeks full
Thinking that plug would cushion my teeth
As I crawled down on that bull

Now, I know what you are thinking
But it weren't that way at all
You're thinking that after a jump or two
I swallowed that big old chaw

Nosirree, that tobacco worked
Kept my teeth and tongue intact
As that bull warmed up to bucking
I just chewed and hugged his back

Since I'd never been a chewing man
Real quick I had to expectorate
I was smart enough to spit downwind
But I lost the wind back at the gate

Now, I know what you are thinking
But it weren't that way at all
You're thinking I swallowed all that juice
I'd worked up from that big chaw

Nosirree, I just puckered up
Thought, where it goes, it goes
Looking back, it was pure bad luck
That I spit on that bull's nose

Now, you'd think a cud-chewing critter
Would be more tolerant than a horse or mule
But that big bull just went plumb wild
When he inhaled the juice I'd chewed

The next jump I went flying high
Kinda sailplaned through the air
I was searching for soft ground to land
But where I lit, it wasn't there

Now, I know what you are thinking
But it weren't that way at all
You're thinking I swallowed that big old quid
But I had it locked tight in my jaws

Yessirree, my plan had worked
I'd protected my tongue and teeth
I couldn't wait to tell my friends
About my new, and safe, mouthpiece

It stayed with me through each spin and jump
Even lasted through the fall

Then they announced my ride scored ninety-one
And I swallowed that big old chaw"

John D. (Jay) Jones

TEMPORARY INSANITY

Kid leaped up off the dusty ground,
glanced left and right, then raced around
the bull-fighter in loud apparel:
Fright wig, red nose and sturdy barrel.
Spied his brother on the fence,
a dang rough ride; Bro's lookin' tense
until the Kid makes one last dash
and clambers up before the crash
of deadly horns smack in the chute.
"Good grief," Kid shrieked, "what did I do?"
"Ya rode that bull," his Bro did say.
"Or almost did. He tossed ya waaaaaaaay
up in the air. Ya fell plumb flat.
I'll betcha ruint your cowboy hat."
"You're worried 'bout the goldang hat?
I'm worried 'bout much more than that.

"Like why I feel compelled to climb
up on these monsters, each dang time.
My head was once screwed on quite tight.
But now I think I ain't quite right.
My vertebrae? Shoot, plumb detached.
My legs? I reckon once they matched.
Ain't real durned sure. But this I know:
This dang bull-ridin's got to go.
Don't recollect even climbin' on.
I must'a, though, 'cause stomped right on
my brand new shirt and safety vest
huge tracks that should'a caved my chest.
I guess I must'a grabbed the rope.
S'pose I had'a have some hope.
But oh-good-gosh my face is sore.
I must'a slammed into a door."

"A wooden door?" Bro laughed "Lord, no!"
A door, mebbe, like mighty Beau.
That bull beaned you like Beau beaned Tuff.
I guess you're feelin' kinda rough."
"Rough?" Kid squalled, "ain't half of it.
I'll tell ya what: I feel like...well, I feel **BAD**, kid **REAL** bad!
Can barely set here, head's plumb dizzy.
Gotta think, get my brain busy
Comin' up with some excuse
So that next bull won't cook my goose."
"Hey, Kid," it's time to climb on down
 To start our final go-around."
"Uh, jest a minute, I'll be there.
Quick, Bro, think fast, ya s'pose I dare?
Approach them judges with my plea
Of temporary insanity?"

K. T. Etling

SHORT CUT

Short Cut is a bucking horse,
and about as mean as anything you've ever seen.
He always starts and he stays the course
totally rank and every second in the saddle obscene.
Side winding sucker'll switch to pile driving and then go spinner,
separating you from saddle and proving you're no gold buckle winner.
Laying there, all those stars floating around,
you getting real intimate with that rodeo ground,
knowing you're at least half dead,
and wondering if they can reattach your head,
then you hear the bull fighters start to pray
cause old Short Cut is coming back your way
to stomp you into the fairground sod
and put you up face to face with God.
At first you think it's just a nightmare you're dreaming
that is 'til you hear the buckle bunnies screaming
and last you saw of that horse he was up in the saddle with the pickup man.
Though you've been dusted and everything is busted, you can stand!
And run! No one in the stands would've believed you could run.
And fly! Over the fence an eye blink ahead of that son of a gun.
No moral tales. No tales of gold buckle glory.
Just simple description and simple prescription:
You draw Short Cut and the story gets gory.
Listen up lad! My advice is worth trusting.
Give 'em back that number and throw in for the mutton bustin'.

"Doc" Dale Hayes

THE RIDE

The cowboy climbs on the big black horse
He can feel him quiver with rage
This horse called Fury NO cowboy's rode
But tonight that's gonna change

He checks his riggin', nods to the crowd
As if to say "Don't worry, I'm a COWBOY
And tonight's the night—I'll ride this horse called Fury.

He gives the signal—the gate opens wide
Fury bursts from the chute with a scream
Buckin', Snortin', Sunfishin' high
In his eyes a menacin' gleam

The cowboy spurs from front to back,
Fury responds with a leap
The cowboy's holdin' his own on this bronc
But that buckle ain't gonna come cheap

Then the sound every cowboy longs to hear
The bell says 8 seconds has passed
He jumps from the bronc,
Waves to the crowd—
THEN WAKES FROM HIS DREAM AT LAST...

Then grandma's cowboy climbs out of bed
Dons his boots and jeans
They'll go to the rodeo, he'll ride the sheep
And ride the broncs in his dreams.

Peggy Coleman

THE BULL RIDE

I pull up to the rodeo grounds, I'm runnin' really late
"Hurry up partner," I heard calling from the gate
"You drew the pick," shouts a cowboy from the chutes above
The tension burns as I whip out my glove

"The bulls are meaner than a junk yard dog,
Cody found out, He's still in a fog."
I grab my rope and put on my vest
Say a little prayer and hope for the best

The crowd's applaudin' for the last bull ride
As I climb the chutes to find my bull inside
I straddle the critter so big and strong
Surely I can stay for eight, it ain't that long

"Come on, you can do it,'" shout the boys near the gate
"Buckle down on that critter, you'll be good for eight."
I nod my head, the gate busts open
I spur the bull good, I'm still a hopin'

That bull spins me around and jumps in the air
I'm gasping for breath, but that bull don't care
Around and around I spin like an ol' tire
I hope eight seconds goes by before I expire

I can feel the rope start to release from my fist
Six seconds, seven seconds; "Please don't let me miss."
I hit the ground running, gettin' gored ain't no fun
The judges say, "Sorry kid, it's over and done."

Back to the truck and out the gate I go
There's another rodeo tomorrow, I'll give 'em a show
Tomorrow I'll put on my gear and ride
Ain't no bull goin' to take away my pride.

L. M. Larson

THE DEATH'S HEAD BULL

The Death's Head bull
Was a tremendous brute
Who'd never been rode
Three jumps from the chute!

Fifteen hands high,
And half as wide—
A full ton of dynamite
In a black bull hide.

A bone jarring bucker
With a cyclone's whirl.
A neck snapping twister,
With a sunfishing curl!

From Texas to Montana,
He'd bucked his way to fame.
(And killed five good cowboys
Whilst livin' up to his name.)

But, his day of reckoning arrived,
(As it must, indeed)
When Ol' Shorty drew his number
At the Miles City Stampede.

From somewhere "south of yonder"
Ol' Shorty had been grown.
And he'd earned a rep for ridin' bulls,
And he'd done it on his own!

With steel coils in his muscles
An' no bigger than a pint of gin,
Shorty rode his share of bad 'uns
But he never lost his grin.

And so it came at Miles City
At the big Stampede and rodeo
That Shorty drawed the Death's Head Bull
With the crowd screamin' fer' a show!

His buddies slapped him on the back
An' wished him lots of luck,
While the Doc got out his stretcher.
('Cause he'd seen ol' Death's Head buck!)

They rosined up the bull rope
An' Shorty gripped it tight.
The Death's Head bull just snorted
An' Shorty grinned, "All right!"

The starter hollered, "Let 'er go!"
And the gate man swung it wide.
And in a swirling cloud of dust,
The bull and Shorty went outside.

The Death's Head bull stood on his nose
An' Shorty raked 'im high.
The Death's Head bull then spun like a top
('Til Shorty toed 'im in the eye!)

The Death's Head bull next sunfished
An' Shorty hung on with his hooks.
That ol' bull next done some things
What ain't yet been wrote in books!

But somehow Shorty rode him
An' even fanned his hat!
An' raked him high an' hooked 'im low
Quicker'n' a scalded cat!

The buzzer fin'ly blasted loud
An' the clowns come runnin' out;
When that little cowboy left that big bull's back
The crowd rose up with a shout!

They cheered him back to the chutes!
(The judges called his ride a win.)
And while that entire arena broke out in pandemonium,
All Shorty did was grin...

His buddies come 'round him hollerin'
"How you done it, I dunno'!"
"Yer the only one, ever rode him out!"
"Shorty, you gived that crowd a show!!!"

Shorty cocked his big hat back,
And his grin split his face in half.
"Well, I knowed ol' Death's Head from before...
Ya' see my Dad raised him from a calf.

"Now, I rode 'im out fair and square!
But stickin' wasn't just dumb luck—
That ol' bugger's picked up some purty mean tricks,
Since that summer I taught him how to buck!!!"

Don McCrary

THE BULL RIDER

Sittin the chute, waitin to pull the gate
This bull's gonna buck, I'm ridin for eight
Pull on the rope, warm it up slight
Adjust the riggin, give it a twist to the right

Got to make a check, to get down the road
Takes a lot of fuel, to carry my load
Traveling the circuit, riding here today
Be gone tomorrow, no time to play

Contractor says, "You bout ready to go"
For the bull's a pawing, he already knows
Turn out them toes, pull my hat down tight
Got to stay in the middle of this one tonight

With a nod of my head, and a pull of the gate
I have to keep up, can't afford to be late
The clown is ready, looking for a fight
Need to ride this bull in the bright arena light

With a leap and a spin, the crowd starts to cheer
I'm counting and counting, is eight seconds near
Got to get up and run, when I hit the ground
I surely thank GOD, for that rodeo clown.

Tony Blisard

THE DAY THAT TUFF JUST CAME TO RIDE

Bad Bulls of the P.B.R.,
Break hearts and heads with ease,
Like two-ton cats they strut their pride,
To wait their turn, the crowds to please,
The banging and clinging of bells and heads,
Says they're here and ready to ride.

But one, just one, the Yellow Whale,
Bodacious, with the yellow hide,
Stubby horns of wicked curl,
Broad back and shoulder wide,
Knew tonight would be the night, for he knew he was,
The only one, that Tuff had come to ride.

Then came this man, a homely male,
With heart and pride abound,
Came this man, to ride the whale,
Bodacious was and always is,
The one, that Tuff had come to ride.

Hedeman came and was Tuff enough,
Bodacious came to show his stuff,
The match was made, the line was drawn
One would win, while one would 'bide,
And everyone knew, the one that Tuff had come to ride.

Tuff slid down to top this beast,
With hands of nervous sweat,
Cotton mouthed and jaws clinched tight,
This moment now, as time stands still,
The world will never know, the thoughts that pass,
Between man and beast, in moments drawn like this.

The chutes got quiet, as the bulls drew still,
Skol's Gold and Locomotive Breath,
Watched with smiles of shown delight,

As Bodacious settled, and the crowd grew quiet,
This was no test, no real just test,
Because, he knew, he was the one, the only one,
That Tuff had come to ride.

He'd been before and would be again,
This rider he knew well,
He'd dumped him once in Tampa Bay and again in Memphis town,
He smiled a wicked smile that brought a wicked frown,
But what he didn't or couldn't guess,
Was the Tuff man, was now in town.

The world explodes with rockets glare,
This Bull on his head would stand,
Bodacious, who this cowboy knew,
With down force strong as sin,
Would try like Tampa and Memphis town again,

The ride that day, Californian's say,
Was the best for beast and man,
The first man out, first to score, a ride, that had no score,
Tuff just smiled and sailed his hat,
Shot holes with thumb and pin, he'd ridden and beaten the best there was,
And lived to ride again.

Freckles Brown smiled down that day,
As Tornado shook his ugly head,
Lane Frost still rode the bitter ride,
And Red Rock hooked the sky,
All that was said, that fateful day,
Was everyone knew, Tuff was here to ride.

Bodacious, now his time retired, still young for sire and seed,
Knows well the stories, and well the daring deeds,
Bested by the very best, still walks with head held high,
He piled him off in Tampa Bay and again in Memphis Town,
Tried his best, but time cut short, the ride of rides that day,
The whale was spiked and ridden down,
The day Tuff Hedeman, came to town...

Jim Kitchens

GENTLEMAN JIM

I never saw a horse I couldn't ride, why I
even rid Sky Ball Paint.
But with Gentleman Jim that all changed at
first glance he made you want to faint.

Jim was big and strong, and he'd stand with
all his muscles so tight.
It was like he was saying, "come on
cowboy, let's me and you fight."

So I pulled down my Stetson and
looked at Jim with a big Texas grin.
Ol' Dan Says, "He'll buck you off in 3
seconds, I'll bet ten!"

So I jump on and tuckers down,
and slaps him with a hide.
Gentleman Jim looks back at me, one time,
then we're off for the ride.

The first buck wasn't so bad,
but the second seemed we'd never come down.
We were up real high, you could look around,
I swear I could see a far off town.

What happened next is, I can't remember much,
it's sort of a blur.
But it happened when I got Ol' Jim
With a brand new silver spur.

Jim took the grand tour, all
around the farm,
With me holdin' on and a prayin',
"Lord keep me from all harm."

It's amazin' how much you can say, so fast,
Hopin' the Lord will hear.
While you're on the back of a buckin' bronc,
and you think the end is near.

I never knew you could live so much
in two seconds' of time.
But that's how long Dan said it was.
I paid him ten, with one silver dime.

Bobby Cohoon

THE WEST THAT WAS

⊷ A WESTERNER ⊷

I knowed he was a Westerner
    I knowed it by his talk;
I knowed it by his headgear,
    I knowed it by his walk.
His face was bronzed and fearless;
    His eye was bright and keen,
That spoke of wide, vast ranges
    I knowed that he had seen.
Somehow I knowed he'd ridden
    The range-lands of the West;
His speech was bunkhouse patter—
    The kind I love the best.
He brought a hint of prairies,
    Of alkali and sage;
Of stretches wide and open—
    The Western heritage.
I knowed he was a Westerner
    Just from the way he done;
His footgear, too, proclaimed him
    A stalwart Western son...
He had "the makin's" with him,
    And I could not forget
His bed-ground from the manner
    He rolled his cigaret.
He brought with him the freedom
    Of that great Western land;
Where grassy billows, endless,
    Sprawl out on ev'ry hand.

The city noises chafed him,
    And each skyscraper tall
Seemed like grim barriers risin',
    Or some deep canyon wall.
He seemed a part and parcel
    Of countries wide and far,
Where great herds dot the mesas,
    Out where the cowmen are.
I knowed he was a Westerner
    Becuz he was so free
In yellin' "Howdy pardner!"
    When he was passin me.

                    E. A. Brininstool, 1914

⇥ HERITAGE ⇤

The ranch on which I hung my hat, though short on most the frills,
Was thirteen sections, give or take, of Texas' rollin' hills.
We called it home, our little world, our very own frontier,
Amongst the cattle, sheep an' goats; the varmints, hogs an' deer.

It's did right well in Nature's care, withstood her angry rage,
Survived extremes of drought an' flood: an' made me earn my wage.
The land has taught me what I know, that livin' life's an art,
That all you need is common sense, resolve an' gentle heart.

One day I watched the breakin' dawn an' whiffed the mornin' air,
A time I often set aside for things like thought an' prayer.
A Mockin'bird an' Mornin' Dove, an' other birds at play,
Were there to sing an' set the mood to start another day.

That mornin' saw the strangest thing, like time itself had merged,
An' all the souls who once were here, appeared an' then converged.
In swirlin' clouds of mist an' fog, right off the bluffs they rolled,
Till all had gathered in the glen, the modern an' the old.

The Indians, conquistadors, an' other ancient men,
The soldiers from this country's wars, an' cowboys from back when.
They all had come from yesterday to help me understand,
The reasons to perpetuate our heritage an' land.

A crazy notion, so I thought, that they could just appear,
But let me tell ya' something now, the reason soon got clear.
They rode with me throughout the day an' showed me things I'd missed,
Some things I'd seen a thousand times an' some I'd just dismissed.

The wagon roads of long ago, still evident today,
Are carved in rock an' rutted earth, not apt to wash away.
They linked the missions, forts an' towns those many years gone by;
An' left their mark for all to see, as modern times grew nigh.

The artifacts an' weathered ruins attest to yesterdays,
When others came an' lived their lives in very different ways.
We've seen their skill in arrowheads they honed from fired stone,

At ever turn and trail we took was something to remind,
The Maker must have had a plan laid out for humankind.
The Earth, He made, has fed us all a half-a-million years,
An' used her constant states of change to challenge pioneers.

Well, now our home is long since gone; the ranch is laid to rest,
Divided, sold an' fenced in lots; the owner thought it best.
That time is ours to always keep; those souls have not returned,
But I recall that breakin' dawn an' all the things I learned.

I do not know if they'll be back or if they'll feel the need,
But I'm prepared to ride the trail, wherever it may lead.
I'm just a spirit ridin' time, whose body's from the Earth,
An' feel it's time I took the reins an' offered-up my worth.

The land has been the legacy we cultivate an' reap,
The life has been the heritage our fathers fought to keep,
An' we are bound throughout our time with those who came before,
To give our hearts and souls to it, and make it something more.

Jim Fish

⚊ OUT HERE AT BUTTE STATION ⚊

I am out here on the desert alone,
Just me and the horses at Butte Station,
Where the only shade is devised by man
And the water's always on short ration.

There was a blacksmith and extra rider,
Which meant a little more food on the shelf,
But, the last days of the Pony Express
Find me running the station by myself.

Twice a day, for only two minutes each,
An express rider comes burning on through.
There's only time for a couple of words,
Then he's on a new mount and out of view.

This job is like no other I have known,
And to choose it again would be insane,
Though lessons of life and about myself
Have been my reward, and also my pain.

It takes discipline to be on your own,
To feed the horses, do all of the work,
Take a bath when it's time, or wash the clothes,
And the duties of the station not shirk.

There is pride in all these productive things,
And the feelings, they help bring me some joy,
But, out here there are a few darker woes
That can instill mighty fear in a boy...

Like when the sky comes clear down to the ground,
And it seems I'll be squashed in between,
Or when the silence roars like a cannon...
That is when I break the spell with a scream!

There are times I am overcome with fear...
Imagination's a weakness of mine.
I have heard sounds that I cannot describe,
And seen shapes at night I cannot define.

The lowest thought is that of dying here...
Just fading away and no one knowing
That I am gone, or where I lay to rot,
Nor the circumstances of my passing.

Once in a while though, I get a great swell
And am overwhelmed by the endless plain.
While looking at this creation so large
I believe it is the whole of God's domain.

A few times I heard Him talking to me
When I had been trying to think things out.
His voice was as soft as the desert breeze...
I always thought'd be more like a shout.

There are beautiful sights in the desert,
And other things that bring peace to the heart,
Like the sun that's going down forever,
Or the smell of the sage 'fore the rains start,

And the owl working the mice in the grass,
A coyote yelp in the bright moonlight,
Or the colors that take time to notice...
Sometimes, everything can seem all right.

But, most of the time out here is empty...
A magnified sense of being alone...
Out here next to the alkaline desert.
What a miserable place to call home.

The loneliest stop on the express trail,
The station with the worst reputation,
Where the only shade is devised by man,
And the water's always on short ration.

Dave Rhodes

⊷ IN THE DAYS OF GRANVILLE AND JOHN ⊷

Oh the days of Granville and John have passed
Never to come again,
And we won't see the likes of times like theirs
In the current affairs of men.

Now Granville and John were bachelor brothers
Who lived high up Middle Creek,
Where the grass grows tall and the steers get fat
And the streams run clear and deep.

Their daddy had helped to fence the Flint Hills
At the end of the open range
When cattle that once trod the Old Chisholm Trail
Now arrived on the Santa Fe trains.

Shipped up from Texas or New Mexico
Or the swamps of Louisianne.
Lean, five year old steers as tall as a horse,
But no wider than your hand.

Tail up the sick ones out of the cars,
Get them out in the pastures and sun,
By the Fourth of July they'd be fat as a pup
On the grass of the Hundred and One.

John rode the pastures and looked out for strays
While Granville hauled salt and kept house
And cooked in a skillet of cold bacon grease
All filled with the tracks of a mouse.

"Nothing at all to worry about,"
He'd say in a slow kind of way.
"Just turn on the fire and let her get warm
And those tracks will soon go away."

No, fine dining was not what you'd get at their house
And to them their work was their fun
With no call to spend much of the hundred a month
They were paid by the Hundred and One.

For what better life than a cowboy's life,
Plain, without any frills?
And what better life for a single man
Than a horse and a song in the Hills?

Squeeze chutes were unknown to Granville and John;
They worked with a horse and a rope.
It was a pleasure to see them drag calves to the fire,
Or ride along home at a lope.

Shipping time was when Granville and John
Were at their peak and their prime.
They could round up a pasture of the spookiest steers
And never leave one behind.

They could ride across pastures on the darkest of nights
And always come out at the gate,
And if you helped ship, I'll tell you for sure,
You sure didn't get to sleep late.

On shipping mornings they'd gather a crew
And start for the pasture at three,
Then sit on their horses an hour, or two,
'Til there was enough light to see.

Now why they didn't just wait at the barn
Or stay a bit longer in bed
Is a question you might as well not even ask;
They'd be jogging too far ahead.

They'd round up the cattle on top of a hill
And cut out five loads of the best,
Then head 'em for Hymer with John in the lead
While Granville counted the rest.

Their horses weren't fancy; their saddles were plain,
But they always got the job done,
And owner or buyer, you got a fair count
In the days of Granville and John.

Now the trains no longer haul cattle to grass
And the stockyards have all been torn down,
Replaced by goosenecks and portable pens
That would have made Granville frown.

For how can you train a horse to watch cows
If he rides in a trailer all day?
And how can you have any worth to your life
 If you use a machine to load hay?

If your work is your life, then what better life
Than to ride the Flint Hills in the dawn?
And what better time to have lived in the Hills
Than the days of Granville and John.

But the days of Granville and John have passed
Never to come again,
And seldom today will anyone see
The likes of these good men.

Jim Hoy

⇒ IT'S FINISHED (SUVATE) ⇐

This was the beginning of the end,
    At Prairie Dog Fork of the Red, at its bend.
March 1875, the night it was cold,
    Old McKenzie's strategy, cruel and bold.
He'd chased the Comanche far and wide,
    Now no place to go, no place to hide.
He'd chased them for one whole year.
    The Comanche had nothing in heart, nothing but fear.
He'd run out of time, run out of heart,
    To stay and fight, was never smart.
In the Palo Duro, they wanted to stay,
    Now they had no time, not even to pray.
Quanah Parker, leader of this band,
    Gave them his heart; gave them his hand.
Wrapped in his blanket, head held low,
    Ran out of blessings, no place to go.
Old McKenzie, on his way down,
    From the top of the rim, to the lower ground.
Hooves of horses, wrapped in burlap to muffle,
    The troops ready to fight, or a scuffle.
To kill the Comanche, to make him bend,
    To settle for all time, to bring the end.
Quanah's scouts, out on the land,
    Had missed McKenzie and his band.
McKenzie's orders, spare the women and kids,
    To do it honorable, to make his bids.
The troopers were on them sure and fast,
    To do it right, to make it last.
They hit the lodges at first day light,
    Burned them, tore em' up, a terrible sight.
The women and kids, trying to run,
    All became visible with the rising sun.
Comanche warriors, trying to battle,
    The troopers herded them, just like cattle.
The coming of the sun, terrible to see,
    Quanah saw, knew it was not to be.
With feet he could hardly drag,
    With rifle and cloth, raised the white flag.

The battle was fought, came to an end,
 All the Comanche ponies, put in a pen.
With rifle fire, all 1200 paid the price,
 Terrible, like the roll of bad dice.
The troopers hung their heads in shame.
 Who was guilty; who was to blame?
All the Comanches walked to Ft. Sill,
 Without a good horse, a bitter pill.
McKenzie to Quanah, with held out hand;
 With misty eyes, beheld the whole band.
He shook the hand, held it fast,
 SUVATE—It's finished at last.

Bert Lloyd

⊷ BLACK SUNDAY ⊷

The world was surely coming to an end that day.
Everyone who lived it really felt that way
As the dust cloud rolled in the sky
While ahead birds of all kinds commenced to fly.

We had all seen the pesky duster many times before
And learned to live with dirt crunching on the floor.
We knew how to push torn rags around the window frame
And wake up with pillowcase and dust looking the same.

Sometimes the sun shone weakly through a murky haze
Long before we heard of pollution's smoggy days.
We feared the dreaded cough of dust pneumonia's curse
And some wore dust masks for nothing could be worse.

That Easter Sunday of April, 1935, dawned bright and clear
And we rejoiced that we were spared the dogged fear
Of day after day dust gritting between our teeth,
Layering over the land, covering all that lay beneath.

Now the sky in the west bore a kaleidoscope threat
Rolling, tumbling, devouring all that it met.
"We were playing outside when we first saw that cloud.
'Mama! Come look!' we hollered real scared and loud.

"Mama took one look and told us to get inside fast.
It got dark and Mama said, 'This surely can't last.'
Then she lit a lamp but she still couldn't see.
She stuck her finger right in my eye trying to find me."

"That cloud rolled and rolled just like smoke.
We got under a wet sheet so we wouldn't choke.
You know, we often slept at night that way
And the sheet would be black the next day."

After a dust storm passed and the wind settled down,
It was hard to find a smile behind a worried frown.
Federal Emergency Relief gave us dust masks for one cent
And slaughtered our cattle in a time that seemed hell bent.

Ballgames helped us forget hard times that Black Sunday.
"Boy, it scared the heck out of me when we looked that way
And saw it come rolling half to three-quarters mile high—
There was a funny stillness, then it hit! Oh, my! Oh, my!"

"Yes, we thought a tornado was coming—we tried to leave the ball game.
The car wouldn't start and Jim said static electricity was to blame.
It finally started after he tied baling wire underneath to ground it.
Often you'd see a car bumper dragging a long chain tied around it."

Suitcase farmers came and plowed the sod, sowed wheat, then left.
They came back to harvest and collect, leaving the land bereft.
The first crops were paid for by high prices of 1927-28,
Then 1931 saw low prices, the drought of 1932 sealed our fate.

April 13, 1933, the first big duster whipped across the plain
Bringing in eight years of hopeless work, misery, and destitute pain.
"The big boys down state didn't believe the stories they'd read,
So a bunch came out to see our land, once alive but now dead.

"Our wheat was already buried under four inches of sand.
The men went to look at the fields and pasture land
Then saw the cloud and ran for the fraid hole instead.
I tell you one thing—they became believers with dread!"

Dust from the storm hung over the Panhandle day after day
And was carried on upper air streams a thousand miles away.
"I lived in Florida and two days later a funny red haze
Dimmed the bright sun and hung around for several days.

"As it cleared some we could tell how hard the wind blew.
We had settin' hens tied in gunny sack—there were two—
Hanging over the clothes line swinging wildly forward and back.
I expect they were through with settin' after that ride in the sack!"

People even got lost in the storm and wandered around in it.
Little Marvin was bringing the milk cow home when the storm hit.
He fell down, lost his sense of direction and ran blindly west.
Searchers stretched a rope across the field to help their quest.

"I rode the school bus and sometimes the storms hit without warning.
Often the only way the bus made it to school on a dusty morning
Was for two boys to hold a rope between them from fence row to row
Guiding boys on each side of the bus telling the driver where to go."

Writers felt the discomfort was worse than the damage to people and land
But those of us who lived those years still belong to a remembering clan
Whose lives and times will ever bear the mark of survival glory
As long as there are those left to tell this sad, yet wonderful story.

Barbara Bockleman

(Quotes are from witnesses to Black Sunday, interviewed by Barbara Bockleman.)

ALL THAT IS LEFT

At the mouth of a redrock canyon
Near the base of a sandstone cliff
She stands there, a skeleton sentinel
With branches arthritic and stiff.
And those upturned fingers appear to pray
For water, though now, it's too late.
Not far from her roots lies a rusty stove lid,
And the remains of a barbed-wire gate.

Not much, you might think, of a legacy,
Not much to remember them by.
Yet this site speaks readable volumes
To the wise and experienced eye.
And the tree, though now dead, says something,
An echo from a waterless grave.
For it tells of the hope of a homesteader,
And of the sacrifice somebody gave.

She stands enshrined, a personification
Of dreams and desires and grit.
For that old cottonwood was the first thing planted
When the flame of faith was lit.
Thriving under a pan of daily dishwater,
Her leaves a light color of jade,
Barefoot children swung from her branches
And a mother snapped beans in her shade.

But drought sucked the life from the homesteader,
Who eventually had to move on.
And within a few years, the tree had also withered
When its daily washwater was gone.
So, today, she stands guard in the canyon
And each storm brings a new limb to the ground,
And every spring, during the desert roundup
Weary cowboys delight in the kindling they've found.

Virginia Bennett

⇥ THE GREAT DIVIDE ⇤

There's a warm wind blowing
beneath the prairie skies tonight.
My bones are tired and weary
I won't run—don't want to fight.
My pony stands restless on these hills.
Connected to the land, she always will be.
There's a warm wind a-blowing
through the prairie skies tonight.

There was a time when the land
was a pure and peaceful place.
When bees came to the clover,
and the land held God's own grace.
When you could drink from rivers
with the cup of your own hand.
Hear the deer running
in the shade of woodland stand.

A time when arm in arm
We were terraced with belief
In step with one another
in our joy and in our grief.
And there was dawn breaking
through the woodland trees beneath.

And the stars held out a beauty
in the blanket of the sky.
A dream for every dreamer,
a tear for every eye.
My pony could graze
without post or fence in sight,
And with a warm wind blowing
beneath the prairie skies at night.

But now my pony
lifts her head into troubled air.
Her hooves paw the ground
and her nostrils flare.

What's in the wind
holds a blank and sterile stare.
My spirit turns
Upon the prairie land, so fair.

Where can my children
ever call the stars by name?
Or know the sparkling waters
from where their spirits came?
In that lonesome valley
where they must walk alone,
what God will they talk to
if the earth is torn and blown?

Freedom is never free.
It costs the changing of the heart.
If no one asks for it to stay,
soon it will depart.
My voice may be a whisper
echoing in din
but the weight of being silent
is a mortal sin.

By my deeds I am written,
and to them I will return.
How I'll be remembered
are through my actions and concern.
And what I have done
for the sake of my children
and their home to come.

Now I cross the great divide.
The still small voice of something,
sounding deep inside.
For the sake of those who follow
I won't forget what's true,
and ride the foothills of my conscience,
doing what I must do.

Dan Kantak

⫸ THE HOME PLACE ⫷

I stopped at the old home place today to pass a little time;
Both of us now show our age—a long ways past our prime.
Since Grandad put his roots down here, a hundred years have passed;
Three generations called it "home"; mine will likely be the last,
Though not the first to claim this place; the Cheyenne and the Sioux
Loved this land and danced their dance, and they must miss it, too.
Our souls are joined in this good earth where no one really leaves,
Yet Time rolls on, the sands run out, the generations grieve.

Abandoned and neglected now, the living here is done,
No one keeps the home fires burning to greet a wandering son.
It sees the seasons come and go, silent and alone,
A ghost ship adrift in a sea of grass, now tossed and overgrown;
Its windows stare out vacantly, and no light shows within,
To light the night or warm with pride for the home it once had been.
The sunburned paint is peeling; once tidy rooms now gather dust,
Where in bygone days our family thrived on faith and love and trust.

Inside, I wander through the rooms, awash in memories;
The fun and laughter I still recall with clarity and ease.
I can hear my mother humming as she went about her chores,
Cooking, mending, and polishing those worn linoleum floors.
The kitchen was her palace where she reigned as sovereign queen,
And we ate like kings on simple fare, not knowing times were lean.
She lent courage, grace, and comfort to our simple way of life,
And held her tears and hid her fears, good mother and good wife.

My dad worked hard from dawn to dark and did it every day,
Broad shoulders in a rancher's world of horses, cows, and hay.
With stubbornness and steady hand he steered our family's course
Through Depression, drought, and other fits of Nature's fickle force.
Where Dad's chair sat, a patient spider plays a waiting game,
As Grandad did for forty years, and then Dad did the same,
Until my brother took it up as keeper of the trust;
Their unraveled dreams now lie among the cobwebs and the dust.

In the bunkhouse where we brothers slept I hear a keening noise,
The mournful moan of prairie wind grieving for those missing boys.
The calving shed is falling down, in its roof a gaping hole;
As snow and rain and sun and wind exact their steady toll;
Where new-born calves in decades past drew first breath safe within,
And stood on trembling legs to fall and struggle up again,
Now only relics of those days remain as memories pale;
A burlap bag, a tattered rope, hang stiffly from a nail.

The horse barn stands in protest and with false hope bravely waits
For return of horse and rider through the sagging corral gates.
In muffled cadence hoofbeats mark the life I left behind,
Where now Champ and Snips and Rocket gallop only in my mind.
Today I stand between two worlds, as different as white from black;
One beckons me to turn around; the other calls me back.
But memories change...are milled by Time...as the river wears the stone,
And I know nothing stays forever, when it's too long left alone.

Roger L. Traweek

⊷ UNDERSTANDING ⊷

By now his gear is all loaded,
But he's having trouble saying goodbye;
He'll watch the flight of a red-tail
As it soars in the evening sky.

He'll stand by the corral in wonder,
Watching the calves mother up,
While his horse paws the ground, restless,
Tied at the end of the truck.

The fire is down to just embers
There where they cooked the last meal.
They've all promised to come back,
Shook hands two or three times on the deal.

But gone are the days of the trail drive,
The bunkhouse and chuck wagon too
Now there's just times he can go help out,
Part of a volunteer crew.

He'll hate to head down the mountain,
He'll linger as long as he can
For it's there where the fir trees surround him
That he truly feels like a man.

When he finally hits the freeway
That's when he's really alone
Even though I'm always here waiting
Anxious to welcome him home.

He doesn't look much like a cowboy
Dressed for work in a business suit,
But the man behind that computer
Really can ride, and rope, and shoot.

He's too old now for the rodeo circuit,
He says that was just life on the fly.
He quit after he won the buckle,
Afraid real life would pass him by.

But always, it's back to the mountains.
I think, in his heart, they're his home.
And he rides there in silent wonder
Where the elk and the cougar roam.

Oh, sometimes I go with him,
And we sleep under a moonlit sky
And watch from the comfort of bedrolls
While centuries of stars march by.

But sometimes at home I am lonely,
Then I turn to the video screen
And watch in teary remembrance
My days as a rodeo queen.

Charlene Schilling

⇥ BRANDING ⇤

The time for branding calves rolled 'round, and Dad was short a crew.
My brother said, "Don't worry Dad, I'll find some help for you."

Bill went around the neighborhood recruiting here and there.
His neighborhood was Country Club, and they said, "Do what? Where?"

"I know that you'll have lots of fun," he told those city folks.
"The ranch is like Bonanza where you all can be cowpokes."

He promised them a beer or two and food fit for a king
If they'd agree to go along and do the branding thing.

Bill could have earned a living selling ice to Eskimos,
So when he took a final count, the yeses beat the nos.

The Greyhound stage that Bill engaged left town at 5 A.M.
Though some did grouse this mid-night roust came much too soon for them.

They reached their destination in an hour and a half,
And those on board were ready to go out and brand a calf.

Dad met them at the pasture gate, and he laid down the rules.
He clearly didn't trust his cows to all these city fools.

"We'll start by walking cattle from the pasture to the pen."
He emphasized the "walking" part, repeating it again.

"Don't get the cows excited now," he warned the eager group.
"This isn't any John Wayne show. We will not shout or whoop."

They fin'lly got the bunch corralled and cows and calves apart.
The calling and the bawling meant the time had come to start.

Les Hoff, a neighbor, branded while the greenhorns held 'em still.
But when they got both hot and tired, they cursed my brother Bill.

Les quickly burned the CU brand onto the calves left side,
While hands inhaled the dust and smoke that smelled of hair and hide.

They struggled with the calves they held, and some of them were tough.
No matter how they did it though, Dad thought they were too rough.

"Now take it easy with those calves," he told them with a frown.
"I don't want you to stress 'em none. Watch how you take 'em down."

"Hey, get your butt down in the dirt." He came on pretty strong.
I figured, whew, his new cow crew just might not last that long.

These bankers, brokers, businessmen weren't used to such abuse,
But Dad went right on yelling if they gave him an excuse.

Bill fin'lly couldn't stand it, so he took our Dad aside.
"You cannot talk to folks like this. These people have their pride."

"I think you should remember, Dad, they came as volunteers.
You'll never get them back again, not in a hundred years."

So dad kept quiet 'till he saw a fellow on his knees.
"Hey, get your butt down in the dirt!" Then he remembered..."Please."

Now in this world of haves and nots, these people were the haves.
Dad didn't think it mattered when it came to branding calves.

They broke for lunch and feasted on baked beans and bar-b-que,
On apple pie and chocolate cake and bowls of chili stew.

'Course balls and shots and horns and ears were also done that day.
By time hands held 300 head, no calves hurt worse than they.

It was a quiet bunch that rode the bus toward home that night,
And those bone-weary cowpokes were a sad depressing sight.

The calves had kicked and stepped on them. Their every muscle ached.
New jeans were smeared with mud and blood, new boots manure-caked.

As they departed for their homes when that long day was through,
They told Bill, "Pardner, don't call us. The next time we'll call you."

And every time that whole year long they needed something done,
Guess who they called. You're right, my friend. My brother was the one.

But next year when the days warmed up, Bill did receive some calls.
"We'd like to help on branding day. Please tell us when it falls."

And when the crowd became so large that things got out of hand,
You had to be invited if you wanted to help brand.

That worked as in the story of Tom Sawyer and the fence.
Folks vied for invitations to the branding day events.

From Canada and Cayman Isles they came by car and plane.
Some came by bus from Littleton. Some came to entertain.

They even came to like our Dad. They said that he was real.
I guess that being tactless was a part of his appeal.

All those who helped year after year had gotten pretty good,
Although in the beginning nobody thought they would.

It doesn't happen anymore. Dad's gone. The ranch is leased.
But this is how it used to be before the brandings ceased.

Jane Morton

WINDMILL MAN

I creak and I groan like an old cowboy's bones
And I have stood here for many years
I did the job that was intended
Seeking only to be mended
Serviced and repaired
But when I was new and shiny
I stood far out on the plains
Converting wind to water
Where there wasn't any rains
And I was never lonely
Watching over sand and hill
Listening to the empty when the wind and I were still

And when the west began evolving
I bore the winds of change
Faithfully revolving above the disappearing range
And when all the land was subdivided
Still I stood my ground
Though my need had long subsided
And I moved further into town
Sometimes I miss that emptiness
Though I still have earth and sky
And the curious attention
Of the kids that pass me by
They say I am the windmill man
So that is what I'll be
If not an object of affection
Then one of curiosity

Oh I still have that yearning
To be out there whirling and twirling
Feeling the wind between my vanes
To be that solitary edifice
Far out on the plains
But like all things made by man
Time has passed me by
Now I creak and I groan
Like an old cowboy's bones
The windmill man am I

Richard Elloyan

THE OLD EMPTY HOUSE

The Old Empty House stands alone on the prairie
The shingles are weathered, the siding is worn
The front step is missing, the wallpaper torn
The glass is all shattered, there is no front door

Old Empty House, what a story you might tell
Of the great western movement and a family so well
They drove your first nail and set the front door
They settled down here to live forever and more

That family is still here out under the grass
Please, Old House, tell me the story of what came to pass
They settled here in eighty-eight with dreams of life and the future to come
The prairie was hard and there was no future for some

The struggle was great with the terrible winter cold and snow drifts piled high
Then, blazing heat from the summer clear sky
The creek ran low and fields were so dry
The locust swept down and they watched their crops die

Old Empty House now so weathered and worn
You stand alone for what they have borne
Their footsteps are gone, their voices long still
But you will remember the unbroken will
They beat this old prairie and changed things around
They made it a land of sound and song

They are out there now under the grass
The great depression came and the dust bowl too
Their friends most left, there was nothing to do
They were too old to go yet too tired to stay
Nothing for them but to wait and pray

Then time came to pass as it always must
And they were buried there beneath the prairie dust
Old Empty House, you molder away
The story you could tell is only yours this day
I stand here now in your empty door
And dream your dreams of what has gone before.

Flavis Bertrand

EMPTY HOUSES

A family once lived there,
Now all that remains
Is an empty little building
Standing lonesome on the plains.

And I'm thinking, as I drive by
That the place looks kinda sad,
And I think about who built it,
And the kinds of dreams they had.

The house itself is still standing,
Though the back porch has fallen down,
Sagebrush took over the doorstep
That the children gathered 'round.

The garden has gone back to grass,
And gooseberries grow in clumps
Around what's left of the Beaverslide
Where the old workhorses scratch their rumps.

Somebody new had bought the place,
And they built them a house of their own,
Nobody else came to live here
After the first ones had gone.

Now, only the breeze wanders through the rooms
Where the children used to play,
But that old house was full of love
Before its family went away.

Denise McRea

HOW LONG WILL THE COWBOY LAST?

Who will I be
Ten thousand years from now?
If someone digs up
What's left of what I am now.

Will they think I'm a soldier
Or a fighter of some kind
from the scars of
Broken bones I'll leave behind

Will they know I'm a puncher
Who spent a lifetime on the range?
Will they know what a cowboy is?
Is this word due so much change?

I guess it don't matter
for I know what I am today.
But will my descendants know
What a cowboy is in their day?

So when I die
Place me in the ground
Don't worry 'bout flowers
Or friends gathered round

Wrap me in a blanket
With spurs on my booted feet
A book by Will James
And my rope rolled up neat.

Send me to meet the Lord
With the tools of my trade
I sure hope I'll need them
In the heaven He's made

But if this world lasts long enough
And the cowboy way is lost.
Maybe, if they dig me up
They'll remember what progress cost.

Robert D. Beene

⇥ NOT WITHOUT A FIGHT ⇤

The price of cows, is mighty low,
The price of feed is high,
The cowman shakes his weary head,
And looks up to the sky,
He prays he'll make another year,
Altho he don't know how,
The bank won't loan no money,
On one more head of cow,
It's been a way of life for him,
This family operation,
He hoped that he could make it thru,
Just one more generation,

He'd seen it when the years were good,
And he'd managed things just right,
But now, no matter where he turns,
It's more and more a fight,
He wonders, should I sell it?
Or just dig my heels in,
He knows he came out good before,
But his patience is runnin' thin,

There's government regulations,
They change it every day,
Why, there's things he can't do on his own damn place,
At least that's what they say,
Then there's all these big investors,
That's buyin' up the land,
They're makin' bird preserves and such,
Now isn't that just grand!

Hell, most of his neighbors sold and left,
or lost it and went belly up,
"What should I do?" he wonders,
As he takes a sip from his cup,
He's never quit before,
Why should he do it now?
Even tho prices are up,
Except of course for cows,

Why can't the cowman take a stand?
It's time to change this mess,
It's time he tells 'em just how he feels,
Instead of bein' depressed,
Stand up, by god, it's time they knew,
What they're doin' isn't right,
If they think they're gonna get this place!
It won't be without a fight...

T. J. Cantin

⇥ TIMES CHANGE ⇤

When I put on my dusty ol' hat, I seem to drift off in time,
To a place where six guns ruled the land, 'round 1859.
Ridin' high, on my pony Ty, we dance across the plains,
Headin' down to a Texas town, words just can't explain.

I feel so proud... Mighty and Loud, to be so Open and Free,
Open Range and Farmlands spread as far as the eye can see.
Outlaws and Indians roam the land, Lawmen and Bounty Hunters too,
A gentle breeze blows through the trees and the Sky is a baby blue.

Things have changed so much since then, but in some ways they never will
I wish I lived when times were simpler, when I could've rode with Wild Bill.
But being a Cowboy, means being Free, workin' hard and workin' good,
And never letting go of that Dream, like no Cowboy ever should.

And though the Twenty-first Century is here,
The Cowboy still lives on,
Living Free, and without Fear,
His Legacy will never be Gone.

Ryan Krantz

OLD HANDS

I RIDE AN OLD PAINT

I ride an old paint and I lead an old Dan,
Goin' to Montana to throw the houlihan.
Feed 'em in the coulees, and water in the draw,
Their tails are all matted and their backs are all raw.

Ride around, little dogies, ride around them slow,
For the fiery and snuffy are a-rarin' to go.

Old Bill Jones had a daughter and a son,
Son went to college, and his daughter went wrong.
His wife got killed in a free-for-all fight,
Still he keeps singin' from mornin' 'till night.

When I die, take my saddle from the wall,
Put it onto my pony, lead him out of his stall.
Tie my bones on his back, an' turn our faces to the West,
We'll ride the prairies that we loved the best.

I've worked in the town and I've worked in the farm,
All I got to show's just this muscle in my arm,
Blisters on my feet, callous on my hand,
And I'm a-goin' to Montana to throw the houlihan.

traditional

AN OLD HAND

He's working in the kitchen of a little cafe
this guy I knew, who was a good hand in his day
back in younger years we'd worked the O bar K
and another spread off to the East, called the Circle Jay
but after being stove up by a rank bull in his way
he hired on to cook instead of cuttin' cows for pay
it's been some years since he used to say
"Gather round the coffee boys, drink n' eat n' pray."
he's over there, I see him, smiling in a friendly way
serving eggs and hash to folks who never may
know this guy's a cowboy
right here in this cafe

Steve Dirksen

LIFE GOES ON

I guess it was his eyes that caught me
As I looked down at his wrinkled skin;
The more than 90 years had taught them
To show pleasure where pain had been.

"Tell me how it used to be Old Timer,"
His eyes lit up as he remembered back;
"I came to this ranch in '68," he said,
"This place was known as Tiger Track.

"We didn't know about modern things.
I was 18 when the end of the war came;
The jingler boss took me on my word.
I stayed and worked at every job the same.

"We ran wild horses ever now and then,
Branded cattle for shipping to the East;
Me and Acey and some boys I forget rode
Night and day. Tough on man and beast.

"We made a hand, though, so I'm told
And didn't mind we never struck it rich;
Many times we talked about leaving here
But, we forever got rid of that itch.

"A man needs roots, my pappy used to say.
So we stayed to work for the DOUBLE T;
We rode hard for the Brand too, Son
They don't make spreads better, you see.

"Times are a changing, Son. It's clear
That things'll never be like they usta be;
Why last year, we rode to camp in a truck
Pulling a trailer of horses. Can you see?

"The Longhorns are gone, faded years ago
And Herefords now graze in their place;
They are brown, red, and yellow and big
And have white hair all over their face.

"I miss the Texas Longhorns too, Son,
They was sturdy and tough on the trail;
I've took 'em to Dodge several times
They managed to survive without fail.

"I'm like them Texas Longhorns, Son,
I too will soon be just out of step;
The sun rises, the sun sets as well
The body once useful no longer has pep.

"Don't fret at my passing, just look ahead,"
He said in a voice that was fadin' low;
"There's a time for going, time for staying
And I reckon its time for me to go."

"I thank you Old Timer." I called his name
As his eyes watered for just one last time;
"You've made my trail easier for work today"
And he passed to his new world sublime.

You see, I've since learned a lesson:
The Lord planned his world this way;
For some, it's leaving, some it's staying,
Right now, seems it's my time to stay.

While here, I've learned a lesson as well
About making life easier for those to come;
Cowboy Poets pour their hearts out in rhyme
To make life happy and pleasant for some.

Tim "Doc" Mason

THE OLD MAN

Every waddie's had an old man,
in his younger days.
That's how he came to learn the truth,
about the cowboy's ways.

He told you tales about stampedes,
when the rain was pouring down,
and how it was, with the ladies,
when you brought the herd to town.

He talked about the early times,
when mean cattle roamed the range.
Said the whole world was going to Hell,
if they didn't make a change.

He showed every thing he knew,
but you still didn't know.
Just when you thought you had it figured out,
you found, it wasn't so.

Then he'd pick you up and dust you off,
and help you down the trail.
Told you, if it was in your heart,
you would never fail.

He was quick, mean and ornery,
but way down deep inside,
there was a big chunk of gentleness,
he just couldn't hide.

He could raise his voice across the remuda,
and quell a nippy mare.
When his cuss words tumbled out,
you'd best not be there.

He kept his reputation clean,
was honest without doubt,
A handshake was all he needed,
to keep the wolves locked out.

He told you to take the time,
to thank the good lord up above.
He's the only one you have,
when the pushing comes to shove.

He taught you it's not what you have,
it's how you passed along the way.
That trouble always came pass,
it never came to stay.

He was sore, lame and staved up,
from rougher younger times.
His tired worn out body,
was just a prison for his mind.

Old men have to ride on,
I hope through heaven's gate.
I hope Saint Peter tips his hat,
and they don't have to wait.

I hope they find a little spread,
out on the cloudy plains.
Where the sun shines down on them,
where it never rains.

When a young man comes along,
who's what I used to be.
I hope I leave, something behind,
like my Old Man left for me.

Ezra Spur

BANKIN' WITH AN OLD COWBOY

I met an old cowboy in front of the bank today,
He was acting hesitant, and unsure of himself
In an old-timer's kind of way.

I could tell that he knew about cattle and horses
and keeping pastures green...
But he didn't have a clue about working that ATM machine!

Now, I thought about minding my own business you see,
But that old peeler was fast losing his dignity.
Cowboys are my heros, Rough, Tough and Strong,
And watching him fumble around, well, it was just wrong!

So I said, "Could I help you out old pard?
These here new fangled machines can be tricky and hard!"
"Well," he said slowly, "I just come to get some of my pay,
I've got my card here but..." Then his voice just trailed away.

I asked if he knew his P.I.N., as I pointed to the slot for his card to go in.
He slowly poked in those digits while I politely stared at the ground.
And...
For that moment there was silence between us with nary a sound.

Then he said, "I usually do my banking with the ladies inside,
But, my pickup had a flat and it slowed down my ride."

I sensed his embarrassment as he reached for his dough,
So I quickly changed the subject and asked,
"Do you think its going to snow?"

He spit some chew, and looked at the sky
He paused, shook his head and let out a sigh.
I knew it was his turn to teach and to shout, for weather in the West
Was a topic this old puncher knew something about!

"Naw!" he said, almost with a bawl,
"first snow won't fly till later this fall...
Them clouds are too light, they'll just be drifting on by."
He paused for a bit and let out another sigh.

Then we talked of breakin horses and best ways to treat cattle,
Then we even talked about the right way to care for your saddle!
As we talked about ranchin and country ways,
I heard the proud old cowboy speak of better days.

He talked of cold mountain mornings, roaming meadows and streams,
And driving the great herds of cattle and chasing a young man's dreams.
This cowboy's voice was now ringing steady and true
As he recalled the glories and struggles that he'd been through.

Seems he started punchin when he was just thirteen.
He worked for his old man and the neighbors
And got his schoolin in-between.

He wanted me to know that he saddle-bummed for a few years just to
      make his way,
That there were lots of long hard hours and not too much pay!

Then he spoke of learning the lessons of a cowboy's life.
"Some smarts," he said, "come pretty easy and others, only with some
pain and strife."

The rancher said, "Cowboy knowledge can come from the strangest sources,
and son, I've learned from the best of men and the sorriest of horses."

I asked him of all the lessons he'd learned each day
if he had a bit of wisdom to throw my way.
He paused, as he thought, "Well shucks," he said,
"You're a sharp young man who's found his head,
I can see you're well on the road,
But, since you asked, here's a thought I might unload...

"It's not important if what you learn makes you rich or poor,
But just ask yourself...What's this learning really for?

"If it has a purpose and heeding it will make you a better man,
then learn it well, for it's part of the maker's plan."
His voice again was steady and did not sway.
"Some things you learn can come back," he said, "in a funny kind of way.

"Now, I'm sure your modern skills with this bank machine are no big deal,
But son, you don't know how good your help made this old cowboy feel."

He shook my hand and climbed into his pickup door.
He said, "Thanks for your patience and teachin me what all those gizmos
and buttons were for."

I watched as his old truck slowly pulled out of the lot,
but I couldn't help thinking what my time may have bought,
Yea, I helped the old fella you could say...
But, I wondered, Who really did the teaching today?

Dan Faught

RIDE FOR THE BRAND

The dismounted young cowboy asked the old hand,
"What does it mean when they say 'Ride for the brand'?"
The grizzled old-timer's age seemed to drop years,
And he sat straight up in the saddle as he surveyed the steers.

"It means a lot of different things, son.
It has a lot to do with what's lost and what's won.
I ain't talking about gambling, but earning a living,
Hard work, trust, respect, taking, and giving.

"It means you don't never foul up the land,
And you don't take unfair advantage or rob.
You work hard, even when the work's rough as a cob.
That's part of what it means to ride for the brand.

"It means you help your neighbors and your friends,
And you help even strangers just passing through.
It means you hire on a hungry saddle-tramp
Who needs a place to winter past the cold and damp.

"It means you don't let the poor folks go hungry
Just 'cause they're down and short on grub and luck.
And it means that you don't work just for a buck,
But 'cause you need work like water's needed by a tree.

"It means you can be trusted, and that you trust each pard,
To do the chores that are needed, no matter how hard,
'Cause you're all riding for the same outfit,
And you're all striving together to benefit it.

"It means you keep searching for that one last stray,
Even though it's the end of the day,
Even though you'd rather stop and go to town.
It means you don't lay your responsibility down.

"It means you give an honest day's work for an honest day's wage,
Whether you're in the corral or out riding the range.
Every job's important, and there ain't none that ain't.
It's not the cowboy way to quit though it'd be easier to say 'I cain't.'

"It means you'll not complain when you help dig a well,
Nor even have to be asked to spell a tired cowpoke who's stove-up.
It means you'll work with others as well as you'll work alone,
And that even when you're tired to the bone, you'll cowboy-up.

"That's what it means, that, and a whole lot more.
It means that you've got pride in yourself, your job, and the land.
So saddle-up. Toughen-up. Cowboy-up. Be a man.
Ride for the brand."

Paul Harwitz

A BOY'S DREAM

As I see him sittin' there on the edge of that bed
I think of all the wisdom and knowledge gathered in his head
All the experience from hard lessons learned
Rough horses, hard work, and the women that left him burned
As I see him reach for his boots off to the side
I know he wears them and his hat all with pride
He walks into the tack house and picks an old saddle up off the floor
He walks over to the grey and throws it on like he's done a thousand
    times before
He isn't puttin' on a show, he sure ain't actin'
Everything he does is like a natural reaction
He was born a cowboy and will go out the same way
I know his day is comin' but when, no one can say
He's lived a long life and done a lot of things you see
I just hope I listen and learn when he talks to me
I admire him for everything he's done
Lord knows it's been tough and not all fun
Sittin' round the house with really nothing to do
Brother says he wants to be a cop, then asks me, "How about you?"
I think about it long and hard, again and again
Then I turn towards the old cowboy and say "I want to be just like him."

John Cook

SONGS LESS TRAVELED

When I was young our dad would sing a song
of Cowboys, horses and love gone wrong.
He'd take us back in time the stories we'd hear,
We rode along as he sang knowing he was near.

And we'd ride that Bad Brahmer Bull and the Chisholm Trail,
We went to Cowboy Heaven, Tied a Knot in that Devil's Tail,
Rode the Strawberry Roan, wore that Continental Suite,
Heard the Jingle Jangle Jingle, and saw the one they called the Brute.
We'd hear that Coyote Song, and the Cattle Call,
Take me back to my boots and saddle when the work's all done this fall.

When it was time for bed or I was feeling low,
I'd ask my dad to sing a song, a song of long ago.
And before he'd finish a smile would cross my face,
As we rode off together, another time, another place.

And we'd ride that Bad Brahmer Bull and the Chisholm Trail,
Go to Cowboy Heaven, Tie a Knot in that Devil's Tail,
Rode that Strawberry Roan, wore that Continental Suite,
Heard the Jingle Jangle Jingle and saw the one the called the Brute.
I'd hear the Coyotes song and the Cattle Call,
Take me back to my boots and saddle when the work's all done this fall.

Now when I am traveling alone and there is nothing but time
A tune comes drifting in and gathers in my mind,
I hum along as the words are unraveled,
Then start singing a song of long ago,
those songs less traveled.

Though time may be different from the wild west then
there is a magic and a wonder of how it all had been,
So let the stories live and your imaginations bring,
A distant memory as you hear a cowboy sing.

And ride that Bad Brahmer Bull and the Chisholm Trail,
Go to Cowboy Heaven Tie a Knot in that Devil's Tail.
Ride that Strawberry Roan, wear that Continental Suite,
Hear the Jingle Jangle Jingle and see the one they call the Brute
Hear that Coyote song and the Cattle Call
Take me back to my boots and saddle when the work's all done this fall.

So hum along as those words are unraveled
So you can sing a song of long ago,
Those songs now less traveled.

A. Kathy Moss

HOME ON THE
AUSTRALIAN RANGE

❧ THE MAN FROM SNOWY RIVER ☙

There was movement at the station, for the word had passed around
    That the colt from old Regret had got away,
And had joined the wild bush horses—he was worth a thousand pound,
    So all the cracks had gathered to the fray.
All the tried and noted riders from the stations near and far
    Had mustered at the homestead overnight,
For the bushmen love hard riding where the wild bush horses are,
    And the stock-horse snuffs the battle with delight.

There was Harrison, who made his pile when Pardon won the cup,
    The old man with his hair as white as snow;
But few could ride beside him when his blood was fairly up—
    He would go wherever horse and man could go.
And Clancy of the Overflow came down to lend a hand,
    No better horseman ever held the reins;
For never horse could throw him while the saddle-girths would stand,
    He learnt to ride while droving on the plains.

And one was there, a stripling on a small and weedy beast,
    He was something like a racehorse undersized,
With a touch of Timor pony—three parts thoroughbred at least—
    And such as are by mountain horsemen prized.
He was hard and tough and wiry—just the sort that won't say die—
    There was courage in his quick impatient tread;
And he bore the badge of gameness in his bright and fiery eye,
    And the proud and lofty carriage of his head.

But still so slight and weedy, one would doubt his power to stay,
    And the old man said, "That horse will never do
For a long and tiring gallop—lad, you'd better stop away,
    Those hills are far too rough for such as you."
So he waited sad and wistful—only Clancy stood his friend—
    "I think we ought to let him come," he said;
    "I warrant he'll be with us when he's wanted at the end,
    For both his horse and he are mountain bred."

"He hails from Snowy River, up by Kosciusko's side,
　　Where the hills are twice as steep and twice as rough,
Where a horse's hoofs strike firelight from the flint stones every stride,
　　The man that holds his own is good enough.
And the Snowy River riders on the mountains make their home,
　　Where the river runs those giant hills between;
I have seen full many horsemen since I first commenced to roam,
　　But nowhere yet such horsemen have I seen."

So he went—they found the horses by the big mimosa clump—
　　They raced away towards the mountain's brow,
And the old man gave his orders, "Boys, go at them from the jump,
　　No use to try for fancy riding now.
And, Clancy, you must wheel them, try and wheel them to the right.
　　Ride boldly, lad, and never fear the spills,
For never yet was rider that could keep the mob in sight,
　　If once they gain the shelter of those hills."

So Clancy rode to wheel them—he was racing on the wing
　　Where the best and boldest riders take their place,
And he raced his stock-horse past them, and he made the ranges ring
　　With the stockwhip, as he met them face to face.
Then they halted for a moment, while he swung the dreaded lash,
　　But they saw their well-loved mountain full in view,
And they charged beneath the stockwhip with a sharp and sudden dash,
　　And off into the mountain scrub they flew.

Then fast the horsemen followed, where the gorges deep and black
　　Resounded to the thunder of their tread,
And the stockwhips woke the echoes, and they fiercely answered back
　　From cliffs and crags that beetled overhead.
And upward, ever upward, the wild horses held their way,
　　Where mountain ash and kurrajong grew wide;
And the old man muttered fiercely, "We may bid the mob good day,
　　No man can hold them down the other side."

When they reached the mountain's summit, even Clancy took a pull,
    It well might make the boldest hold their breath,
The wild hop scrub grew thickly, and the hidden ground was full
    Of wombat holes, and any slip was death.
But the man from Snowy River let the pony have his head,
    And he swung his stockwhip round and gave a cheer,
And he raced him down the mountain like a torrent down its bed,
    While the others stood and watched in very fear.

He sent the flint stones flying, but the pony kept his feet,
    He cleared the fallen timber in his stride,
And the man from Snowy River never shifted in his seat—
    It was grand to see that mountain horseman ride.
Through the stringy barks and saplings, on the rough and broken ground,
    Down the hillside at a racing pace he went;
And he never drew the bridle till he landed safe and sound,
    At the bottom of that terrible descent.

He was right among the horses as they climbed the further hill,
    And the watchers on the mountain standing mute,
Saw him ply the stockwhip fiercely, he was right among them still,
    As he raced across the clearing in pursuit.
Then they lost him for a moment, where two mountain gullies met
    In the ranges, but a final glimpse reveals
On a dim and distant hillside the wild horses racing yet,
    With the man from Snowy River at their heels.

And he ran them single-handed till their sides were white with foam.
    He followed like a bloodhound on their track,
Till they halted cowed and beaten, then he turned their heads for home,
    And alone and unassisted brought them back.
But his hardy mountain pony he could scarcely raise a trot,
    He was blood from hip to shoulder from the spur;
But his pluck was still undaunted, and his courage fiery hot,
    For never yet was mountain horse a cur.

And down by Kosciusko, where the pine-clad ridges raise
    Their torn and rugged battlements on high,
Where the air is clear as crystal, and the white stars fairly blaze
    At midnight in the cold and frosty sky,
And where around the Overflow the reedbeds sweep and sway
    To the breezes, and the rolling plains are wide,
The man from Snowy River is a household word today,
    And the stockmen tell the story of his ride.

A. B. Paterson, 1890

⚜ I HAVE SEEN THE LAND ⚜

I have been to where the sun sets with a vengeance,
And burns the sky with red and ochre hues.
I have lived where man and his dependents
Take solace from the best of nature's views.

I've seen the open plain of the Savannah,
Where brolgas dance and jabirus take flight.
I've watched the white corella in the evening,
Summon in the darkness of the night.

I've searched the water-holes of northern rivers,
Before the wet awakes the mighty flood,
Where crocodiles have gathered in their numbers
To moisten skin where all that's left is mud.

I've watched the summer storms create the fires
That glow as night-time falls upon the land.
I've walked the blackened ground where man aspires
To forge a living where the ant-hills stand.

I've listened to the rolling sound of thunder
As lightning strikes the ground with awesome power.
While raging storms advance across the landscape
Renewing life with every passing hour.

And I have seen the rivers as they're rising,
Pounding banks; re-shaping at a whim.
Yes, I have heard the rumble of the flash flood
And had that rush of fear from deep within.

I've flown across a landscape etched with beauty,
Where rivers snake their way towards the sea.
I've watched as waves sweep clean the endless beaches,
Fuelled gently by the early evening breeze.

I've been to where the wedgetail soars intently,
Watched as they, for movement on the ground.
And as I've floated high above Australia,
I've come to know this country's glory bound.

And I am everything they call Australian,
For I am every soul upon this land.
And for all time, as nature is my soul-mate,
For my country proudly will I stand.

Graham Dean

❧ AFTER THE WET ❧

While I'm working at the coal face deep down below the ground,
and hear timber cracking with a sharp and tortured sound,
I peer into the darkness through the cap lamp's feeble glow,
thinking of the stock camps on the stations I know.

Where grass is waving stirrup high out on the black soil plains,
and the creeks and gullies brimming full from the yearly rains.
for now the wet has ended on the stations in the north
and it's time for mustering camps to once again go forth.

There's a feeling of excitement and air is full of sounds
as station camps are starting out on their yearly rounds.
From the plains of Coorabulka to box scrubs on Loraine,
they're running in fresh horses to station yards again.

Gates and panels rattle as the horses are drafted out,
they're stirring up the dust and dirt as they mill about,
and horses that are fat and fresh will test the stockmen's skills,
but ringers look forward to the challenge and the thrills.

The camp cooks call the ringers when the morning star is bright
and they're saddled up and riding before the sky is light.
They're rounding up fat bullocks from the river on Nardoo
and running in big pikers from scrubs at Manbulloo.

Where branding fires are glowing in the yards at Eight Mile Camp,
they're pulling up big micks to the bronco-branding ramp,
mixing in with smoke and dust and the smell of scorching hair,
the sound of bawling cows and calves comes floating on the air.

The sound of stockwhips echo from scrubs on Inverleigh,
where along the Flinders River cattle still run free
And out there on The Barkley mirages shimmer on the plains
where on the air there's music of bells and hobble chains.

So when this shift is over and my cap lamp's in the rack,
I'll draw my pay and tell them I won't be coming back.
For I'll be heading up to Queensland's cattle camps once more,
to some outback station where I used to work before.

For stockmen are a nomadic lot who cannot settle down,
we have good intentions when we get a job in town.
But when the Wet's over and grass is high out on the plain,
we roll our swags and head out to stock camps once again.

Jack Sammon

❧ JUST A DANCE ☙

I saw him at a local dance in an outback country place,
And was immediately attracted to his strong and sunburnt face.
A stockman, tall and rugged, in his brightly patterned shirt,
A contrast to his jeans and boots with a touch of outback dirt.

His laughter rang across the hall as he chatted with a mate,
A haunted sort of laugh—and I could only contemplate
The kind of life this stockman led, of cattle, dust and flies,
The spirit of the outback, as seen through distant eyes.

The country band struck up a jive and his boots tapped to the beat,
And then the first of many girls was swept upon her feet.
His energy exploded into a rhythm fast and sure
That left his partners gasping; and clearly wanting more!

He was popular on the dance floor as each girl took their chance,
Hoping for a sign that this was more than just a dance.
But when the song was over, he moved on again once more
To whisk another hopeful to his realm upon the floor.

For he was searching for a partner to end his lonely days,
A companion to make his life complete in, oh, so many ways.
And one with spirit to match his own, to hold within his heart
And walk beside him down the track to make a brand new start.

And so I watched this stockman, and I could not understand
How a man with much to offer could still hold an empty hand.
And just as I was wondering how fate had kept him free—
He was suddenly beside my chair with his hand outstretched to me.

My surprise soon turned to pleasure, and we danced away the night
And talked about all sorts of things to make the world all right.
But soon I came to realise that he hadn't left my side
To go in search of others—and in my heart I cried

'Cos, through all the fun and laughter he'd surely lost another chance—
You see, I was just a stand in. To me, t'was just a dance!
For on my hand, a band of gold was there for all to see,
And more than just a friendship between us could never be.

I left him at the local dance in an outback country place.
A man in search of someone—haunted look still on his face.
And I wonder where he is today, has he found his one true chance
To hold onto a treasure found, when it's more than just a dance.

Louise K. Dean

EVER FAITHFUL
AND MAVERICKS

BALLAD OF THE DROVER

Across the stony ridges,
Across the rolling plain,
Young Harry Dale, the drover,
Comes riding home again.
And well his stock-horse bears him,
And light of heart is he,
And stoutly his old packhorse
Is trotting by his knee.

Up Queensland way with cattle
He's traveled regions vast,
And many months have vanished
Since home-folks saw him last.
He hums a song of someone
He hopes to marry soon;
And hobble-chains and camp-ware
Keep jingling to the tune.

Beyond the hazy dado
Against the lower skies
And yon blue line of ranges
The station homestead lies.
And thitherward the drover
Jogs through the lazy noon,
While hobble-chains and camp-ware
Are jingling to a tune.

An hour has filled the heavens
With storm-clouds inky black;
At times the lightning trickles
Around the drover's track;
But Harry pushes onward,
His horses' strength he tries,
In hope to reach the river
Before the flood shall rise.

The thunder, pealing o'er him,
Goes rumbling down the plain;
And sweet on thirsty pastures
Beats fast the splashing rain;
Then every creek and gully
Sends forth its tribute flood
The river runs a banker,
All stained with yellow mud.

Now Harry speaks to Rover,
The best dog on the plains,
And to his hardy horses,
And strokes their shaggy manes:
"We've breasted bigger rivers
When Hoods were at their height,
Nor shall this gutter stop us
From getting home tonight!"

The thunder growls a warning,
The blue, forked lightning's gleam;
The drover turns his horses
To swim the fatal stream.
But, oh! the flood runs stronger
Than e'er it ran before;
The saddle-horse is failing,
And only half-way o'er!

When flashes next the lightning
The flood's grey breast is blank;
A cattle-dog and packhorse
Are struggling up the bank.
But in the lonely homestead
The girl shall wait in vain
He'll never pass the stations
In charge of stock again.

The faithful dog a moment
Lies panting on the bank,
Then plunges through the current
To where his master sank.
And round and round in circles
He fights with failing strength,
Till, gripped by wilder waters,
He fails and sinks at length.

Across the flooded lowlands
And slopes of sodden loam
The packhorse struggles bravely
To take dumb tidings home;
And mud-stained, wet, and weary,
He goes by rock and tree,
With clanging chains and tinware
All sounding eerily.

Henry Lawson, 1889

⌒ FROM HELL TO HEART ⌒

We'd watched the herd for weeks on end and learned their habits good.
Lead mare was smart and cunning, the stallion extra shrewd.
His chest was wide, his legs were black from knees down to his hooves.
His eyes were wise and his blood bay coat was scarred with scrapes and grooves.
"He's all your'n," my pardner said, with a crooked half-way grin,
"But just in case this don't work out, I'll notify your kin."
Bay 'peared to be 'bout 5 'r 6—with wild ones ya just cain't tell.
His image was hard and he was sly. He was the stud from hell!
Ol' Jake 'n me, we dogged that herd for nigh on 4 'r 5 days.
We took turns keepin' 'em movin' and when they were water crazed
We eased 'em to the canyon where they'd always gone to drink.
They all were tired and thirsty, their flanks a showin' shrink.
We'd built a brushy rampart near the narrows goin' in.
The canyon walls would hold 'em fast and make a dandy pen.
The stud was actin' wary, he knew it wasn't right
But the water scent was in his nose and almost in his sight.
Lead mare was sippin' from the spring, the herd was closin' fast.
The needed water cold and clear was their reward at last.
My prize stepped forward, rattled his nose—we rushed to fill the gate.
He whirled around to get away, eyes filled with fear and hate.
He tried the fence, we waved and yelled, hopin' it wouldn't fail.
The air grew thick as the whole herd spooked creatin' a dusty gale.
Ol' Jake's a hollerin', "Git the ropes, Catch 'im b'fore he drinks!"

We roped the stud midst all that dust hopin' the ropes don't kink.
Jake dallied round a cedar stump, the rope smokin' as it slipped
But he dug in with all his might and finally got a grip.
The stud hit the end and flipped around, bawled and tried again.
The ropes held fast and the horse went down but leaped up fit to win.
His ears laid back, he gnashed his teeth, white foam of anger flyin'.
He chose to fight an get away or damn sure die a tryin'!
We got 'im down and tied his legs and gave ourselves a rest.
Those weary days of doggin' herd had put us to the test.
We let Bay up and snubbed 'im close and tied up one of his feet.
Threw on the kack an' cinched 'er down as he quivered in the heat.
"OK Slim," ol' Jakey says, "Git ready fer a ride
I'll drop the poles to let ya out and keep the herd inside.

That hoss'll go who knows how long, but he's yourn' when he's done.
Hang on to whatever ya can. That hoss is gonna run!
 Step up and take yourself a seat, then I'll cut 'im loose
God have mercy on your soul!"
 I did my part, Jake dropped the poles
And the stud saw the hole!
 He stood there for an instant as he felt me fork his spine
Then hell broke loose as he bawled and bucked and raced for timberline.
 I don't recall the course we took but that cayuse gave his best.
He bucked and run and run and bucked without a second's rest.
 I was a hangin' onto whatever I could grab
Hopin' he didn't stumble or we'd both be one big scab.
 Ol' Jake was follerin' some behind to gather me if I blew
But I stayed put a hearin' his words, "That hoss belongs to you!"
 After what seemed eternity and I felt my body spent,
That wild horse stopped in his tracks and to his side he went.
 I rolled aside and let him lay, he closed his eyes with a moan.
I laid there stiff, too tired to move. Jake jogged up on his roan.
 "Is he daid?" Jake drawled as he reached me his canteen.
I shook my head, Bay flicked an ear as I swallered down a stream.
 I rubbed his face with my wet kerchief and wet his lips and gums.
He wanted more and his tongue licked out so I rubbed it with my thumb.
 I held him down and wiped him more and talked to him real soft.
He was so tired and thirsty he couldn't even cough.
 At last he gained a bit of strength and stumbled to his feet.
He stood there kind o' wobblin' but still a true athlete.
 I coaxed him with the water to take a step or two.
He fought the lead half-heartedly but knew that he was through.
 That was back eight years ago and the memory's clear as glass.
We've been a team most every day and he's turned first class.
 Some of his mares and colts we kept to give the ranch a start,
And the stud we thought had come from hell turned out to be all heart.

Lynne Hendrickson

⇜ THE APPALOOSA ⇝

Where arctic winds howl
And sweep the Palouse,
The brave Nez Perce Indian
Bred a Spotted Cayuse.

"A gift of the wind?"
They whispered in wonder.
Sired by the lightning,
Born of the thunder.

Eyes wide and wild
They could see all around,
one orb cold blue
Its partner dark brown.

The face powdered white
By the hard driven snow,
Its mane looked like smoke
The tail black as coal.

Ayeee! This one's rump
Stands many hands high
with freckles as thick
As stars in the sky.

Sprung from those roots
Came "Frosty," my horse,
A knot head Appaloosa
The devil its source.

I groomed and fed him
He stared with wild eyes,
And faster than lightning
His temper would rise.

His ears pinned back
his nostrils held wide,
He whirled round and bit me
Right in the side.

I led him to pasture,
I put out his lick,
I curried his coat
Until shiny and slick.

He kicked me and dumped me,
Scraped me out of the saddle
On low hanging limbs,
I was losing the battle!

At last I decided
to give him his head.
I'd ride Frosty out
Until he was dead!

With the bit in his teeth
and his wild crazy eyes,
He bucked, then he screamed,
And reared t'ward the skies.

Just when my seat
was incredibly sore
from slapping the saddle,
He crow-hopped some more.

I flew through the air,
I soared like a bird.
His pawing the ground
was the last thing I heard.

Our wrangler named Payute,
Asked for that horse
"Take him," I said,
"I've sure had the course."

The next time I saw them
I watched from the porch,
A proud, handsome Indian
Sittin' tall on that horse.

I knew as I watched them,
That some ancient force
Reunited that Indian
and Frosty, his horse.

Rusty Calhoun

⇌ BACKWARD R DOUBLE BAR D ⇋

There is a rancho way out West,
that's where I want to be.
It's a spread that's like no other,
and it was made for you and me.

There the water's pure the grass is sweet,
and the hay always newly mown.
You'll never have to leave this ranch,
until you're fully grown.

Yep, that's what I tell all the dogies,
so they're happy while they're here.
Just drink the water, eat the grass,
and forget that you're a steer.

Just live your life in neutral,
because neutered is what you are.
And don't buy in to all that bull,
about someday being a star.

A bull has to fight for all he gets;
he has to always be the best.
He never can be off his guard,
nor can he ever rest.

A bull's life isn't all that grand,
though it's filled with matrimony.
When an old bull has to cash it in,
he winds up as baloney.

Steers always get to laze about,
eating grass and drinking water.
And a steer is never traumatized
by the behavior of his daughter.

If you were a bull, just think about
the things you'd have to do.
You'd be driven from the cows in section one,
to the cows in section twenty-two.

And when you've done your service there,
there's that bunch down by the creek.
When they're all taken care of,
you'd best not be feeling weak.

Cause there's still the heifers in section twelve,
and the matrons in section seven.
Then the 3-year olds in section eight,
and the 8-year olds in eleven.

Then start again in section four,
move on to section five.
Hey Bull you better shake a leg,
come on, let's look alive!

The cows in section twenty-six
are sure a muddy mess,
But you can't wait for them to shower,
nor for them to undress.

Now jump in the back of the truck,
get chauffeured to section two.
You better hurry up Bull,
there's still a lot to do.

So many cows, so little time,
I always hear them say.
That old bull's resting on his knees;
he probably stopped to pray.

But as a steer you just stroll about,
your life is never hustle-bustle.
Your body's nice and tender,
no knots of sinew and of muscle.

I see you're growing up real nice,
I think you're in your prime.
If you'd like a long vacation,
try a French-Mediterranean clime.

I'll send you to an abattoir,
I'm sure you'll think it grand.
An abattoir? Just wait and see,
then your life you'll understand.

Though the grass is always greener,
don't envy the old bull in the palace.
Cause the foreman told me yesterday,
he went to a slaughterhouse in Dallas.

David J. Dague

❧ BLIZZARD CALF ❧

late spring storms are deadly
much like a loaded gun
clouds burdened like a pregnant cow
before her birthing's done
snowflakes fell at a frantic pace
rushing headlong to the earth
when we looked out we realized
there was little cause for mirth

trapped as we were in my hideaway
this tiny dugout made of sod
two miles from the safety of our parents' home
at the mercy of the hand of God
the fangs of the storm that day snuffed out
the life of many a Two Bar cow
as the wind's bitter snarl
chased them off the cliff at Mitchell's Brow

in a three foot drift just outside the door
we found a nearly frozen calf
when Davey brought it in and thawed it out
its antics made us laugh
for three days we ate unsalted beans
burned chips to keep us warm
the two of us kids and that darned calf
but we lasted out that storm

through the quagmire left by melting snow
we finally found the track
but that fool calf had adopted us
followed us all the way back
the Two Bar hands told us to keep him
cause his mama couldn't be found
some said that calf was lucky to find us
but it was the other way around

Bobbie Gallup

⇌ THE CONVERSATION ⇌

This cowboy and his dog
Were travelin in his truck
From a Rodeo
Were they'd left their last buck
The cowboy needed to talk
He was feelin worn and beat
So he turned to his best friend
Sittin next to him on the seat
He said "Dog we've seen better days,
When it seemed I couldn't lose."
"When you were eatin Alpo,
And I didn't have the blues."
The dog let out a moan
And laid his head on his owner's thigh
Then looked up at his pal
With a sad and compassionate eye
As the cowboy stroked his dog
He vented his frustrations of the day
He talked of missed opportunities
And his recent lack of pay
He said, "The things I used to do with ease,
Now make my body sore,
I don't bounce like I used too,
You know, we're not pups anymore.
It seems the simple tasks we do
Get harder with every day,
Shoot, it wasn't that long ago
When our work seemed more like play.
Dog gone it!, I know what you're thinkin,
That nothin stays the same,
And feeling sorry for myself won't stop
Anything from makin change."
And as the dog let out another moan
He rolled over on his back

Then as his owner scratched his belly
He stretched his body out long and flat
The cowboy said, "You know I've tried
To give you the best life that I could,
And when things weren't the greatest,
It seemed you always understood
So hold on to your understanding ways
While I enter this next go-round
And we'll find out together what happens next
And which new road we'll travel down
Yea, I know, quitin this way of life
Doesn't mean my life's at an end
It's just I feel sad, like at a funeral
Where I'm sayin good-bye to an old friend."
Then the dog whimpered, as if he understood,
And pawed the cowboys chest
His compassion made the cowboy feel better
So he scratched his friend's wide breast
"Relax old friend and be calm," he said,
"You know, sometimes change is good
Heck maybe now our lifestyle will improve
Like we always knew it could
Come to think, we've been kinda bored
With this danged ole' rodeo trail
Shucks, it seems like here lately
That we've both been chasin our tail
And besides it's not like we have to completely quit
There's still plenty of fun to be had
You know the more we talk about it
Being a weekend warrior doesn't sound half-bad."
The cowboy took a long deep breath
And let out a bittersweet sigh
Then smiled down at the friend
Laying a-sleep, upside down on his thigh
"I think it's a good thing we had this talk"
He said as the dog exhaled a loud snore
"I see it did you some good,
And you're not so worried anymore."

Risky Betts

⇜ THE GOOD MOTHER ⇝

It was time to fetch the cattle home
From off the Flint Hills grass,
We strung up a panel catch pen
And hoped that it would pass,
We saddled up the ponies,
All day we rode 'em hard
To gather all the cattle in
And pen 'em in that yard.
Amid the blowing and bawling
We sorted big from small,
And loaded up according,
'Till we thought we had 'em all.
Back home on winter pasture
We turned the trailers out;
One little heifer stuck around,
Couldn't budge her with a shout.
She watched as little babies
Hopped and paired with mom,
Then eyed the empty trailer
And promptly lost her calm.
All night she stood and bawled
Her grief 'till it would break your heart:
It didn't take a genius
To know we'd torn a pair apart.
The only place the babe could be
Was back there in the Hills,
So we loaded up and headed back,
Me and Danny Wills.
We rode that pasture half a day
'Til Danny sighed and said,
"If she left a calf behind her here,
It's more than likely dead."
We'd sat ourselves to rest a spell
In the shadow of the truck
When of a sudden Dan sat up,
Said, "Can you believe the luck?"
He pointed to a clump of grass
That sported two red ears;

Said, "That's just the darndest thing
That I have seen in years!
He's stayed right where she put him,
He never made a sound;
But thanks to her persistence
Her baby has been found!"

Margo Udelle Imes

THE LAST OF THE HERD

The old buffalo walked slowly
Looking for a place to settle down
To hunker down and rest a bit
On a warm patch of ground

Out in the distance the storm clouds
Were building up again
Looking dark and forbidding
And as ugly as sin

It had been a rough winter
All the way from last fall
But this old bull had seen more rough winters
Than he cared to recall

Right now the old fella
Just wanted to lay for a spell
He was old and tired
And he wasn't feeling real well

He found himself a spot
That seemed extra warm and dry
And let himself down
With a grunt and a sigh

As he lay, he let his mind wander
Back to the journey that had been his life
All the days he had lived
Through good times and strife

The warm summer days
Spent grazing on grass
The long cold winters
That never seemed to pass

The rituals of spring
The mating and the fights
The brisk winds of fall
And the ever-longer nights

He had seen it all
Had this old guy
Many, many moons
He had seen pass by

He used to run with others
His friends and his kin
But they were all gone now
Taken by bloody men

They used to cover the plains
And they sounded like thunder
But now he's alone
All the rest had gone under

He had watched them all die
In bunches and ones
Slaughtered by those hunters
With their big roaring guns

So now he's the end
The last of his kind
And the only place he saw them
Was in the back of his mind

So he laid there and thought
Of the times he had known
A solitary warrior
Living all alone

The wind suddenly grew colder
As the snow started to fall
But over the rising wind
He heard a familiar call

It was the call of the Herd
Home he knew he must go
It would be warmer there
There would be no more snow

So he closed his weary eyes
Laid down his grizzled head
And in just a few seconds
The old buffalo was dead

He's free to roam forever
With his family and friends
On a prairie with no winter
Where the grass never ends

The old bull lives now
In the fields of the past
And I can still see him
When my mind I cast

They say that the buffalo
Were big, dumb brutes
But to me, they're America
They're a big part of my roots

I love those big creatures
And I know they're not all dead
But there used to be millions more
Close to extinction they were led

Sometimes I wish I lived
In those olden days of yore
So I could see those vast herds
The way they were before.

Ron Loof

⌒ IN DEFENSE OF DONKEYS ⌒

I've bailed off 'a horses and bucked off 'a mules
Been stove up and fed up. I'm wantin' new rules!

So I hitched up my trailer and gassed up my truck
Went and bought me a donkey, I'm changin' my luck!

See, a donkey descends from a sensible lot.
Snorty and snuffy or broncy he's not.

He gives each situation no more than it's due.
He's cautious and careful. He thinks a thing through.

A donkey is calm where a horse comes apart.
Why, even a mule's only half as smart!

But beware: He's a tough and shrewd character judge.
If he finds you unworthy, why, he just won't budge!

And hold to yur temper, or Mr. Long-ears will hold you a hostage.
(You'll be there for years.)

'Cause he takes no truck with the volatile sort.
You think you can force him? HA! Don't sell him short!

But prove he can trust you. Be patient and fair...
And a better trail pardner ain't found anywhere!

He'll pack you through country that's brushy and rough.
Might even cross creeks (If he likes you enough.)

So just pay no mind to them horse and mule folks.
When they laugh and poke fun. Let 'em tell their "ass" jokes.

'Cause your day is comin'. Be certain! It will!
Maybe crossin' a ridge or ASScending a hill.

When something will spook 'em. Some trivial matter
Will cause 'em to blow up, get wall-eyed and scatter.

They'll unload their riders and packs, flatten fences.
A coffee pot rattles and the buckin' commences.

Now all this just might catch your donkey off guard
But he won't run real fast and he won't go too far.

Most likely he'll startle, then walk on real quiet.
A' leavin' behind all that wreckage and riot.

Oh, they'll get 'em gathered and drug into camp
Their eggs will be busted, their bedrolls all damp.

Meanwhile, you've had your supper. Your bed will be dry.
You'll watch the repairs, then ask with a sigh...

Why would anyone deal with so much grief and care
When a better trail pardner ain't found anywhere.

Than this faithful feller a' standin' right here
A' eatin' your shirt while you're scratchin' his ear.

That was some wreck today! But he went on despite it!
You smile. Why a donkey? Why NOT is more like it!

Connie Rossignol

⌁ TEXAS LONGHORN ⌁

I am the Texas Longhorn
With horns big and bold
My ancestors came from Mexico
Columbus' cattle I am told

We swam the Rio Grande
A new land to arrive
A territory called Texas
And there we learned to thrive

There was no quarter given
From this harsh terrain
It made us strong and smart
O'er this wasteland we did reign

We bore our calves with ease
Within minutes they did stand
We were ready to face together
Pests and predators of this land

Our numbers grew to millions
Our life seemed so complete
But one predator we would face
That we never could defeat

The cowboy came with horse and rope
To put his mark upon our hide
North we went for many miles
Crossing rivers deep and wide

Songs were sung to soothe us
As we were bedded for the night
Legends were told about us
When we stampeded, from our fright

Many footprints we did leave
Upon the Chisolm Trail
Driven to Dodge City
To ride the miles upon the rail

Loaded up on the cattle cars
The steel rails we did ride
A growing country needing more
Of our meat, tallow and our hides

Our numbers dwindled fast
After twenty years of cattle drives
They mixed us with imported breeds
We were on a downhill slide

But in 1927
Your government stepped in
And now after many years
We're on the rise again

I've been roped, branded and rustled
Many a Cowboy has cursed my name
But it's Me that made them famous
TEXAS LONGHORN is my name

Kathy and Phil Grady

⇌ SHORTY ⇋

We all just called him Shorty,
And everyone knew why.
He'd helped to raise many a kid,
And was never short on try.

When it came to working cattle,
Or just loafin' away the day.
He wasn't one to rattle,
And had his own easy way.

Well Shorty passed away last spring,
The Good Lord called him home.
To his pasture up in heaven,
Where he'll be free to roam.

For Shorty was our pony,
And we all miss him so.
But we know that we will see him,
When it's our time to go.

Where the grass is always green,
And the sky is always blue.
There will be our amigo,
Waiting for us too.

Tim Graham

⌁ THANKS BILL ⌁

You might not guess to see him now, but I recall a time
Bill done his work ahead of me; but I was always close behind.
And Bill agrees we done just fine, without that new machine
with its air-conditioned, cushioned ride, in that John-Deere shade of green.

We worked in mud and sun and rain, and when I'd ride, he'd still walk!
Y'know that ol' boy never once complained, but then, Bill never talked.
So I told him all my secrets, all my hopes and dreams and fears,
and he listened, nodding now and then, in fact, Bill seemed to be all ears.

I still recall that time we hauled the cream cans after dark;
Bill's leg went down that badger-hole, and dang near upset the cart!
When he swung left and I dodged right, cream went everywhere;
...I had it down inside my boots, and Bill had it in his hair!

He looked scared that I'd be mad as hell, and send him packin'
But by the time the noise died down, well, I could only lay there laughin'!
And here and now, twixt you and me, I'm glad Bill never knew
just before he hit that badger hole...one wheel broke plum in two!

Yeah, we worked side by side, ol' Bill and me, so I give him half the ranch,
my only stipulation was, he wouldn't change the brand.
so I set off for the Lawyer, thought I'd make things right official,
and I didn't bat an eye when that Gent asked Bill's middle initial.

'Cause there weren't one thing I wouldn't do, to tell Bill "Thanks a Million"
But on every piece of paper that there Lawyer'd written William!
...William E...for Edward...Muleshoe, named after my dead brother;
(And to tell the truth, I'd ruther have ol' Bill than any other!)

Yessir, field by field, and crop by crop, we built this place together.
and to them that thinks I slipped a cog, I got two words..."mule feathers!"
'Cause there weren't no finer hired hand, none better than ol' Bill,
And I never had to pay him much...just keep his oat sack filled!

Stevie "medicinedog" Raymon

⇐ THE HORSE WE BOUGHT FOR DAD ⇒

I was expecting something tall,
Lean, and prolly solid bay,
With a pretty head, and about ten,
So as not too old to play.

Well, we got tall, he's 16.1,
Chestnut, lots of chrome, flaxen mane.
Sure looks nice from a distance,
Nineteen years old, and built like a train.

Well, all right, we'll take him home,
And try him out for awhile.
He's to be my dad's horse, you know,
And we paid up with a smile.

The man had hundreds of stories
To tell about this great old horse,
Endurance races, won against odds,
And he's hunted and packed, of course.

The man owned him for 15 years,
And there were tears in his eyes
As we loaded that old horse,
And he said his last good-bye.

We brought him home, introduced him to
That little Arab mare I had.
He didn't like her, beat her up good,
He knew what he liked, that horse of Dad's.

Turned out, he was hard to ride,
You had to stick on pretty good.
He scared dad, and mom fell off,
So, in the pasture he stood.

Until one day, I had to ride
And go somewhere with my pals.
I wanted control, so we fought,
For at least a hundred miles.

Took me a while to figure out
It's best to give him his head.
He'd go along faithfully,
Just like the other man had said.

After that, all was merry
I pointed him at everything
He ran barrels, swam ponds, jumped logs
And in my eyes, he was the king.

We ran up hills, dodged gopher holes,
As I threw back my head and laughed.
On his back, I sang, I cried,
And sometimes we'd chase a wayward calf.

From his back, the world looked better.
It was there I had my first kiss.
I look back, and think to myself,
Those are the days that I miss.

Racing home from school every day,
To ride with friends until the night,
And hang up saddle and bridle
When the sun slipped out of sight.

Then it was college, and jobs far from home,
But I kept his picture with me.
The horse stayed with my parents,
Enjoying pasture and good feed.

Someone tried to ride him once,
But he lay down and wouldn't go.
It worked, no one rode him but me,
When we'd relive the times of long ago.

Dad came to love him, though he never rode,
He fed and groomed him loyally,
Until I had my own farm and house,
And a husband to take care of me.

Dad brought me his horse, now twenty five,
To live with me until the end,
And there were tears in his eyes
When he said good-bye to his friend.

So, we are together once more,
And he's going a little blind.
But he eats all he likes, grass and oats,
And tidbits of apples I find.

In his eyes, I can still see,
He longs for a good, hard ride.
Instead, in the pasture he waits,
Nickers, and comes to my side.

I wonder if it's food he wants,
Or if he's begging for a run,
To ride until the sun has set,
And join together, as one.

Until then, he waits for me,
And teaches the new colt I bought
What to eat and where to run,
When to walk and when to trot.

I know he'll always wait for me,
And come to my side when he sees.
Begging for treats, a hug and a kiss,
With his eyes, he silently pleads.

He doesn't want to retire,
Still wants to work every day,
Doesn't want to stand idle,
Needs to earn his oats and hay.

How do I tell him, I'm saving him for
The time when I have my own kids?
So they learn to ride atop his back,
The way their mother did.

This horse has touched so many lives,
When his time has finally passed,
There won't be a soul with dry eyes.
I know he'll always be happy, at last.

He'll gallop into the sunset,
Leaving all of us, so sad.
When we say good-bye, tears in our eyes,
To the horse we bought for Dad.

Jenn Jacula

COME SIT BY MY SIDE

RED RIVER VALLEY

From this valley they say you are going,
We will miss your bright eyes and sweet smile,
For they say you are taking the sunshine
That brightens our pathway awhile.

Come and sit by my side if you love me,
Do not hasten to bid me adieu,
But remember the Red River Valley
And the girl that has loved you so true.

For a long time I have been waiting
For those dear words you never would say,
But at last all my fond hopes have vanished,
For they say you are going away.

Won't you think of the valley you're leaving?
Oh how lonely, how sad it will be.
Oh think of the fond heart you're breaking,
And the grief you are causing me to see?

From this valley they say you are going;
When you go, may your darling go too?
Would you leave her behind unprotected
When she loves no other but you?

I have promised you, darling, that never
Will a word from my lips cause you pain;
And my life,—it will be yours forever
If you only will love me again.

Must the past with its joys be blighted
By the future of sorrow and pain,
And the vows that was spoken be slighted?
Don't you think you can love me again?

As you go to your home by the ocean,
May you never forget those sweet hours,
That we spent in Red River Valley,
And the love we exchanged 'mid the flowers.

There never could be such a longing
In the heart of a pure maiden's breast,
That dwells in the heart you are breaking
As I wait in my home in the West.

And the dark maiden's prayer for her lover
To the Spirit that rules over the world;
May his pathway be ever in sunshine,
Is the prayer of the Red River girl.

traditional; adapted from "The Bright Mohawk
Valley" by James Kerrigan, 1896

⤝I WAS THE LADY⤜

I was the lady, that loved the Old Timer,
The one who everyone knew,
We traveled the trails, of trouble together,
Creatin' a legend or two,
Sometimes we lived, in a tough Texas cowtown,
And he'd keep the peace on the street,
The town women acted, like they did not know me,
If ever by chance we would meet.

Rode stages to Denver, up in the high mountains,
A city that everyone knows,
I remember mud streets, froze hard in the winter,
And houses, all covered with snow,
Cook stove a'smokin', livin' on coffee,
And bacon at six bits a pound,
And my young Old Timer, brought me a red ribbon,
When there wasn't no ribbons around.

We lived in a square tent, held up by some guy ropes,
And a dozen wood tent pegs or two
I had to bake biscuits, in a cast iron Dutch oven,
Long before daylight broke through.
I washed on a washboard, and dried on the bushes,
And bathed in creek water ice cold,
And slept on a pallet, with my give out prospector,
Exausted, from searchin' for gold.

I helped with the hayin', branded the yearlin's,
I even helped him build a fence,
And when he was ailin', I doctored and nursed him,
A patient who paid not a cent.
He did what he wanted, went where the trail wandered,
And me?, he left sittin' at home,
I did the raisin', of the kids we created,
And learned to live lonely, too long.

As time moved along, kids grown up and married,
People would stop by to see,
If the Old Timer'd tell them, a tale about old days,
Back when the West was still free.
We'd set on the porch, in the cool of the evenin',
And writers would write and take notes,
About the old places, we lived in the old times,
And all the tough trail towns he broke.

Sometimes they'd ask questions, and mem'ry would fail,
At me, he would cut his grey eyes,
I'd say "You remember," and clear all the cobwebs,
As my Old Timer went back in time.
We weathered the hard times, we didn't have nothin',
And the times when the blessin's were free,
Then the winter of livin', finally took my Old Timer,
And nobody misses him, like me.

Now in the evenin', I sit in the rocker,
And sometimes I'll look down the road,
I'm lookin' for someone, someday to come ridin',
And tell an old lady, "Get on."
Right up behind him, holdin' on to whatever,
Knowin' where this trail will wind,
Sittin' forever, on a solid gold front porch,
Me, and that Old Timer, of mine.

T. R. Stephenson

SHE TIED HER HEARTS TO TUMBLEWEEDS

She looks out of the window,
At the ranch he brought her to.
Newly married, full of love,
By and by, the years they flew.

In time, she learned to love this land,
Even the winters, cold and raw.
For the flowers that bloomed in springtime,
Made up for it all.

Then came the time when her husband left,
She'll not forget the day.
He just went to town, to fetch some seed,
Some sixty miles away...

His horse shied from a rattler,
But, this, she'd never know.
For his life was spent, as his horse did jump,
Into a canyon, far below.

Never did she find him,
For several years she tried.
Most of the time, she worked the ranch,
And late at night she cried.

She started stitching little hearts,
For hers was aching so.
She tied those hearts to tumbleweeds,
And then she let them go.

Writing poems, in her spare time,
To keep her from feeling worse.
Then she'd take those little hearts,
And sew to them each verse.

Carrying hearts out to the wind,
For it always seemed to blow.
She tied her hearts to tumbleweeds,
And then she let them go.

Rafe, worked for the Rafter 7,
Building fence, and riding line.
Nothing in his life to prepare him for,
What he was about to find.

Something caught his eye one day,
Just a little speck.
A heart tied to tumbleweed....
He wondered, "What the heck?"

He read the little poem inside,
And in his heart he felt her pain.
And he started gazing north,
Across the windswept plain.

What manner of woman did this?
He knew he had to know.
She tied her heart to tumbleweeds,
And then she let them go.

He rode down to the main house,
Just to draw his pay.
He didn't try to explain to them,
What made him act this way?

For several months he searched,
Every canyon, every draw.
Searching hard for little hearts,
On every tumbleweed he saw.

Old Rocket, pulled up lame one day,
And he got off to let him rest.
When a tumbleweed, blew by,
A brand new heart, there on its crest.

He dropped the reins, and chased it down,
The ink, it wasn't dry.
Then he knew the one he longed for,
Was bound to be close by.

Walking o'er the next rise,
From the way the tumbleweed came.
He saw the woman in the yard,
He knew he'd never be the same.

As he howdy'd to the house, he saw
The ranch, in need of a man.
He said "Ma'am, my horse could use some rest.
Looks like you could use a hand."

She looked him up and down, and said,
"I can't afford the pay,
But there's hay, there for your horse
I'll turn no animal away."

He said, "Ma'am, this might be forward,
But I don't know no other way"
And he reached inside his saddlebag,
And the hearts he did display.

"Ma'am, I believe that these are yours
I've been searching for you so.
You've tied your hearts to tumbleweeds,
Why did you let them go?"

Dozens of tiny hearts, he held,
So gently in his hand.
In his eyes she saw such tenderness,
And a heart big as this land.

"Come inside," said she,
"Let's get out of this wind
And I'll tell you all about it
While your horse begins to mend."

They talked all evening,
Way after the sun went down.
And they were still conversing,
When morning rolled around.

She asked "How long you been searching?"
He said, "Since early fall.
Reckon, what day it really is?"
She got the calendar from off the wall.

"Oh my," said she, in surprise,
As she looked up the date.
"It's February 14th,"
She thought it must be fate.

Now, nearly twenty years have passed,
Since Rafe, and her first met.
And if you ride out toward Big Springs,
Their ranch is the biggest yet.

Now many a passerby, has wondered,
About the sign on the gate, and the words below.
Under a crimson heart, and a tumbleweed,
The words "and then she let them go."

Don Gregory

COWBOY IN LOVE

Ya got a smile thet's big as Texas,
an' jest as sunny bright.
Yer eyes is purty as all outdoors;
all sparkly like the night.
Yer hair is soft as a feather bed.
It floats on summer air
like a billowin' cloud above the range,
an' honey, I do declare!
thet you've stole my heart strings clean away,
from whar I had them hid,
to keep them safe from love's wild ways,
an' then thet thing you did
when ya rode yer hoss up to the barn;
jest the way you hopped right down,
with a look and a shake of yer ridin' skirt,
wal, the bobwar I'd strung 'round
my heart to keep it safe from wemmin's ways
jest fell to pieces then,
an' now thet I've seen the likes of you,
I'm in love all over ag'in.

Davey Lee George ("McCloud")

COWBOY CHRISTMAS

THE COWBOYS' CHRISTMAS BALL

Way out in Western Texas, where the Clear Fork's waters flow,
Where the cattle are "a-browzin'," an' the Spanish ponies grow;
Where the Northers "come a-whistlin'" from beyond the Neutral Strip;
And the prairie dogs are sneezin', as if they had "The Grip";
Where the cayotes come a-howlin' 'round the ranches after dark,
And the mocking-birds are singin' to the lovely "medder lark";
Where the 'possom and the badger and rattlesnakes abound,
And the monstrous stars are winkin' o'er a wilderness profound;
Where lonesome, tawny prairies melt into airy streams,
While the Double Mountains slumber, in heavenly kinds of dreams;
Where the antelope is grazin' and the lonely plovers call—
It was there that I attended "The Cowboys' Christmas Ball."

The town was Anson City, old Jones's county seat,
Where they raised Polled Angus cattle, and waving whiskered wheat;
Where the air is soft and "bammy," an' dry an' full of health,
And the prairies is explodin' with agricultural wealth;
Where they print the *Texas Western*, that Hec. McCann supplies
With news and yarns and stories, uv most amazin' size;
Where Frank Smith "pulls the badger," on knowin' tenderfeet,
And Democracy's triumphant, and might hard to beat;
Where lives that good old hunter, John Milsap, from Lamar,
Who "used to be Sheriff, back East, in Paris, sah!"
'T was there, I say, at Anson with the lovely "widder Wall,"
That I went to that reception, "The Cowboys' Christmas Ball."

The boys had left the ranches and come to town in piles;
The ladies—"kinder scatterin'"—had gathered in for miles.
And yet the place was crowded, as I remember well,
'T was got on this occasion, at "The Morning Star Hotel."
The music was a fiddle an' a lively tambourine,
And a "viol came imported," by the stage from Abilene.
The room was togged out gorgeous—with mistletoe and shawls,
And candles flickered frescoes, around the airy walls.
The "wimmin folks" looked lovely—the boys looked kinder treed,
Till their leader commenced yellin': "Whoa! fellers, let's stampede,"
And the music started sighin', an' awailin' through the hall
As a kind of introduction to "The Cowboys' Christmas Ball."

The leader was a feller that came from Swenson's ranch,
They called him "Windy Billy," from "little Deadman's Branch."
His rig was "kinder keerless," big spurs and high-heeled boots;
He had the reputation that comes when "fellers shoots."
His voice was like a bugle upon the mountain's height;
His feet were animated an' *a mighty, movin'* sight,
When he commenced to holler, "Neow, fellers stake your pen!
"Lock horns ter all them heifers, an' russle 'em like men.
"Saloot yer lovely critters; neow swing 'an let 'em go,
"Climb the grape vine 'round 'em—all hands do-ce-do!
"You Mavericks, jine the round-up—Jest skip her waterfall,"
Huh! hit was gettin' happy, "The Cowboys' Christmas Ball!"

The boys were tolerable skittish, the ladies powerful neat,
That old brass viol's music *just got there with both feet!*
That wailin', frisky fiddle, I never shall forget;
And Windy kept a-singin'—I think I hear him yet—
"Oh Xes, chase yer squirrels, an' cut 'em to our side;
"Spur Treadwell to the centre, with Cross P Charley's bride;
"Doc Hollis down the middle, an' twine the ladies' chain;
"Van Andrews pen the fillies in big T Diamond's train.
"All pull yer freight together, neow swallow fork an' change;
"'Big Boston,' lead the trail herd, through little Pitchfork's range.
"Purr 'round yer gentle pussies, neow rope em! Balance all!"
Huh! hit wuz gettin' active—"The Cowboys' Christmas Ball."

The dust riz fast an' furious; we all jes' galloped 'round,
Till the scenery got so giddy, that Z Bar Dick was downed.
We buckled to our partners, an' told 'em to hold on,
Then shook our hoofs like lightning, until the early dawn.
Don't tell me 'bout cotillions, or germans. No, sir 'ee!
That whirl at Anson City just takes the cake with me.
I'm sick of lazy shufflin's, of them I've had my fill,
Give me a frontier break-down, backed up by Windy Bill.
McAllister ain't nowhar: when Windy leads the show,
I've seen 'em both in harness, and so I sorter know—
Oh, Bill, I sha'n't forget yer, and I'll oftentimes recall,
That lively gaited sworray—"The Cowboys' Christmas Ball."

Larry Chittenden, 1890

A COWBOY'S CHRISTMAS PRAYER

The worn and wrinkled cowboy
slowly shaved and combed his hair.
He picked the finest clothes he had
and then he dressed with care.
He stomped into his new bought boots
and shrugged into his coat.
The others would have questioned him,
but his thoughts seemed quite remote.

He stepped out of the bunkhouse,
and pulled his hat down tight,
Then climbed aboard his private horse
and rode into the night.
The single footin' gelding
ate the miles without a pause
And seemed to know the rider
had a most important cause.

Twenty miles on through the night,
with the rider deep in thought,
The stars came out to guide his way
to the goal the ride had bought.
His horse stopped on a gentle rise,
tho' the rider pulled no rein,
And the cowboy raised his head to stare
'Cross the quiet and lonely plain

He crawled down off the weary horse,
loosed the cinch so it could blow,
Then walked a yard or two away
and knelt down in the snow.
He crushed his hat against his chest,
raised his face up to the sky,
And then he started talking
like a friend was standing by.

"Lord, you see I rode a piece tonight
'Cause I knowed that you'd be here.
Course you wuz at the bunkhouse too,
but on this hill ya' seems near.
As I look acrost this prairie
and see the things you've made,
Why, comparin' things us men has done
really puts 'em in the shade."

"I thank you for the love you show
in everything you do,
And I'm proud to be a top-hand
with a loyal happy crew.
I've still got all my fingers,
my legs are bowed, but tough,
Rheumatiz' ain't touched my bones,
and my mind is sharp enough."

"Your spirit gives me comfort,
and I know that when I die,
You'll let me rest forever
at that bunkhouse in the sky.
Forgive me when I wander off,
like a wild jug-headed hoss,
And I pray You'll not give up on me
'fore I learn that you're the boss."

"I've rode out here to tell you
I'm thankful for a Savior's birth,
And to send you MERRY CHRISTMAS
from your folks down here on earth."
Then he mounted up and rode away
with a casual good-bye nod.
A cowboy with his heart at peace
in the palm of the hand of God.

Gail T. Burton

NIGHTWORK

I'd been at the ranch less than a year
I was warm in the bunkhouse when the foreman appeared
He said, "Jonesy, you're low man—this task falls to you
There's a new calf missing—mother is, too
Saddle up Mack; don't forget your maguey
I hate to send you out on this cold Christmas Eve
But coyotes are hungry—This year has been hard
We can't stand to lose even one little pard."

As I rode through the snow in the blustery wind
I complained to myself 'bout the shape I was in
Tonight meant the barn dance...pretty girls, lots of laughs
I'd miss it all, thanks to one snot-nosed calf
My job seemed hopeless, an impossible test
But since I was out here I'd give it my best
We'd start in the open and work towards the rough
I pointed Mack north and hoped for some luck.

We scoured the pastures, the gullies, the hills
But nothing was moving; it was quiet and still
We rode down the canyon and up past the draw
And that's when I saw them...It filled me with awe
Alone in a clearing, not trying to run
Quiet and peaceful, stood mother and son
Slowly they looked up—their eyes all aglow
And I was reminded of a scene long ago.

My throat got a lump; my eyes got a tear
I'm lucky, I thought, to have ended up here
Where hardships are many, but blessings are, too
Where a short draw can lead to a soul-shaking view
I got off my horse and knelt in the drifts
And I said, "Thank you, Jesus, for all of the gifts
By myself, I'm not much, but I'll do what I can
I've got my own saddle; can I ride for your brand?"

Lanny Joe Burnett

293

A CHRISTMAS POEM

Christmas is a-comin' soon!
Pardner, ain't ya seen?
The decorations showed up
In the stores on Halloween!

The papers just plumb fulla ads;
Some days it's three feet thick!
That's good-we got a woodstove,
'N' we're short on kindlin' sticks.

The kids all hope that Santa
Brings 'em ever'thing they chose;
"I want a Nintendo!"
"Please don't bring me any clothes!"

The Sally Army's out in force,
A-tunin' up their band;
I always drop a dollar,
'Cause they once gave me a hand.

There's some who say we've lost the track,
'N' don't know rhyme or reason,
That all this hooraw overlooks
The spirit of the season.

They point 'n' say I don't believe,
'Cause in church ya'll never find me;
But I don't need no hymns, or prayers,
Or crosses to remind me.

This year, I think I'll try
What one ole cowpoke used to do;
I'll saddle up, 'n' leave a note:
"Back in an hour, or two."

I'll ride west outta Reno,
A-followin' the river,
'Way up into the mountains
Where the air's so cold it shimmers.

Far away from stores 'n' crowds,
Where the only single sound
Will be my pony's muffled steps
Through the snow upon the ground.

'N' when I reach the perfect spot
(I'll know it when I'm there),
I'll doff my hat, 'n' feel
The icy wind blow through my hair.

I'll find the brightest star that night,
Gaze up at it, 'n' say,
"Happy Birthday, Boss,"
'N' then I'll softly ride away.

Charley Sierra

MY COWBOY'S NIGHT BEFORE CHRISTMAS

'Twas just before Santy came, the story is told.
Cattle weren't stirrin', fact they's bunched against the cold.
The tack was hung near the chuckwagon with care.
Why, we didn't know Santy was close anywhere.

Cowboys on the ground were wishin' for their beds
While nightmares of wild steers ran through their heads.
'Tween now and the next gather, we needed a nap.
Cookie had just finished, and tied down the flap.

When out past the cavvy, there rose such a fuss,
I sprang to my feet, leavin' the bedroll a muss,
And grabbin' my shotgun and my ragged ol' hat
I run t'ward the racket thinkin' "...what'n thunder's that?"

When thoughts of amazement through my head courses,
It was a buckboard teamed up with draft horses,
A driver in red buckskins, so spry and dainty,
I know'd in an instant, it must be ol' Santy.

Quicker than jackrabbits, them horses they came,
And, he's shoutin' commands to each one by name...
"Get a step, Joe! One more, Prince! On, Big Ed!
Pick it up, Sam! Tighten up, Lou! On, Old Ned!

Don't spook the cavvy, back away from them pens,
You're a pullin' this wagon like a bunch of ol' hens!
Now, when I haul on these lines I mean to stop.
Hold up in this cow-camp like a ton of cow flop!"

They sat down in their riggin', like I knew they would,
With a wagon of goodies...made of leather and wood.
Then, in a twinklin' with no further delay,
He said, "Back it up, boys, this here ain't no sleigh."

I couldn't believe my ears, and lookin' around,
Off that wagon ol' Santy came with a bound.
He was short, and his chinks reached near to his toes.
He was happy and fat, with a little red nose.

There was a ton of packages and some new tack,
And, ol' Santy was carryin' it all on his back.
His eyes sort of bloodshot, much like a cherry,
From "rastlin'" them horses clean across the prairie.

His lips was plumb puckered, his mouth drawn and droll,
(Mine got that way, the day I swallered my Skoal.)
He was holdin' a piggin' string tight in his teeth,
Not fer' tie down, but for tyin' "up" a fine wreath.

His head was too big and he had a round belly,
No doubt derived from eatin' Texas Chili.
He's chubby and plump all right, I'd say quite jolly.
I laughed plumb out loud when I seen him, by golly.

He winked his bloodshot eye, and spat 'tween his lips,
And, it made me to know we were all in the chips.
He weren't much for chatter, just done what was due,
Givin' presents and goodies to the whole durn crew.

Then, he stuck his finger in his wee little ear,
Wallered it around and said, "We're through bein' here."
He fled to the wagon, and his team called 'em up,
"Come on you swaybacks...what's the dad-burn holdup?

We won't be back till next year 'cause we're flat broke.
Merry Christmas, my eye, I just busted a spoke!"

David Kelley

BEAT THE DRUM SLOWLY

⊰ THE COWBOY'S LAMENT ⊱
(STREETS OF LAREDO)

As I walked out in the streets of Laredo,
As I walked out in Laredo one day,
I spied a poor cowboy wrapped up in white linen,
Wrapped up in white linen as cold as the clay.

"Oh, beat the drum slowly and play the fife lowly,
Play the dead march as you carry me along;
Take me to the green valley, there lay the sod o'er me,
For I'm a young cowboy and I know I've done wrong.

"I see by your outfit that you are a cowboy"—
These words he did say as I boldly stepped by.
"Come sit down beside me and hear my sad story;
I am shot in the breast and I know I must die.

"Let sixteen gamblers come handle my coffin
Let sixteen cowboys come sing me a song.
Take me to the graveyard and lay the sod o'er me,
For I'm a poor cowboy and I know I've done wrong.

"My friends and relations they live in the Nation,
They know not where their boy has gone.
He first came to Texas and hired to a ranchman,
Oh, I'm a young cowboy and I know I've done wrong.

"It was once in the saddle I used to go dashing,
It was once in the saddle I used to go gay;
First to the dram-house and then to the card-house;
Got shot in the breast and I am dying today.

"Get six jolly cowboys to carry my coffin;
Get six pretty maidens to bear up my pall.
Put bunches of roses all over my coffin,
Put roses to deaden the sods as they fall.

"Then swing your rope slowly and rattle your spurs lowly,
And give a wild whoop as you carry me along,
And in the grave throw me and roll the sod o'er me,
For I'm a young cowboy and I know I've done wrong.

"Oh, bury beside me my knife and six-shooter,
My spurs on my heel, my rifle by my side,
And over my coffin put a bottle of brandy,
That the cowboys may drink as they carry me along.

"Go bring me a cup, a cup of cold water,
To cool my parched lips," the cowboy then said;
Before I returned his soul had departed,
And gone to the round-up—the cowboy was dead.

We beat the drum slowly and played the fife lowly,
And bitterly wept as we bore him along;
For we all loved our comrade, so brave, young and handsome,
We all loved our comrade although he'd done wrong.

Frances Henry Maynard, 1876

❧ THE WILD CREW ❧

As I rode out just this morning,
There were Four Riders I did see
There in the clouds above Square Butte,
And They come ridin' straight at me.

One Rider forked a chestnut colt
that reared and squealed and blowed.
A buckskin mare, just hide and bones,
a Second Rider rode.

A Third bestrode a haggard black,
Gaunt, sick, and hollow-eyed,
And He used him hard with quirt and word,
And He spurred him, too, besides.

The Fourth One sat a pale horse,
And He seemed the One to note,
And when He looked me in the eye,
The bile rose in my throat,

For then I knowed each sev'ral one
That rode with that Wild Crew
And like They rode at me today,
Some day They'll ride at you.

And a killer rides the red horse
And the horse's name is War.
That buckskin mare, she's Famine,
That the Second Rider bore.

The Third, He topped Black Pestilence,
Vile sickness and disease.
The Pale Rider on the fleabit gray
Pinched Death between His knees.

And if that Rider speaks your name,
Your blood will turn to ice,
For the wages of your sins is Death
And Eternity's the price

To ride the Waste behind Them
And to wear the Devil's brand
For when you wear a heart so black,
You can't make God a hand.

Well, They rode on by and let me be
So's I could bring this tale to you,
But I know dang well I won't ride out
From a second rendezvous.

But when They come, you'll know Them now
They're outlaws—gallows bait.
They're somewheres, a-doggin' our back trail—

And don't you think They ain't.

Jeff Streeby

⇥TO THE BOYS AT CUTTER BILL'S BAR⇤

Me and the boys were cuttin' the dust
at a place known as Cutter Bill's Bar
when the barkeep named Slim
had a note handed him
and he called for us all to retire.

I've got this here message that I need to read
and it's signed by an hombre named Lew
he's written this letter
to all of you fellers
addressed to the Cutter Bill crew.

Well most of the talkin' and music went low
as Slim started readin' aloud
'cause the words that were writ
cast a spell over it
and a hush fairly fell on the crowd.

Dear fellers the message went on to explain
I've had me some bad luck I fear
my cayuse got spooked
and throwed me to boot
'neath the hooves of some mean-tempered steers.

So I'm writin' this letter to you boys
'cause I ain't got a fam'ly or kin
and I don't want to go
without someone should know
and I think on you boys as my friends.

There wasn't no more he had written
a drifter it seemed wrote the end
just before dawn
the old man passed on
then I brung this here note to you men.

The talkin' and music came back then
but none of us boys was the same
a cowboy no doubt
from some whereabouts
had died all alone with his name.

There's a time in a man's life I reckon
when he faces the fact he's alone
and he don't want to go
without someone should know
and a place has to do for a home.

So it was as I stepped from that barroom
that a sense of great loss slowly grew
at the first light of dawn
with the day comin' on
I whispered, "Adios," to old Lew.

Rod Nichols

⋇LIKE IT FINE DOWN HERE⋇

The night was sprinklin' twinklin' stars
in clusters 'cross the sky...
and down below a cowboy lay,
sick...about to die.
The sky above, the earth below...
were foggy and obscured;
but in the cowboy's feverish dream,
a distant voice was heard,

"Heaven, maybe...hell, perhaps,"
declared a distant voice.
"I've weighed the good and bad in you;
and heaven—that's my choice."
Though racked with pain and fever,
the cowboy hadn't died.
Fighting through the fog, the man,
with heavy heart, replied,
"If it's all the same with you,
I like it fine down here.
I'd like t' ride the range again
and rope some racin' steer.

"I like it fine down here, oh Lord!
It ain't for me up there.
I'd miss the crisp Dakota winds
a' combin' through my hair.
I'd miss the cowboy's laughter,
and the frequent barroom brawl;
the ridin' herd on moonlit nights
and hearin' cattle bawl.
The cowboys down at Caseys,
and the mugs a' friendly beer.....
I'd miss 'em! Lord, I'd miss 'em!
I'd like t' stay right here!

"I'd miss ole Cookie's coffee.
I'd even miss his beans.
I'd even miss my worn out boots
and dirty, beat-up jeans.
The mountain mists at mornin',
and the roarin' waterfall,
the thunder and the lightenin'
of the sudden summer squall....
I'd miss 'em! Lord, I'd miss 'em!
I know I'd miss 'em all...
the roundups in the springtime
and the cattle drives each fall."

Pain be damned! The cowboy climbed
a mountain cliff all night;
stumblin' every now and then,
but always clutchin' tight.
When the cowboy reached the crest,
his fiery fever broke;
and in his bedroll on the range,
at daybreak, he awoke.
Never did just wakin'-up
seem such a splendid treat...
not a gray cloud anywhere...
just blue skies, sunshine-sweet.
"Heaven, maybe...Hell, perhaps..."
still echoed in his ear;
and once again the cowboy said,
"I like it fine down here!"

Bette Wolf Duncan

⚜ THE END ⚜

Of life and death,
I've been thinkin' a lot.
But a final decision
I've made not.

'Bout the final disposition
Of this frail human form
That I have enjoyed
since the day I was born.

My pals have a plan
That appeals to me.
The logic is brilliant,
As you will see.

David Wylie's gonna skin me,
Upon my death.
And take my hide to Rick Pinner
And wait with baited breath.

For Rick to tan me
In that stinkin' stuff.
Then remove my hyde
When he's waited long enough.

Then color my hyde
In red, blue or pink.
And take me to Glen Wylie,
When I no longer stink...

Then Glen's gonna pad saddles
For cowgirl folk.
And you can believe it or not,
For it ain't no joke.

'Cause I still want to be here,
As all eternity passes.
Between fast Quarterhorses
And cowgirl........Wranglers!

David J. Dill

⊰ARE THERE HORSES IN HEAVEN?⊱

If I must face an after-life,
don't saddle me with harps and wings
or place a crown upon my head
for golden halos, all such things,
I do bequeath to those who'll find
themselves with saints for company
content to stand before a throne
in adoration, singing praise
to God throughout eternity.
Don't clothe me in an angel's robe
woven on empyrean's loom,
or shoe my feet in sandals meant
for Eden's paths, but give me room
to freely roam the universe,
find new worlds and chart my course
where I may spend eternity
astride a swift Arabian horse
that can't be bribed with silken tent
nor fenced-in pastures, clover grown.
Give me a steed who scorns the bit,
who's hot of blood and freedom-prone.
Let me and some Arabian mare
become as water, earth and air—
two rebel spirits spurning fences,
walls and heavenly Eminences.

I have no wish for Paradise
if horses are forbidden there
and golden New Jerusalem
is a city thoroughfare.
Though I'm now bound and restrained by
nature's law of gravity,
my soul, at times, takes wings to soar
and heaven means a horse to me!

Mary A. Gallagher Kaufman

⇥ SAM'S REMEDY ⇤

The ranch old Samuel lived upon was fifty miles from town
so he couldn't run in there for parts when machinery broke down.
But Samuel had a remedy for emergencies so dire—
if anything would fall apart, he'd mend it with baling wire.
His pickup, year of '49, would get him into dutch,
but Samuel only tugged a bit on the wire on the clutch
and off he'd go in a dusty cloud, sputtering and jingling wire.
Yep, he could fix 'most anything with rusty baling wire.
His fence gates all were wired up with loops of varying size.
When one wore out he'd push it down and hurriedly devise
another loop to fix it with and then went on his way.
He fixed his front door with it too and used it on his hay.
And when old Samuel came to die and they put him in a box—
what do you know, the lid went down but had no kind of locks.
Old Samuel roused from his final rest and said, "Don't just stand around—
close her up with baling wire 'fore you put me in the ground!"
And when he got to the pearly gate he saw all he could desire—
for holding it shut efficiently was a loop of baling wire!

Jean A. Mathisen

⊰ COWBOY HEAVEN ⊱

My uncle went to Cowboy Heaven, before I was ever here,
and ol' Hank made his way too, with just his guitar and a beer.
There's a place up there for cowboys, where Lane Frost holds on for eight,
and you can talk to pure bred cowboys, from all of our great states.
The ladies ride 'round golden barrels, with their buckles shinin' bright,
and folks thank God each day, for sendin' down that light.
So if you lose a cowboy, just remember this one thing,
he's there in every lyric, that Hank and Lefty sing.
He's under every Stetson hat, and on every bull or bronc
he's on the arm of redneck girls, at the local honky tonk.
He's watchin' from behind the chutes, and he pulls your rope so tight,
and when you lay your head down, he's that star that's shinin' bright.
He's up there with my granddad, and with all your granddads too,
and every step you take, he'll be watchin' over you.
The final buzzer sounded, and he's taken his last ride,
but on earth he still remains, in every cowboy's pride.
So cowboys don't give up, and ride your horses 'till the end,
for at the gates of Cowboy Heaven, awaits your western friend.
Ride in memory of the man, who wears the Stetson halo,
and keep him in your heart, at every rodeo,
and when your life just gets you down, and you're feelin' sad and blue,
remember...Cowboy Heaven, and your angel wait for you.

Jennifer M. Bain

❧INTROSPECTION❧

He felt the soft evening breeze reach out and caress his tired old body
    And upon that breeze there came to him the soft note of an old
        cowboy rhapsody
His old memories flickered and then burned brightly as he recalled the past
    And he began to chuckle as remembered how his life had been cast
His chuckles soon turned to laughter that joined with the notes of
    that rhapsody
    And then they rode away together on that soft evening breeze

The old cowboy had been away for many years from the old home place
    Time had caught up with him, you could tell by the wrinkles on his face
But he had finally returned home again to that barren South Dakota plain
    If only with a small hope that he could revive old memories again
His mind was totally stunned by the sights that met his old eyes
    Sadly, there was very little left that he could recognize
There was very little left of the old place that he used to know
    The house and barn had been taken down by sixty years of Dakota snow
The land was now just so many acres of dirt filled with weeds
    Could this really be the same place that had fulfilled his family's needs
The old windmill had long ago stopped turning and then had fallen down
    The relatives had all passed away or had moved to some town
But, a small ray of hope, when he saw where his mother's back yard used to be
    He knew that it was the same tree his mother had planted on the old
        home place
And, he knew too that the tree was also a sign of God's good grace
    So it was, beneath that tree the old man sat until the darkness of night fell
He was listening to all the stories that the old tree had to tell
    And it was there, that the old man died while listening to that old tree
But there should be no sadness, for the old man died happy, that you could see

When they found him, there was a smile on the face of the old man
    Because he had been able to return to the place where his life had began
We buried him there, beneath the branches of that old tree
    Figuring it was as good a place as any for him to spend eternity

He felt the soft evening breeze reach out and caress his tired old body
    And upon that breeze there also rode the soft notes of an old
    cowboy rhapsody

J. D. Reitz

313

QUIET STARLIGHT
ON THE PLAINS

A COWBOY'S PRAYER
(WRITTEN FOR MOTHER)

Oh Lord, I've never lived where churches grow.
    I love creation better as it stood
That day You finished it so long ago
    And looked upon Your work and called it good.
I know that others find You in the light
    That's sifted down through tinted window panes,
And yet I seem to feel You near tonight
    In this dim, quiet starlight on the plains.

I thank You, Lord, that I am placed so well,
    That You have made my freedom so complete;
That I'm no slave of whistle, clock or bell,
    Nor weak-eyed prisoner of wall and street.
Just let me live my life as I've begun
    And give me work that's open to the sky;
Make me a pardner of the wind and sun,
    And I won't ask a life that's soft or high.

Let me be easy on the man that's down;
    Let me be square and generous with all.
I'm careless sometimes, Lord, when I'm in town,
    But never let 'em say I'm mean or small!
Make me as big and open as the plains,
    As honest as the hawse between my knees,
Clean as the wind that blows behind the rains,
    Free as the hawk that circles down the breeze!

Forgive me, Lord, if sometimes I forget.
    You know about the reasons that are hid.
You understand the things that gall and fret;
    You know me better than my mother did.
Just keep an eye on all that's done and said
    And right me, sometimes, when I turn aside,
And guide me on the long, dim, trail ahead
    That stretches upward toward the Great Divide.

Badger Clark, 1906

～ A COWBOY'S PRAYER ～

A cowboy rode alone one day, a roundin' up some strays.
When he paused atop a gentle rise, where he could see for quite a ways.

There was hills and valleys, and trees and clouds, as far as the eye could see.
And he began to quietly contemplate, just how this came to be.

It didn't look like no accident, like some folks tried to teach.
To believe that would take believin', against what his mom had
    always preached.

So he listened to the gentle wind, that rustled through the trees,
And watched a deer go runnin' by, as pretty as you please.

He marveled at the hawk up high, a ridin' in the air.
Removin' his hat, he bowed his head, and spoke this simple prayer:

"Sir, I don't know much about, how this ol' world came to be,
I just know you made a place, for cowboys just like me.

"So thank you, Sir, for givn' me, a place to work and ride,
Where I can see your handiwork, with you right by my side.

"And thank you for that simple book, that tells us of your Son,
You must be really proud of Him, and what He went and done.

"I'm really proud and humble, 'bout what your Book does say,
About how I can also be your son, yours showed us the way.

"I know how much you love this place, I really love it, too.
So I'll do my best to care for it, in everything I do.

"Thanks is not near enough, to say how I truly feel.
But I know you can see my heart, and know these words is real.

"I gotta go now, Sir, and finish out my day.
Thanks again for all you've done, and givin' me this day!"

Lloyd Shelby

— A PRAYER FOR MAN AND HORSE —

Now I lay me down to sleep
in this bedroll on the ground,
and I pray the Lord my soul to keep
if tomorrow I ain't around.

But Lord, if it's my time to join you
in the great by-and-by
well, sir, can we bring my horse
for your remuda in the sky?

I've had him since a child
and he was just a colt,
and I long to ride him through the skies
and chase a lightnin' bolt.

We'll work hard, Lord
ride your fences all day long,
and I promise not to rope no angels,
I'll try hard to do no wrong.

It's just that me and Ol' Roan are pardners
and we will be 'til the end,
So please Lord, don't take me
unless you take my friend.

But, if You should choose
in all Your wisdom and sage
to take one before the other
for bad health or old age

Well, keep us busy
'til the other's time has come
so we won't miss too much
the other one

And we'll wait for our reunion
and go ridin' through the skies
chasin' them longhorn cattle
with Your brand upon their sides.

Well, thank you Lord for listenin'
to this simple cowboy's prayer,
and I'll talk to You tomorrow
though I know not from where

But I'll lift my heart to Heaven
and pray to You of course,
as I do 'most every night—
a Prayer For Man And Horse.

Amen and Goodnight.

HJ "Hoss" Peterson

About the Poets

The Classic Selections

E. A. (Earl Alonzo) Brininstool, born in New York in 1870, was a Western historian, best known for his writings about Native Americans. He wrote extensively about Custer and he helped Standing Bear write his autobiography, *My People the Sioux* (1928).

"A Westerner" by E. A. Brininstool from *Trail Dust of a Maverick*, 1914

Legend holds that Arthur Chapman, born in 1874, dashed off "Out Where the West Begins" for his *Denver Republican* column when the Western states' governors were arguing about where the West begins. He was surprised at the attention it received; it was widely circulated, taken up by politicians, and it hung in the office of the Secretary of the Interior in Washington.

"Out Where the West Begins" by Arthur Chapman from *Out Where the West Begins and Other Western Verses*, 1917

William Lawrence "Larry" Chittenden, a New Yorker, wrote about a Cowboy Christmas dance he attended in Anson, Texas in 1885. Chittenden later settled in Anson, and the event he helped make famous still takes place annually.

"The Cowboys' Christmas Ball," by William Lawrence "Larry" Chittenden from *Ranch Verses*, 1893

Charles "Badger" Clark, born a minister's son in 1883, wrote "A Cowboy's Prayer" for his mother. Clark wrote his mother regularly from the West, and said that he "found prose too weak to express his utter content..." His mother submitted his poems to the *Pacific Monthly*, and the rest is Cowboy Poetry history.

"A Cowboy's Prayer" by Charles "Badger" Clark from *Sun, Saddle, and Leather*, 1915

Curley W. Fletcher's original version of "The Strawberry Roan," written in 1915, had 15 verses. The popular 1930's songwriters and radio personalities Fred Howard and Nat Vincent ("The Happy Chappies") reworked the lyrics and the tune quickly became one of the most frequently recorded cowboy songs, performed by singers from Gene Autry to Red Steagall.

"The Strawberry Roan" by Curley Fletcher, 1915 as represented in *American Balladry From British Broadsides*, G. Malcom Laws, Jr.

GAIL I. GARDNER wrote the "The Sierry Petes (or, Tying Knots in the Devil's Tail)" in 1917. It became so widely known and frequently performed that it is often mistakenly cited as a traditional piece by an anonymous author.

"The Sierry Petes (or, Tying Knots in the Devil's Tail)" by Gail I. Gardner, from *Orejana Bull* © 1935, reprinted with the kind permission of grandson Gail Steiger

BREWSTER HIGLEY's poem, "The Western Range," evolved into the popular American song, "Home on the Range." The first version of the song, written by Brewster Higley with Dan Kelley, and Clarence, Eugene and Virgie Harlan is included in this volume.

"The Western Home" by Brewster Higley et al., 1873 from Harlan/Kelly descendant Mary Barr Norris, who also provided additional information

HENRY LAWSON, born in New South Wales in 1867, was a frequent contributor to *The Bulletin*, a Sydney newspaper where he and A. B. "Banjo" Paterson ("The Man From Snowy River") often debated their views of bush life. Lawson, the son of a Norwegian fisherman and an early feminist writer, suffered from deafness and personal difficulties throughout his life. He worked in the bush and traveled throughout Australia and New Zealand. His poetry and short stories are beloved Australian classics.

"Ballad of the Drover" by Henry Lawson from *In the Days When the World Was Wide*, 1896

FRANCIS HENRY MAYNARD's classic "The Cowboy's Lament" (also known as "Streets of Laredo") borrows from the Irish and Scottish folk tunes "The Bard of Armagh" and "The Unfortunate Rake." Maynard was born in 1852 in Iowa City, Iowa, and left there at age 17 for Kansas, where he had many adventures accounted in his unpublished book, *The Winning of the Wild*. He died in Colorado in 1926.

"Streets of Laredo," by Francis Henry Maynard, 1876 (Don White, relative by marriage, provided biographical information.) *The Winning of the Wild: the Adventures, in Prose and Poetry, of F.H. Maynard, An Old-time Cowboy,* by Professor James F. Hoy ("In the Days of Granville and John") of Emporia State University is forthcoming from the University of Oklahoma Press.

A. B. (ANDREW BARTON) "BANJO" PATERSON was born in 1864 in New South Wales. He grew up in the Australian bush and immortalized its people and places in poems such as "The Man from Snowy River," "Waltzing Matilda" and other verses.

"The Man from Snowy River," by A.B."Banjo" Paterson from *The Bulletin*, 1890

ROBERT SERVICE, an inveterate traveler and adventure seeker, was born in England in 1874 and grew up in Scotland. He found himself in the Yukon during the height of the gold rush and there he wrote stories of the prospectors and poems such as "The Shooting of Dan McGrew" and "The Cremation of Sam McGee." His work met with immediate acclaim and his poetry remains widely read and performed.

"The Cremation of Sam Magee," by Robert Service, from *The Spell of the Yukon and Other Verses*, 1907

RHODA SIVELL was born in Ireland in 1874. She lived in Canada and published the book of poetry that includes "The Cow-Girl" in 1912.

"The Cow-Girl," by Rhoda Sivell from *Voices on the Range*, 1912

CONTEMPORARY POETS' BIOGRAPHIES
*Additional information and poems are available
at CowboyPoetry.com*

ROSE MARY ALLMENDINGER lives near Colorado Springs, Colorado. She owns and operates the historic Hitch Rack Ranch, has been a breeder of registered quarter horses for 30 years, and is involved in the real estate industry. Her poetry and political commentary have been published in numerous periodicals.

"When the Old Yella Bus Comes Down the Lane"
© 2001, Rose Mary Allmendinger

JIM R. ANDERSON is a storyteller, poet, guitarist and singer. He was born and raised on family owned farming and ranching operations in Texas and Colorado. Part of the group Palo Duro, and a member of The Southwest Cowboy Poets, Jim is deeply committed to the preservation and promotion of Western heritage.

"Imprints" © 1999, Jim R. Anderson

JENNIFER M. BAIN is an Iowa native who enjoys attending rodeos and writing poetry. Her works have appeared in several publications.

"Cowboy Heaven" © 2001, Jennifer M. Bain

ROBERT BEENE has "cowboyed" on several ranches in Nebraska and Oklahoma and is currently a full-time farrier. His poetry has been published in *The Christian Ranchman*.

"How Long Will the Cowboys Last?" © 1995, Robert D. Beene

VIRGINIA BENNETT has been writing and performing Cowboy Poetry since 1988. She has been featured in many major anthologies, is the author of two books, and edited the recent *Cowgirl Poetry* (Gibbs Smith). She and her husband manage a ranch east of Paso Robles, California.

"All That is Left" © 1991, Virginia Bennett

FLAVIS BERTRAND's family homesteaded in the Dakota Territory and he was born and raised in Clark, South Dakota. After living in California for a number of years, he returned to his roots and lives today in Newell, South Dakota. His wife Eleanor Bertrand illustrated his book of poetry, *Whispering Wings*.

"The Old Empty House" © 1975, Flavis Bertrand

RISKY BETTS writes from true life experiences on the road as a rodeo Cowboy and his life on ranches around the country. He trains horses and instructs riding lessons in Moorpark California. He continues to gather new material from competing in rodeos and jackpot team ropings, and performs his poetry at gatherings and other functions.

"The Conversation" © 2000, Risky Betts

DAN BLAIR is a life long lover of nature and the great outdoors. A professional wildlife/Western artist and author with 16 Best Of Show wins, Dan calls Utah home. Western history and heritage are his secret loves. His unique poetry style is a tribute to that love affair.

"The Origin of a Good Cowboy" © 2001, Dan Blair

TONY BLISARD is a fourth generation Cowboy and Texan. He says "Riding horses and bulls came natural after being taught by the best. Traveling different states working with horses proved valuable experience." Tony now owns a small thoroughbred race horse farm where he breeds his horses and writes his poetry.

"The Bull Rider" © 2001, Tony Blisard

Utah native PAUL BLISS heads the Utah Western Heritage Foundation, well known for its fall Western Legends trail ride, and he oversees his own Bliss Cattle Company with his wife Stacy. Paul lectures and performs throughout the country.

"Cowboy Poetry in Motion" © 2000, Paul Bliss

BARBARA BOCKELMAN lives in the Oklahoma Panhandle. Her personal experiences and interviews are included in her book, *Black Sunday*. She has performed her poetry at The National Cowboy Hall of Fame, Oklahoma City, as well as the National Cowboy Symposium, Lubbock, Texas, and is a member of The Cowboy Storytellers of the Western Plains.
  "Black Sunday" © 1996, Barbara Bockelman

RON BRINEGAR, Gentleman Cowboy Poet, lives in Scottsdale Arizona, and writes a "Bucky and Nate" monthly humor column for the web magazine *ReadTheWest.com*. He's been a regularly featured poet at many of the Cowboy gatherings in Nevada, California and Wyoming.
  "Graduate" © 1999, R. L. Ron Brinegar

"BUCKSHOT DOT" *see* DEE STRICKLAND JOHNSON

SCOTT BUMGARDNER lives in Houston, Texas where he has been sharing Texas and Cowboy history with thousands through the Houston Rodeo's Speakers Committee and the Cowboy History and Performance Society (CHAPS). He specializes in bringing history to life through the words of those who lived it, spiced with his original poetry.
  "A Time to Thaw" © 2001, Scott Hill Bumgardner

DEBBIE BURDIC lives in Elko, Nevada. She writes stories of her husband's family in poetic verse. Some of the stories are true and some are just tall tales. Debbie prefers to leave that interpretation to her readers.
  "The Rat Pack Mine" © 1998, Debbie Burdic

LANNY JOE BURNETT was raised on a ranch in Fannin County, Texas, the son of fourth generation Texans. He uses his talents to "illustrate the spiritual as well as the sometimes questionable philosophical ideals of the Cowboy." He has performed at gatherings from Central Asia to West Texas.
  "Nightwork" © 1999, Lanny Joe Burnett

GAIL T. BURTON, a native of Temple, Oklahoma, has written poetry about Cowboys for over forty years. He is the creator of "The Adventures of Randy Jones & Booger Red," carried monthly in *The Tombstone Epitaph*. Now living at Benton, Arkansas, he presents his brand of poetry at gatherings throughout the West.
  "A Cowboy's Christmas Prayer" © 1998, Gail T. Burton

RUSTY CALHOUN lives in Chandler, Arizona. She was born and raised on a working cattle and horse ranch, and is a fifth generation member of her family to continue that tradition. She is the poet wrangler for several Cowboy Poetry gatherings in the West, where she presents her original poetry.

"The Appaloosa" © 1999, Rusty Calhoun

T. J. CANTIN works a large southeastern Montana ranch, taking care of "a big part of 4,000 head of mother cows, plus water lines and building fences." He says "900 sections of land is a lot to cover in a day, so we stay pretty darn busy."

"Not Without a Fight" © 1996, T. J. Cantin

JESUS CERVANTES lives in Eloy, Arizona and is twelve years old. He was the 2001 first place winner in the Council of Western Spirit's "Write 'em Cowboy" student poetry contest. He likes to write poems and short stories. Jesus was recently named a Little League all-star for the second year.

"I Seen John Wayne" © 2001, Jesus Cervantes

JANICE N. CHAPMAN was born and raised in Oklahoma and currently lives in Enid. She has received several poetry awards and has published her own book of poetry, *Hello Out There*. She maintains the *1LuckyLady.net* poetry web site.

"Curse the Winter Ride" © 2001, Janice N. Chapman

MICKEE CHEEK raises yearlings on the Bar LC Ranch south of Arnold, Nebraska. "Sandhills Seasons" took first place at the 1999 Laramie, Wyoming Cowboy Poetry Gathering.

"Sandhills Seasons" © 1999, Mickee Cheek

BOBBY COHOON lives in Poplar Branch, North Carolina. He is a musician, playing and singing the traditional songs in addition to writing Cowboy Poetry. He says "We should do all we can to keep tradition alive in all things. Letting tradition die would be the easy way, but it wouldn't be the Cowboy Way!"

"Gentleman Jim" © 2001, Bobby Cohoon

PEGGY COLEMAN has entertained crowds across the country with her music and comedy—Cowboy style. She is working on a children's book and a children's album of Cowboy songs, always inspired by her grandchildren. Peggy resides in Pawnee, Oklahoma where she can enjoy the Cowboy way of life firsthand.

"The Ride" © 1998, Peggy Coleman

John Cook works on a cattle ranch near Tensleep, Wyoming, where he enjoys living and writing the Cowboy way of life.

"A Boy's Dream" © 2001, John Cook

A California ranching native, David J. Dague now resides in Chicago, Illinois and is Director of Operations for a national printing firm. He has performed country and Western music and his original poems in Chicago saloons for over 25 years.

"Backward R Double Bar D" © 2001, David J. Dague

Graham Dean is "the Poet, the dreamer, the idealist" who left the city to be with his country born wife and decided that the little town of Prairie in North West Queensland, Australia, population 50, was just the right place to write and perform his bush poetry.

"I Have Seen the Land" © 1999, Graham Dean

Louise K. Dean lives in the town of Prairie in North West Queensland, Australia where she devotes her time between the performance of her poetry, her art, organizing poetry festivals and looking after her husband, all of which she could not see herself without.

"Just a Dance" © 1999, Louise K. Dean

David J. Dill retired from the USDA after 34 years and resides in Hillsboro, Texas where he commutes to his ZD Ranch at Hubbard, Texas and pastures cattle on his Conservation Award Winning ranch. He is an avid student and teacher of Natural Horsemanship, and he wrangles horses and writes Cowboy Poetry.

"The End" © 1996, David J. Dill

"California Steve" Dirksen lives in Southern California with his wife and two children. He has been published in *American Cowboy* and *Desert Cowboy* and *ReadtheWest.com*. He is an educator, poet and artist who also recites his poetry at gatherings.

"An Old Hand" © 2001, Steve Dirksen

Bette Wolf Duncan is the author of the Western-Cowboy book of poems, *Russell Country* (Hancock House). One of her poems was awarded first prize in the annual contest sponsored by the Canadian Poetry Association, B.C. Chapter. She has been featured in numerous publications including *The Dogwood Express*, and her poetry appears extensively across the internet.

"Like it Fine Down Here" © 2001, Bette Wolf Duncan

DIANE DURRILL is a native of Los Alamos, New Mexico. Her formative years were spent in Idaho. She has published *Up Country* and *Passage to the Inside* and appeared in numerous anthologies. Loving the mountains, ocean, and desert, her travels have inspired many scribbles of the pen. Diane owns Passage Publishing in Boise, Idaho.

"Each Line" © 1999, Diane Durrill

JOHNNY D. EATON is a proud Missouri Cowboy, truck driver, and published poet who lives in Steelville, Missouri.

"Missouri Cowboy" © 1999, Johnny D. Eaton

RICHARD ELLOYAN was raised in the historic mining town of Virginia City, Nevada, where he had the opportunity to walk the same streets as his boyhood hero, Mark Twain. Richard says "A good story, a good laugh, a heartfelt tear—those are the basic elements of life I strive to inject in my songs and poetry."

"Windmill Man" © 1999, Richard Elloyan

K.T. ETLING has cowboyed in Wyoming but lives in Missouri close. Some of her best friends are horses, including her current favorite, *bint bint Sahanade*, an Arabian mare. She is a charter member of the Missouri Cowboy Poets Association and has been extensively published in *American Cowboy* and other magazines.

"Temporary Insanity" © 1998, K. T. Etling

PETE EVANSON was raised in Wyoming in the 40's and 50's and is retired and now living in Salem, Connecticut. He says "writing poetry (exclusively with rhymes) and songs provides some escape from the realities of living in present times, but allows me to enjoy the luxury of using modern technology during the creative process."

"The Odyssey" © 2000, Pete Evanson

DAN FAUGHT is a school principal from Roseburg, Oregon. He grew up on ranches and farms in Southern Idaho and has an appreciation for the traditional "Cowboy wordsmiths." He says the goal of his Cowboy Poetry is "to connect the history of the Cowboy with the modern world we experience today."

"Bankin' With an Old Cowboy" © 2001, Dan Faught

JODY FERGERSTROM, Hawaii born and raised, lives on the Big Island of Hawaii. She credits her brother Moki and his Oregon Buckaroo pards for getting her started on Cowboy Poetry.

"The Horseman and the Cowboy" © 2000, Jody Fergerstrom

SHERROD L. FIELDEN says he "is pleased when his work can bring enjoyment to others." His poetry has been published in various newspapers and collections of poetry. He is semi-retired and resides, with Sue, his wife of 39 years, in Meridian, Texas.

"Stampede" © 2001, Sherrod L. Fielden

JIM FISH is a third-generation Cowboy living in Junction, Texas and pursuing a career with the NeWest MultiMedia Group. Though he hangs a shingle at an office, he has thirty-five years as a ranch Cowboy and more than a hundred years of his family's ranching heritage on which to call.

"Heritage" © 1998, Jim Fish

It seems FRENCH CAMP RED, being dead, depends on this guy, BRAD SMITH, to write down his story—the Cowboy, the legend, the myth. Smith's a boring guy with a wife and two kids living the American dream in Elk Grove, California. It's not clear who makes it all rhyme.

"Dog Swamp Stranger" © 2000, Brad Smith

DENNIS GAINES is a former working Cowboy with roots in West Texas. He is now a full-time writer and entertainer helping to preserve Cowboy culture. In July, 2000, the Academy of Western Artists named him the Cowboy Storyteller and Humorist of the Year.

"Ty Murray—Eat Your Heart Out" © 1991, Dennis Gaines

BOBBIE GALLUP is an interpretive planner and songwriter, living in northern Colorado. Her work with scenic and historic byways across the West often uncovers stories from earlier times deserving of songs and poetry, which she writes to help preserve fragments about the people, places and events of our history.

"Blizzard Calf" © 2000, Bobbie Gallup ASCAP

DAVEY LEE GEORGE is a retired USN Hospital Corpsman and retired Chesapeake Bay Waterman who writes Cowboy Poetry under the name of McCLOUD. His book *Sailors, Lovers and Cowboys* is published by Writer's Club Press.

"Cowboy in Love" © 2001, Davey Lee George

KAY HOLMES GIBSON farms and writes near Watson, Missouri. Her work has been published by McGraw Hill, Eldridge Publishing, *Backhome*, *Bird Watcher's Digest*, *Almanac for Farmers & City Folk*, and numerous publications for children. She is a member of the Society of Children's Book Writers and Illustrators.

"Gopher Holes" © 2000, Kay Holmes Gibson

JANICE GILBERTSON lives in the foothills of the Santa Lucia Mountains in the Salinas Valley of California. She was raised with, and has been around cattle and horses all of her life. Most of what she writes comes from real experiences and she likes to make folks laugh a little. She writes when the notion strikes and says "you never know when that may be."

"Line Dance Lesson" © 2000, Janice Gilbertson

RUDY GONZALES is one of the nation's most requested Cowboy entertainers, a real working Cowboy turned professional Cowboy entertainer. Rudy has entertained U.S. Presidents, prisoners, lumberjacks, legislators, cowpunchers, congressmen, sheepherders, Senators, international diplomatic conferences, and at Cowboy Poetry gatherings, fairs, rodeos, and big game conventions. He was the first Cowboy ever to entertain at the Kennedy Center.

"Rudy's Handlebar Moustache" © 1993, Rudy Gonzales

KATHY AND PHIL GRADY were born and reside in North Carolina, and "the Cowboy way" has always been a part of their lives and in their hearts. Certain times of the year you might meet them traveling with a couple Texas Longhorns and a little stray dog whom they love dearly.

"Texas Longhorn" © 2000, Kathy and Phil Grady

TIM GRAHAM's poetry and songs tell about the things he knows and loves. He was raised on a farm in the Midwest, where they raised cattle and did custom hay baling. Tim began training horses in the late 70's. He now makes his home near Weatherford, Texas where he day works.

"Shorty" © 1998, Tim Graham, All Rights Reserved

DON GREGORY lives in Fort Worth, Texas with his two kids. While having a hand in raising a few cattle, he says he has never been a Cowboy as such. His poetry is mainly romantic in nature, and "She Tied Her Hearts to Tumbleweeds" is one of his first efforts at Western poetry.

"She Tied Her Hearts to Tumbleweeds" © 2001, Don Gregory

"WILD BILL" HALBERT was so named at an early age for his prowess at breaking wild horses. He has "broke, trained and high schooled" many horses. He says he "wrote his poetry and hid it away until about 1990," when he started to get published. He now is a publisher in his own right.

"Runnin' fer 'is Life " © 1994, Wild Bill Halbert

DIANE HARPER lives in a coastal village in Massachusetts, with her husband, two horses, a dog and cat. Diane grew up loving horses and Cowboys. From Roy Rogers to John Wayne, they symbolized the life she hungered for, and still does.

"Midnight Cowboy" © 2001, Diane E. Harper

LYNN HARWELL, a native Texan, combines farm and ranch experience with a career in academia to spin tales in rhyme, mostly of the West. He runs a small cow and meat goat outfit near the Blue Ridge in upstate South Carolina.

"Bear Tale" © 2000, Lynn Harwell

PAUL HARWITZ was born on the East Coast, spent a number of years on the West Coast, and now lives in Wyoming. His poems cover a wide variety of Western subjects.

"Ride for the Brand" © 1999, Paul Harwitz

DR. DALE HAYES, a story teller, writer, and poet in the "Cowboy" style is also a university professor. He believes "...good pasture, good water, a good woman, and a few head make life what it ought to be..." He lives in the Manitoba bush where he is proving that maxim.

"Short Cut" © 2000, "Doc" Dale Hayes

MICHAEL HENLEY is a businessman, rancher and outdoorsman from Cabot, Arkansas. He has shared his poetry and songs around the campfires as he has hunted the Western U.S. for the last 25 years.

"The Guide" © 1995, Michael Henley

LYNNE HENDRICKSON grew up at the foot of Wyoming's Wind River Mountains and has always had a great love for horses. She says "I appreciate their abilities and great sense of freedom yet the loyalty that can be won. Cowboy Poetry is my newly discovered second love."

"From Hell to Heart" © 2001, Lynne Hendrickson

JEFF HILDEBRANDT is the "Boss Wrangler" for the Westerns Movie Channel. He lives just outside of Denver and has been writing range rhymes for about 3 years. He appears regularly at the Colorado Cowboy Poetry Gathering and at the National Cowboy Symposium and Celebration.
 "Nadacowboy" © 1999, Jeff Hildebrandt

DEBRA COPPINGER HILL manages the 4DH Ranch where her family raises cutting horses. She's a proud member of the Charley Russell Western Heritage Association and is a Top Five Academy of Western Artists performer. Her work is included in *Cowgirl Poetry* (Gibbs-Smith), *American Cowboy* magazine, and she appears in "Cowboy Corral," a PBS Cowboy Poetry series.
 "Wild Stickhorse Remuda" © 2000, Debra Coppinger Hill,
 Old Yellow Slicker Productions

ALLAN HORTON, a Florida native, owns Myakka Valley Ranch, a commercial Brangus/Braford cow-calf operation in Manatee County. Personal experience guides his poetry. He is married, a grandfather and an editorial writer for the *Sarasota Herald-Tribune* who builds boats, plays guitar, sails solo and paints watercolors.
 "Brothers At Heart" © 1991, Allan H. Horton

JIM HOY, a folklorist at Emporia State University in Kansas, was reared on a Flint Hills ranch near Cassoday. He has written or edited nine books, including *Cowboys and Kansas* (University of Oklahoma Press, 1995) and *Prairie Poetry: Cowboy Verse of Kansas* (Wichita Eagle Publishing Co., 1995).
 "In The Days of Granville and John" © 1995, Jim Hoy

MARGO IMES has captured her experiences raising kids, calves, and colts on a south central Kansas farm in her poems, some of which are collected in her book, *Pony Tales*. She enjoys horses, trail riding, and Cowboy Poetry gatherings, and particularly likes to do benefit shows.
 "The Good Mother" © 2000, Margo Udelle Imes

S. A. JACKSON was born in central Utah and raised on a ranch. He began writing poetry at age 64, and because of the diversity of his subjects he refers to his work as "Western" rather than "Cowboy" poetry.
 "Reel vs. Real Cowboys" © 1999, S. A. Jackson

Jenn Jacula lives north of Vermilion, Alberta and enjoys living and working on her mixed farming operation with her husband and his family. She draws her inspiration from everyday life.

"The Horse We Bought for Dad" © 2001, Jenn Jacula

Billy James was born in Howland, Texas. He became interested in writing Cowboy Poetry after visiting the Rex Allen Days in Wilcox, Arizona. He now lives in Sacramento, California with his wife, Lou Ann, where he works as a grain inspector for the State of California.

"Who's There?" © 2000, Billy James

James H. "Jim" John is a third-generation Kansas native who lives in Wichita, "a big town, not a city, with pure Cowtown roots." Jim says "I've always been a Cowboy at heart. It just comes with having your roots in the West."

"A Real Cowboy" © 1997, James H. "Jim" John

"Buckshot Dot" (Dee Strickland Johnson) is an Arizonan who grew up on Navajo and Hualapai reservations and at Petrified Forest. She has taught school, raised cattle in the Ozarks, and been named the Academy of Western Artist's Female Cowboy Poet of the Year. She enjoys singing, writing and drawing about the West.

"Tomboy" © 1994, Dee Strickland Johnson

Jay Jones is a native Missourian who resides in Columbia and is a member of the Missouri Cowboy Poets Association. As a young man he competed in amateur rodeos as a bull rider and calf roper. Experiences from those early days still appear in much of his work.

"The Mouthpiece" © 2000, Jay Jones

Tom Jones lives in Liverpool, England. Many of his kin settled in the West 140 years ago, so he has always been "Cowboy affiliated." Instead of riding a bronc, he chose a fire engine, and has been writing poetry ever since he retired.

"The Immigrants, 1858" © 2000, Thomas Vaughan Jones

Dan Kantak lives in Lafayette, Louisiana. He manages the safety department of an oceanographic/geophysical survey company. In his non-working hours he manages his avocation, writing. His spoken word performances "are something to see."

"The Great Divide" © 2001, Dan Kantak

MARY A. GALLAGHER KAUFMAN, says she was "born over 80 years ago with a love for horses." She lives and writes in Florida.

"Are There Horses in Heaven?" © 2001, Mary A. Gallagher Kaufman

DAVID KELLEY was born in the Panhandle of Texas. He has been writing Cowboy Poetry for over twenty years. He says "It just came natural to write the way I talked." He adds, "While the Cowboy is not perfect, he certainly embodies the spirit of goodness and fair play that we could all use in this imperfect world we live in."

"My Cowboy's Night Before Christmas" © 1998, David Kelley

LINDA KIRKPATRICK's roots reach deep into the soil of Texas. The ranch that she grew up on was 20 sections of rocky Texas Hill Country and was the foundation for the poems that she writes about today. She writes and recites about what she loves best: Texas.

"My Cowgirl Life" © 1999, Linda Kirkpatrick

JO LYNNE KIRKWOOD is descended from pioneer settlers of southern Utah, and her family has been involved in the ranching and farming industry since they first arrived in the area in the mid-1800's. She now teaches writing and art in central Utah, and lives on her family farm with her husband and four children.

"A Cowboy Season" © 2001, Jo Lynne Kirkwood

JIM KITCHENS lives and works in a part of Texas that is famous for Cowboy Poetry: Marfa, Texas in the Big Bend Area. He has worked as a Cowboy on various ranches in this area. He has been published by Western Reading Services, American Collegiate Poets, and in the *Bellingham Review* and other publications.

"The Day that Tuff Just Came to Ride" © 2000, Jim Kitchens

RYAN KRANTZ lives in Sunrise, Florida, where he competes at rodeos in the exciting event of Bullriding. He also has a love for breaking and training horses.

"Times Change" © 2000, Ryan Krantz

LAURA LARSON grew up on a small farm near Clarks, Nebraska. Thanks to her father, she learned to appreciate the land and the country way of life. Laura has won numerous awards for her poetry.

"The Bull Ride" © 2001, Laura Larson

ERIC LEE is 45, and Texas-born. He's written poetry since he was 12, ridden horses since he was 5, and been a Cowboy from birth. He now lives in the Northern Arizona mountains with his wife, Vicki, and continues happily to do all three.

"Just Another Calf" © 2001, eric lee

BERT LLOYD's passion for American history has been the inspiration for much of his poetry. He lives on a small farm near Lubbock, Texas where he runs bird dogs, raises a few quail, and a lot of Cain.

"It's Finished (Suvate)" © 2000, Bert Lloyd

RON LOOF lives in Colorado Springs, Colorado. He writes poetry as a way to stay connected with the rich traditions and history of the American West. His inspirations are his two daughters, as well as the beauty and grandeur of Colorado.

"The Last of the Herd" © 2001, Ron Loof

MCCLOUD *see* DAVEY LEE GEORGE

DON MCCRARY is a native Kansan who learned to write poetry at the knee of his father, a master wordsmith in his own right. The poem "Death's Head Bull" was a collaboration between Don and his late father, William Donald McCrary 1924–2001. Don says, "This one's for you, Pop!"

"The Death's Head Bull" © 1979, William Donald McCrary

MARK MCMILLAN lives in the Cariboo region of British Columbia, Canada where he owns and operates a small working guest ranch with his wife. Mark is a Director of the BC Cowboy Heritage Society. In his poetry, he shares his stories, adventures and experiences on the ranch.

"Hayin' in the Cariboo" © 2000, Mark McMillan

DENISE MCREA of Leadore, Idaho has been a member of the Cowboy Poets of Idaho for 10 years. She says "I write about my life, and the people, places, and animals I know, and things that have happened over the years."

"Empty Houses" © 1999, Denise McRea

TIM "DOC" MASON lives near Stephenville, Texas and has written poetry since 1947, with 215 poems to his credit. He has published three poetry books, and texts and articles on veterinary nutrition. He spent 19 years in university teaching and 19 years in the feed industry.

"Life Goes On" © 1995, Tim "Doc" Mason

JEAN MATHISEN is a native of Lander, Wyoming and comes from a seven-generation ranching family in the Lander Valley. She is the author of 6 books of poetry and nearly 500 historical articles about Wyoming and the West.

"Sam's Remedy" © 2001, Jean A. Mathisen

ROD MILLER lives in Sandy, Utah, where he writes about Cowboys and the West. He is a member of Western Writers of America.

"The E. S. L. Ranch" © 1998, Rod Miller

JANICE MITICH, Wyoming ranch-raised, now lives among the saguaros east of Tucson, Arizona. Her poetry has been published in *Cowboys Are Part Human* and other publications. She is a member of The Society of Southwestern Authors, and performs at Cowboy Poetry Gatherings in Arizona, New Mexico, California, and Utah.

"Queen of the West" © 2001, Janice E. Mitich

JANE MORTON writes from her memories of the historic Ambrose family ranch near Fort Morgan, Colorado. The author of ten children's books, she has had Cowboy poems published in *Fence Post* magazine. A performer at Cowboy Poetry gatherings, she now lives in the Black Forest near Colorado Springs, Colorado.

"Branding" © 2001, Jane Morton

A. KATHY MOSS lives in Canyon City, Oregon. She has been performing her own work for the last three years and has been published in *Cowgirl Poetry* (Gibbs Smith), *North American Hunter* and other publications. She has published three books of poetry and is a member of the Charley Russell Western Heritage Association and of the Academy of Western Artists.

"Songs Less Traveled" © 2001, A. Kathy Moss

JIMMI NAYLOR calls Agnos, Arkansas home. She is an 8th grade teacher and barrel racer. She writes contemporary Cowboy Poetry about the life she lives and knows best.

"Sweet Thing" © 1999, Jimmi Naylor

LEE NEILL lives near Monett, Missouri, where he pastors the rural Macedonia Free Will Baptist Church. A former high school Spanish and English teacher and counselor, radio-TV news writer, and dairy farmer, he and his wife, Darline, continue to reside on the family farm and raise grandchildren.

"Cowboys and Country Boys" © 1999, Lee Neill

ROD NICHOLS, originally from Nacogdoches, Texas, now lives in Missouri City, Texas. His "Cowboy" poetry reflects the deep respect he has for the Cowboy and Texas. Rod says that writing "is a way of preserving the values of the Cowboy: hard work, honesty and a sense of humor."

"To the Boys at Cutter Bill's Bar" © 2001, Rod Nichols

LEON OVERBAY, "The Boones Creek Bard," lives near Jonesborough, Tennessee on the same farm where he grew up. His hobbies include story-telling and performance poetry. Most of his poetry is about growing up in the rural south in the 60's.

"The Cross-Eyed Bull" © 1991, Leon Overbay, "The Boones Creek Bard"

JIM PACKARD is a radio personality from Madison, Wisconsin. He's the announcer/sidekick on "Michael Feldman's Whad'Ya Know?" on Public Radio International and producer and often host of Wisconsin Public Radio's daily "Conversations with Larry Meiller." His daddy was born in Coffee Creek, Montana, hence Jim's love of the West.

"The Nightingale" © 2001, Jim Packard

ED PARRISH writes magazines and executive speeches for the Cessna Aircraft Company in Wichita, Kansas. In his street act as The Magic Guy, he alternates magic acts with poetry recitations. Ed says the two fit together like this: "Poetry is magic with words, and magic is wordless poetry."

"The Automatic Rope" © 2000, Ed Parrish

SHAD PEASE was born in Laramie and raised on cattle ranches in Wyoming and Colorado. He has set the stage for Michael Martin Murphey, and shared it with Chris Ledoux, Waddie Mitchell, Don Edwards, and Red Steagall. He has written over two hundred poems and recorded three albums.

"Stampede" © 1997, Shad Pease

HJ "HOSS" PETERSON was raised in Southeastern Wyoming, where he grew to love the Cowboy way of life. Through countless hours in the saddle, he has developed a unique take on the life of the modern Cowboy; a view he explains in his book, *Real Cowboys Don't Line Dance.*

"A Prayer for Man and Horse" © 1994, HJ Peterson

RICK PITT is from Lander Wyoming. He says he "enjoys reading Western history, Cowboy Poetry, and living in Wyoming."

"Hell's Half Acre" © 2001, Rick Pitt

VERLIN PITT is a native of Wyoming and works as a Deputy Sheriff. It
has been stated that he writes the finest, most humorous Cowboy Poetry
ever written. He would like to thank his mother Hazel for making
that statement.
  "Desert Rat" © 1999, Verlin Pitt

TOM POLLARD spent his early years on farms and ranches in Pushmataha
County, Oklahoma. Although he was never a Cowboy, he says he "recalls
with wonder and nostalgia those wonderful early days." He now resides in
Fort Worth, Texas (he adds, "Where The West Begins") and loves writing
and reading Cowboy Poetry.
  "Cowboy's Lament" © 1992, Tom Pollard

MIKE PUHALLO is the president of the Charley Russell Western Heritage
Association. He has spent the last twenty five years of ranching in
partnership with his brother, which provides him with "lots to write and
paint about."
  "Home from the Winter Range" © 2000, Mike Puhallo from *Piled Higher and
  Deeper on the Cariboo Trail*, Hancock House, 2001

STEVIE "MEDICINEDOG" RAYMON is a northeast Oregon native, now residing
in the Ozarks. She is a singer/songwriter and member of the Missouri
Cowboy Poets Association. With a decided interest in Western history,
Native cultures and language, she describes her two greatest passions as "all
that is Wild in Creation" and laughter.
  "Thanks Bill" © 1997, Stephanie Raymon

JK REESE resides in Lexington, Kentucky and says he "has a bodacious time
pickin' 'n' grinnin' (mostly grinnin'), dreamin' Cowboy dreams, and vicari-
ously livin'" the adventures of his characters.
  "Bad Pete's Comin' to Town" © 2001, J. K. Reese

JD REITZ is a retired South Dakota rancher and rodeo Cowboy now residing
in Spokane, Washington. He is a member of the Charley Russell Western
Heritage Association and Alberta Cowboy Poets Association. He says he is
"still goin' the road doin' Cowboy Poetry." His latest book is called
Heartwords And Headtrips.
  "Introspection" © 2001, James David Reitz

DAVE RHODES lives in Cache Valley, Utah. He writes poetry mainly about his ancestors' experiences with the Pony Express and their lives in the early days of the American West.

"Out Here at Butte Station" © 1998, Dave Rhodes

MICHAEL SORBONNE ROBINSON, who was "shoein' and trainin' horses during college," is now one of Utah's top poet/songwriter/performers. His show, "Millennial Cowboy" has charmed thousands. Raucous, warm, or philosophical, Michael rides the ranges of emotion with his award-winning work. He says that his wife Debra, his kids, and horses "are the loves of his life."

"The End of the Drought" © 2001, Michael Sorbonne Robinson

FRANCINE ROARK ROBISON is the Cowboy Poet Laureate of Oklahoma. She says she "didn't walk five miles in the snow to school," but she did "walk down to the cattle-guard to catch the bus, carrying her homework and Roy Rogers lunch box." She has appeared at numerous poetry gatherings.

"North to Abilene" © 2000, Francine Roark Robison

SHERRI ROSS writes poetry for her family and friends at their fifth-generation family ranch in the Western North Dakota Badlands. Her family raises Longhorn, Angus, and Hereford cattle on their working cattle ranch. They have operated Dahkotah Lodge Guest Ranch for the last ten years.

"Seasons" © 1999, Sherri Ross

CONNIE ROSSIGNOL lives with her family in Tomé, New Mexico. There they "grow a little hay to sell with a little left over to feed a few head of jackstock" that they ride and drive.

"In Defense of Donkeys" © 1998, Connie Rossignol

JACK SAMMON lives near Bathurst in Australia. His poetry and stories depict the life he lived growing up and working as a stockman and drover (cowboy) on the vast cattle stations (ranches) of Northern Australia, before the country (range) was enclosed with fences.

"After the Wet" © 2000, Jack Sammon

CHARLENE SCHILLING says she's "a wife, mom and school teacher by choice," who has "identified with Cowboy Poetry, chased a few cows, and even laid on a brand or two." She says her "claims to greatness" are "a 52-year marriage, some fine offspring" and her book, *Times and Places*.

"Understanding" © 2000, Charlene S. Schilling

MICHAEL "COYOTE" SCHROLL of Wyoming is a fourth-generation Westerner. An artist and a poet, his poems give his audiences a glimpse into how the West was, and how it continues to be.

"At the Airport" © 1998, Michael Schroll

LLOYD SHELBY lives on the Rancho Poquito in Crosby, Texas, where he raises horses and mosquitoes. He has performed at the National Cowboy Hall of Fame, Luckenbach, and numerous other venues. He is a member of CHAPS, the Cowboy History and Performance Society, and a Director with the American Jack Rabbit Horse Association.

"A Cowboy's Prayer" © 2000, Lloyd Shelby

CHARLEY SIERRA writes and wrangles in northern Nevada with his wife Jenny, and is "pardner-in-crime" to Chuck Shaddoway, author of the highly acclaimed Mr. Woofer stories. Some folks call Charley a "prevaricator"; others say he's just a liar.

"A Christmas Poem" © 1994, Rip-Snortin' Press

PAULA SISK and her family operate a dairy near Westville, Oklahoma. The rhythm of the milking machines seems to inspire Paula's poetry and prevent milkbarn monotony. Paula's poem "Dust" was featured on Public Radio International. She enjoys writing humorous poems that give others insight into farm and ranch life.

"Sweet Lucille" © 2001, Paula Sisk

BRAD SMITH *see* FRENCH CAMP RED

JAY SNIDER was born and raised in southwest Oklahoma. Born a Cowboy, his poetry offers an insight into personal experiences and stories he's heard through a lifetime of being one. He is a member of the Charley Russell Western Heritage Association and the Academy of Western Artists.

"My Ol' Amigo Lum" © 1999, Jay Snider

BRUCE SOUTH, an award winning poet, has called Red Lodge, Montana home since 1992. His poetry reflects his experiences, from his farm and ranch work to being a teamster and wrangler on guest trips, to riding bulls in some of his younger years. He has appeared at gatherings throughout the West.

"The Rough Ride" © 2001, Bruce South

EZRA SPUR, Western artist and poet, lives in Puyallup, Washington. He says that his poems are "the recollections of his youth on the prairie of middle America." His appreciation "of the working folks" and his love of the land are reflected in his poetry.

"The Old Man" © 2000, Ezra Spur

RED STEAGALL is the Official Cowboy Poet of Texas and one of America's most acclaimed Western performers, whose work celebrates the West and Cowboy values. His Ranch Headquarters at RedSteagall.com includes information about his books, recordings, performances, and more.

"Born to this Land" © 1989, Red Steagall

T. R. STEPHENSON lives somewhere West of San Antonio. He is an ex-outlaw, a reclusive man, "due to several folks who would still try to kill him." He performs poetry, songs and stories all over the USA. He is also a voiceover artist.

"I Was the Lady" © 1997, T. R. Stephenson

JEFF STREEBY grew up in Sioux City, Iowa. He has worked with cattle and horses and done day work throughout the West. Jeff teaches English at Perris High School in Perris, California. His work has been widely published and he performs at Cowboy Poetry gatherings around the state.

"The Wild Crew" © 1994, Jeff Streeby (set to music in 1999 by Ken Overcast, it appears on his *Montana Cowboy* CD under the title "Ride, Cowboy, Ride.")

LARRY D. THOMAS, born and raised in West Texas, has lived in Houston since 1967. He's an active member of Western Writers of America, and his poetry has appeared in *Texas Longhorn Trails*, *The Equine Image* and elsewhere. "Lone Star" was originally published in *Cutting Horse Chatter* in November, 2000.

"Lone Star" © 2000, Larry D. Thomas

DIANE THOMPSON is District and County Clerk of Hartley County, Texas. She's been married to her best friend for 34 years and has two children. She's been published in *Cowboy Magazine*, belongs to the Southwest Cowboy Poets' Association, and has a few horses, two mules and some Corriente cows.

"Movin' On'" © 1999, Diane Thompson

DON TIDWELL resides in Centerville, Utah. He is a retired army officer who enjoys telling "stories in rhyme." He is a Cowboy Poetry enthusiast and a former member of the Utah State Poetry Society.

"Poetic Competition" © 2001, Don Tidwell

NEAL TORREY belongs to the Missouri Cowboy Poets Association and Oklahoma Western Heritage, Inc. He turns actual events into poems, and the results are both historical and hysterical. A former Park Service employee and Special Deputy Sheriff, he is also an accomplished Western artist.

"Western Wear" © 1998, Neal R. Torrey

ROGER TRAWEEK lives in Oregon's High Desert near Powell Butte. He is a retired teachers' union representative and intends to spend his retirement writing prose and poetry. Roger is a volunteer worker for the High Desert Western Arts Gathering in Redmond, Oregon.

"The Home Place" © 1999, Roger L. Traweek

TEX TUMBLEWEED, born in Oklahoma, has spent a lifetime in Texas. Now retired, Tex lives in the White Rock area of Dallas, Texas and says, "The closest I ever get to a horse now is at the Mesquite Rodeo arena, so I spend my time writing about them."

"A Prairie King" © 1997, M. S. Land

LEROY WATTS was born in Southwest Missouri. He lived much of his life in the mountains and deserts of Colorado and Arizona before retiring back to the Ozark hills. His poetic stories are "reminiscin's" of those lifestyles. Leroy is one of the founders of The Missouri Cowboy Poets Association.

"Gateway to the West" © 1999, Leroy Watts

OMAR WEST spent the first half of his life trying to get to the American West, where his heart had always been. He is now found at the BAR-D Ranch, Chief Honcho and resident poet at *CowboyPoetry.com*, the internet's largest collection of Cowboy Poetry.

"Friends" © 2001, Omar West

J.A. (JAKE) WHITE is a native of Missouri, a former Marine Rifleman, and a Viet Nam veteran. He "was raised up" riding horses and working on small farms. He has traveled from Golihad, Texas to Kamloops B.C. doing Cowboy Poetry, always a Cowboy at heart.

"Facsimile Cowboy" © 1998, J. A. (Jake) White

DIANA WRAY grew up in northern Utah spending time on her grandparents' ranch and wishing to be a "Cowboy." She still has that same wish, but now has to be content just to write about it. In her next life, she expects things to be different.

"A Cowboy's Computer" © 2001, Diana N. Wray

BEST OF THE WEST

This directory represents selections of the top events, organizations, publications, museums, and historic sites of interest concerning Cowboy and ranching life.

Current listings for all categories are maintained at *CowboyPoetry.com*, where information is continually added and updated. Submissions are invited.

The following pages include listings in these categories:

ANNUAL COWBOY POETRY AND WESTERN MUSIC EVENTS

ORGANIZATIONS AND ASSOCIATIONS
Cowboy and Western Poetry, Heritage, and Music
Rodeo and Equine
Ranching

PUBLICATIONS

MUSEUMS AND WESTERN HERITAGE SITES

ANNUAL COWBOY AND WESTERN MUSIC EVENTS

Events are organized by month, based on recent annual dates. A list of these and other events with current dates is maintained at CowboyPoetry.com.

JANUARY/FEBRUARY

Cochise Cowboy Poetry and Music Gathering Sierra Vista, Arizona
P. O. Box 3201, Sierra Vista, AZ 85636 www.cowboypoets.com

Colorado Cowboy Poetry Gathering Arvada, Colorado
Arvada Center for the Arts and Humanities, 6901 Wadsworth Blvd.,
Arvada, CO 80003 www.arvadacenter.com

Cowboy Ski Challenge Jackson Hole, Wyoming
Chamber of Commerce, PO Box 550, Jackson, WY 83001

Lewis and Clark Cowboy Poetry, Music and Western Arts Festival Lewiston, Idaho
Western Heritage Corporation, P. O. Box 208, Nezperce, ID 83543

National Cowboy Poetry Gathering Elko, Nevada
Western Folklife Center, 501 Railroad Street, Elko, NV 89801 www.westfolk.org

Picacho Peak Trail Ride and Cowboy Poetry Gathering Eloy, Arizona
Chamber of Commerce, 305 Stuart Blvd., Eloy, AZ 85231

Sagebrush Cowboyography Poetry/Music Gathering Buffalo, Wyoming
543 N. DeSmet, Buffalo, WY 82834 www.cowboyography.com

South Texas Ranching Heritage Festival Kingsville, Texas
Texas A&M University-Kingsville and other sponsors www.tamuk.edu

Trail Dust Days, Cowboy Traditions Festival Tucson, Arizona
Agro Land & Cattle Co., Inc., 6541 E. Tanque Verde Rd., Tucson, AZ 85715

MARCH/APRIL

Cowboy Hall of Fame Cowboy Poetry Gathering Oklahoma City, Oklahoma
1700 N.E. 63rd Street, Oklahoma City, OK 73111 www.nationalcowboymuseum.org

Cowboy Poetry and Music Festival Santa Clarita, California
23920 Valencia Blvd., Suite 120, Santa Clarita, CA 91355 www.santa-clarita.com/cp

Cowboy Songs and Range Ballads Cody, Wyoming
Buffalo Bill Historical Center, 720 Sheridan Avenue Cody, WY 82414 www.bbhc.org

Festival of the West Cowboy Poetry & Storytellin' Scottsdale, Arizona
P.O. Box 12966, Scottsdale, AZ 85267 www.festivalofthewest.com

Kamloops Cowboy Festival Kamloops, B.C. Canada
B. C. Cowboy Heritage Society, Box 137, Kamloops, BC, V2C 5K3 www.bcchs.com

Miracle Ranch Cowboy Rendezvous Port Orchard, Washington
12500 Camp Court N.W., Poulsbo, WA 98370 www.cristacamps.com

The **Missouri Cowboy Poets Association Gathering** Mountain View, Missouri
Route 1, Box 155-A, Verona, MO 65769

Rhyolite Jamboree Rhyolite, Nevada
P.O. Box 958, Beatty, NV 89003 www.rhyolitejamboree.com

St. Anthony Cowboy Poetry Gathering St. Anthony, Idaho
Chamber of Commerce, 114 N. Bridge Street St. Anthony, ID 83445
www.stanthonychamber.com

Shanghai Days Cowboy Gathering Wharton, Texas
Chamber of Commerce, P.O. Box 868, 225 N. Richmond Wharton, TX 77488
www.shanghaicowboys.com

Texas Cowboy Poetry Gathering Alpine, Texas
Sul Ross State University www.cowboypoetry.org

Weatherford Cowboy Poetry Gathering Weatherford, Texas
Chamber of Commerce, P.O. Box 310, Weatherford, TX 76086

MAY/JUNE

Campfire Concerts at Historic Fort Concho San Angelo, Texas
630 South Oakes, San Angelo, TX 76903 www.campfireconcerts.20m.com

Chishom Trail Cowboy Gathering, Trail Ride and Rendezvous Meridian, Texas
P.O. Box 974, Meridian, TX 76665 www.pardners.org/ChisholmTrail.htm

Cowboy Poetry and Western Music Thousand Oaks, California
P.O. Box 1695, Thousand Oaks, CA 91358
www.conejoplayers.org/CowboyPoetry.htm

Cowboy Poetry Festival Brandon, Manitoba, Canada
P.O. Box 57, Nesbitt, MB, R0K 1P0 Canada www.cowboypoetry.hypermart.net

The Cowboy Trade Day Claremore, Oklahoma
www.cowboytrader.com

Dakota Cowboy Poetry Gathering Medora, North Dakota
www.ndtourism.com

Echoes of the Trail Fort Scott, Kansas
Fort Scott Community College, 2108 S. Horton, Fort Scott, KS 66701
www.ftscott.cc.ks.us

The Gathering Pincher Creek, Alberta, Canada
Pincher Creek and District Agricultural Society, Pincher Creek, AB,
T0K 1W0 Canada www.pincher-creek.com

High Desert Western Arts Association Redmond, Oregon
P.O. Box 28, Bend, OR 97709 www.hdwaa.org

Pioneer Wagon Train and Cowboy Poetry Mariposa, California
Chamber of Commerce, 5158 Highway 140, P. O. Box 425, Mariposa, CA 95338
www.mariposa.org

Rutlader Outpost Cowboy Poets Gathering Rutlader, Kansas
33565 S. Metcalf, Louisburg, KS 66053 www.rutladeroutpost.com

Western Colorado Cowboy Poetry and Music Festival Whitewater, Colorado
160 Whiting Road, Whitewater, CO 81527 www.hangingw.com

The Western Heritage Classic Abilene, Texas
www.westernheritageclassic.com

Waltzing Matilda Poetry Festival Winton, Queensland, Australia
P.O. Box 84, Hughenden, QLD, Australia 4821
www.camelraces.asn.au/poetry.html

Wild Bill Hickok Days Deadwood, South Dakota
Chamber of Commerce, 735 Main Street, Deadwood, SD 57732
www.deadwood.org/events.htm

William's Lake Stampede William's Lake, British Columbia, Canada
Box 4076, Williams Lake, BC, V2G 2V2 Canada www.williamslakestampede.com

JULY/AUGUST

The Academy of Western Artists Will Rogers Cowboy Awards Ft. Worth, Texas
P.O. Box 35, Gene Autry, OK 73436 www.workingcowboy.com

Annual Gathering (Old Miner's Days) Big Bear Lake, California
P. O. Box 1044, Big Bear Lake, CA 92315 www.oldminers.org

Arizona Cowpunchers' Reunion Rodeo Flagstaff, Arizona
Flagstaff Convention and Visitors Bureau 211 W. Aspen Avenue,
Flagstaff, AZ 86001 www.flagstaffarizona.org

Arizona Cowboy Poets Gathering Prescott, Arizona
415 W. Gurley Street, Prescott, AZ 86301 www.sharlot.org

Calgary Stampede Calgary, Alberta, Canada
P.O. Box 1060, Station M, Calgary, AB, T2P 2K8 Canada
www.calgarystampede.com/stampede

California Rodeo Cowboy Poetry Gathering Salinas, California
1034 North Main Street, Salinas, CA 93906 www.carodeo.com

Campfire Concerts at Historic Fort Concho San Angelo, Texas
630 South Oakes, San Angelo, TX 76903 www.campfireconcerts.20m.com

Carbon County Gathering of Cowboy Poets Rawlins, Wyoming
Box 603, Rawlins, WY 82301 www.wyomingcowboypoetry.com

Cowboy Festival and Wild West Show O'Keefe Ranch, Vernon B. C., Canada
Box 955, Vernon, BC, V1T 6M8 Canada www.okeeferanch.bc.ca

Festival of the American West Wellsville, Utah
The American West Heritage Center, 4025 South Hwy 89-91, Wellsville, UT 84339
www.americanwestcenter.org

Idaho State Cowboy Gathering Nampa, Idaho
P.O. Box 326, Eagle, ID 83616 www.cowboyrudy.com

Kamloops Cattle Drive Kamloops, B.C., Canada
P.O. Box 1332, Kamloops, BC, V2C 6L7 Canada www.cattledrive.bc.ca

Montana Cowboy Poetry Gathering Lewiston, Montana
408 NE Main, Lewistown, MT 59457 www.lewistownchamber.com/mcpg.htm

Omak Stampede and World Famous Suicide Race Omak, Washington
P.O. Box 2028, Omak, WA 98841 www.omakstampede.org

Red Deer's Westerner Days Red Deer, Alberta, Canada
Westerner Park, 4847A-19 Street, Red Deer, AB, T4R 2N7 Canada www.westerner.ab.ca

Rim Country Western Heritage Festival Payson, Arizona
Rim Country Museum, 700 Green Valley Parkway, Payson, AZ 85541

Taylor Cowboy Poetry & Music Taylor, Arizona
Snowflake/Taylor Chamber of Commerce, P.O. Box 776, Snowflake, AZ 85937

Texas Cowboy Reunion Poetry Gathering Stamford, Texas
P.O. Box 928, Stamford, TX 79553 www.tcrrodeo.com

SEPTEMBER/OCTOBER

Badger Clark Hometown Cowboy Poetry Gathering Hot Springs, South Dakota
www.hotsprings-sd.com

Blanco County Heritage Fest Blanco, Texas
PO Box 504, Blanco, TX 78606

California Cowboy Gathering Dublin, California
P.O. Box 2695, Dublin, CA 94568 www.cowboygathering.com

Campfire Concerts at Historic Fort Concho San Angelo, Texas
630 South Oakes, San Angelo, TX 76903 www.campfireconcerts.20m.com

Cheyenne Cowboy Symposium and Celebration Cheyenne, Wyoming
www.cheyennecowboysymposium.com

Clifton Fall Ranch Round Up Clifton, Texas
Clifton Main Street Program, P.O. Box 231, 115 N. Avenue D, Clifton, TX 76634

Cowboy Symposium & Celebration, San Angelo, Texas
www.sanangelocowboys.20m.com/

The Cowboy Trade Day Claremore, Oklahoma
www.cowboytrader.com

Dalton Days Longview, Texas
Gregg County Historical Museum, 214 N. Fredonia, PO Box 3342,
Longview, TX 75606 www.gregghistorical.org

The Dick Shepherd Memorial Cowboy Poetry & Song Gathering Nara Visa, New Mexico
Quay County Chamber of Commerce, 404 W. Tucumcari Blvd., PO Drawer E,
Tucumcari, NM 88401

Durango Cowboy Gathering Durango, Colorado
Box 2571, Durango, CO 81302

Flagstaff Cowboy Poetry Gathering Flagstaff, Arizona
457 Doney Pk. Lane, Flagstaff, AZ 86004

Gene Autry Oklahoma Film and Music Festival, Gene Autry, Oklahoma
P.O. Box 67, Gene Autry, OK 73436 www.cow-boy.com/museum.htm

Gila Valley Cowboy Poetry & Music Roundup Safford, Arizona
Graham County Chamber of Commerce, 1111 Thatcher Blvd., Safford, AZ 85546

Hell's Canyon Mule Days Enterprise, Oregon
P.O. Box 50, Enterprise, OR 97828 www.wallowavalley.com/muledays

Lincoln County Cowboy Symposium Ruidoso Downs, New Mexico
P.O. Box 40, Ruidoso Downs, NM 88346 www.zianet.com/lccs/

Lone Pine Film Festival and Cowboy Poetry Lone Pine, California
126 South Main Street, P.O. Box 749, Lone Pine, CA 93545 www.lone-pine.com

Maple Creek Cowboy Poetry Gathering & Western Art Show
     Maple Creek, Saskatchewan, Canada
Box 1504, Maple Creek, SK, S0N 1N0 Canada

Michael Martin Murphey's WestFest Steamboat Springs, Colorado
www.westfest.net

Morrison Cowboy Celebration Morrison, Colorado
P. O. Box 293, Morrison, CO 80465 www.town.morrison.co.us/cowboys

The National Cowboy Symposium and Celebration Lubbock, Texas
4124 62nd Drive, Lubbock, TX 79413 www.cowboy.org

Old West Days Valentine, Nebraska
P.O. Box 345, Valentine, NE 69201 www.heartcity.com/owd/

Palouse Country Cowboy Poetry and Western Music Festival
Pullman, Washington and Moscow, Idaho
Palouse Gathering, P.O. Box 416, Pullman, WA 99163

Rafter S Timed Event Championship Roping and Cowboy Reunion
Cyril, Oklahoma
Route 1, Box 167, Cyril, OK 73029

Red Steagall Cowboy Gathering Fort Worth, Texas
www.theredsteagallcowboygathering.com

Superstition Mountain Gathering of Cowboy Poets Apache Junction, Arizona
Apache Junction Main Street Project, PO Box 1747, Apache Junction, AZ 85217

Visalia Round-up Visalia, California
Visalia Cowboy Cultural Committee, 1528 East Noble, Box 168, Visalia, CA 93292

West Texas Ranch Rodeo & Celebration Midland, Texas
Midland Chamber of Commerce, 109 N. Main, Midland, TX 79701

Western Legends Celebration and Cowboy Poetry Rodeo Kanab, Utah
89 S. 100 E., Kanab, UT 84741 www.westernlegendsroundup.com

Wet Mountain Western Days Westcliffe, Colorado
www.custercountyco.com/WesternDays/home.asp

Wyoming Cowboy Poetry Roundup Riverton Wyoming
Chamber of Commerce, 213 W. Main Street, Riverton, WY 82501
www.rivertonchamber.org

NOVEMBER/DECEMBER

Arizona National Stock Show/Cowboy Classics Phoenix, Arizona
1826 W McDowell Rd, Phoenix, AZ 85007 www.anls.org

Cowboy Christmas Poetry Gathering Wickenburg, Arizona
Wickenburg Chamber Of Commerce, 216 N. Frontier Street, Wickenburg, AZ 85390

Cowboy Days Las Cruces, New Mexico
New Mexico Farm and Ranch Heritage Museum, 4100 Dripping Springs Road,
Las Cruces, NM 88011

Cowboy Poetry and Buckaroo Fair Heber City, Utah
Heber Valley Chamber of Commerce, 475 North Main, Heber City, UT 84032

Gilbert Cowboy Poetry and Music Gilbert, Arizona
Gilbert Chamber of Commerce, P.O. Box 527, Gilbert, AZ 85299

Grand Canyon Hole in the Ground Cowboy Poetry & Music Gathering
Grand Canyon, Arizona
www.gcanyon.com/Cowboy_Poets.htm

International Western Music Association Festival Tucson, Arizona
P.O. Box 35008, Tucson, AZ 85740 www.westernmusic.org

Larry Chittenden Cowboy Celebration Anson, Texas
Anson Chamber of Commerce, 1132 Court Plaza, Anson, TX 79501

Michael Martin Murphey's Cowboy Christmas Ball Anson, Texas
(and other locations) www.michaelmartinmurphey.com

Monterey Cowboy Poetry and Music Festival Monterey, California
PMB153, 528 Abergo St., Monterey, CA 93940 www.montereycowboy.com

Storyfest George West, Texas
P.O. Box 660, George West, TX 78022 www.georgeweststoryfest.org

World Championship Ranch Rodeo Amarillo, Texas
www.wrca.org/rodeoin.html

Yerington Cowboy Show Yerington, Nevada
Mason Valley Chamber of Commerce, 227 S. Main St, Yerington, NV 89447

ORGANIZATIONS AND ASSOCIATIONS

Cowboy and Western Poetry, Heritage, and Music

Academy of Western Artists (AWA)
P.O. Box 35, Gene Autry, OK 73436 www.workingcowboy.com

American Chuckwagon Association
1723 E. Tate St., Brownfield, TX 79316

The American Cowboy Culture Association
4124 62nd Drive, Lubbock, TX 794113 www.cowboy.org

B. C. Cowboy Heritage Society
Box 137 Kamloops, BC, V2C 5K3 Canada www.bcchs.com

Charley Russell Western Heritage Association (CRWHA)
230 Ute. Trail, Woodland Park, CA 80863 www.charleyrussell.org

Cowboy History and Performance Society (CHAPS)
P.O. Box 710770, Houston, TX 77271 www.cowboysociety.org

Cowboy Poets of Idaho
111 E. 3000 N, Rexburg, ID 83440 sites.netscape.net/cowboypoetsc/homepage

Cowboy Poets of Utah
665 East Julho St., Sandy, UT 84093 utah_cowboys.tripod.com

Cowboys of Color
2100 Evans Ave., Fort Worth, TX 76104 www.cowboysofcolor.org

High Desert Western Arts Association (HDWAA)
P.O. Box 28, Bend, OR 97709 www.hdwaa.org

Missouri Cowboy Poets Association (MCPA)
Rt 1 Box 155-A, Verona, MO 65769

Southwest Cowboy Poets Association
Box 2192, Amarillo, TX 79105

Texas Cowboy Poetry Association
20 La Nell, Canutillo, TX 79835

Utah Western Heritage Foundation
www.utahwesternheritagefoundation.org

Western Heritage Corporation
Box 208, Nezperce, ID 83543

Western Folklife Center
501 Railroad Street, Elko, NV 89801 www.westfolk.org

Western Music Association (WMA)
P.O. Box 35008, Tucson, AZ 85740 www.westernmusic.org

Western Literature Association (WLA)
Utah State University, 3200 Old Main Hill, Logan UT 84322
http://www.usu.edu/~westlit/index.html

Western Writers of America (WWA)
209 E. Iowa, Cheyenne, WY 82009 www.westernwriters.org

Working Ranch Cowboys Association (WRCA)
P. O. Box 7765, Amarillo, TX 79114 www.wrca.org

Rodeo and Equine

American Horse Council
1700 K Street NW, Suite 300, Washington, DC 20006 www.horsecouncil.org

American Junior Rodeo Association (AJRA)
4501 Armstrong, San Angelo, TX 76903 home1.gte.net/ajra/index.htm

The American Paint Horse Association (APHA)
P.O. Box 961023, Fort Worth, TX 76161 www.apha.com

American Professional Rodeo Association (APRA)
P.O. Box 930, Bellefonte, PA 16823-0830 www.apra.com

American Quarter Horse Association (AQHA)
P.O. Box 200, Amarillo, TX 79168 www.aqha.com

Appaloosa Horse Club
2720 W. Pullman Road, Moscow, ID 83843 www.appaloosa.com

Australian Pro-Rodeo Association (APRA)
PO Box 264, Warwick, QLD, Australia 4370 www.prorodeo.asn.au

Canadian Professional Rodeo Association (CPRA)
#223, 2116 27 Avenue N.E., Calgary, AB, T2E 7A6 www.rodeocanada.com

The Institute of Range and the American Mustang (IRAM)
P.O. Box 998, Hot Springs, SD 57747 www.wildmustangs.com

National Barrel Horse Association (NBHA)
P.O. Box 1988, Augusta, GA 30903 www.nbha.com

National Cutting Horse Association (NCHA)
4704 Hwy 377 South, Fort Worth, TX 76116-8805 www.nchacutting.com

National High School Rodeo Association (NRSRA)
11178 N. Huron, Ste. 7, Denver, CO 80234 www.nhsra.org

National Intercollegiate Rodeo Association (NIRA)
2316 Eastgate North, Suite 160, Walla Walla, WA 99362
www.collegerodeo.com

National Little Britches Rodeo Association (NLBRA)
1045 W. Rio Grande, Colorado Springs, CO 80906 www.nlbra.com

National Pro Rodeo Association (NPRA)
P.O. Box 212, Mandan, ND 58554 www.npra.com

National Reined Cow Horse Association (NRCHA)
4500 S. Laspina St., Tulare, CA 93274 www.nrcha.com

National Reining Horse Association (NRHA)
3000 NW 10th St., Oklahoma City, OK 73107-5302 www.nrha.com

National Senior Pro Rodeo Association (NSPRA)
1963 North First St., Hamilton, MT 59840 www.seniorrodeo.com

Professional Bull Riders Association
6 South Tejon, Suite 700, Colorado Springs, CO 80903 www.pbrnow.com

Professional Rodeo Cowboys Association (PRCA)
101 ProRodeo Drive, Colorado Springs, CO 80919 www.prorodeo.com

Professional Western Rodeo Association (Pro-West)
PO Box 427, Moses Lake, WA 98837 www.pro-west.net

Professional Women's Rodeo Association (PWRA)
1235 Lake Plaza Drive, Suite 134, Colorado Springs, CO 80906 www.wpra.com

United States Calf Roping Association (USCRA)
P.O. Box 690, Giddings, TX 78942 www.uscra.com

United States Team Roping Championships (USTRC)
P.O. Box 1198, Stephenville, TX 76401 www.ustrc.com

Women's Professional Rodeo Association (WPRA)
1235 Lake Plaza Drive, Suite 134, Colorado Springs, CO 80906 www.wpra.com

RANCHING

American Farm Bureau
225 Touhy Ave. Park Ridge, IL 60068
600 Maryland Ave., SW, Suite 800, Washington, DC 20024 www.fb.org

American Farmland Trust
1200 18th St. NW, Suite 800, Washington, DC 20036 www.farmland.org

Center for Rural Affairs
101 S Tallman St., PO Box 406, Walthill, NE 68067 www.cfra.org

Community Alliance With Family Farmers
P.O. Box 363, Davis, CA 95617 www.caff.org

International Texas Longhorn Association (ITLA)
P. O. Box 122988, Fort Worth, TX 76121 www.itla.com

National Cattlemen's Association
5420 South Quebec St., Greenwood Village, CO 80111
1301 Pennsylvania Ave. NW, Suite 300, Washington, D.C. 20004 www.beef.org

National Livestock Producers Association
660 Southpointe Court, Suite 314, Colorado Springs, CO 80906 www.nlpa.org

Ranching Heritage Association
Box 43201, Lubbock, TX 79409 www.ttu.edu/RanchingHeritageCenter/association.html

PUBLICATIONS

Ag Journal focuses on the business of agriculture and includes cultural and equestrian events, entertainment, and columnists, including Baxter Black.
122 San Juan, La Junta, CO 81050 www.agjournalonline.com

American Cowboy Magazine covers western and rodeo lifestyles and features include a regular Cowboy Poetry page.
P. O. Box 820, Buffalo, WY 82834 www.americancowboy.com

Arizona Highways, first published in 1925, is an advertising-free monthly magazine with articles that celebrate Arizona travel and history.
2039 West Lewis Avenue, Phoenix, AZ 85009-2819 www.arizonahighways.com

Australian Farm Journal, published monthly, is Australia's leading agricultural business, farm management, marketing and technology magazine.
10 Sydenham St, Moonee Ponds VIC, 3039 Australia
www.australianfarmjournal.com

Barrel Horse News is the monthly magazine of the National Barrel Horse Association, dedicated to the sport of barrel racing.
P. O. Box 9707, Fort Worth, TX 76147 www.nbha.com

BC Cowboy Heritage Society Newsletter is an on-line publication with information, stories, and poems "from the north side of the Medicine Line." www.bcchs.com

California Cattleman is the monthly publication of the California Cattlemen's Association, published 11 times a year.
1221 H Street, Sacramento, California 95814 www.calcattlemanmag.com

Canadian Cowboy Country, published five times a year, celebrates the Canadian Cowboy culture and western lifestyle and includes news, features and event listings.
50 Street, Edmonton, AB, T6B 2L5 Canada www.canadiancowboy.ca

Cattlemen Magazine is a Canadian monthly filled with features and news about the cattle industry.
P.O. Box 6600, Winnipeg, MB, R3C 3A7 Canada www.agcanada.com/cm/cm.htm

Christian Cowboy Magazine is a bi-monthly magazine with Christian-focused articles, including poetry.
P.O. Box 248, Bandera, TX 78003 www.christiancowboy.org/magazine.html

Chronicle of the Old West is a monthly newspaper for Old West enthusiasts.
P. O. Box 2859, Show Low, AZ 85902 www.chronicleoftheoldwest.com

County Grapevine is a grassroots newspaper covering music, dance, storytelling, Cowboys, rodeos and country entertainment.
P. O. Box 380219, Murdock, FL 33938 www.countrygrapevine.com

Country Line Magazine is a monthly Texas country music, Cowboy and lifestyle magazine
P.O. Box 17245, Austin, TX 78760 www.countrylinemagazine.com

Cowboy Magazine offers fiction, poetry, and more for "people who value the Cowboy lifestyle."
Box 126EP, La Veta, CO 81055-0126 www.datasys.net/edpak/cowb.html

Cowboy Sports and Entertainment Magazine includes articles on rodeos, western art forms, Cowboy gatherings and western heritage events.
16360 Park Ten Place, Suite 117, Houston, TX 77084

Cowboy Sports News is a monthly publication that includes features and a rodeo calendar of events, results and standings.
P O Box 575, Sealy, TX 77474 www.cowboysportsnews.com

Cowboy Times serves Texas, New Mexico, Oklahoma, Kansas and Colorado with the latest news in rodeo, roping and barrel racing.
P.O. Box 1419, Clovis, NM 88101 www.cowboytimesnews.com

CowboyPoetry.com News is a free email newsletter with updates on the latest news, features, events, new Cowboy Poetry, and the Lariat Laureate competition at the Bar-D Ranch.
www.CowboyPoetry.com

Cowboys & Indians is a Western lifestyle magazine published 7 times a year, with a variety of articles including interviews and features on travel, fashion and art.
www.cowboysindians.com

Cutting Horse Chatter is the monthly publication of the National Cutting Horse Association.
4704 Hwy. 377 South, Fort Worth, TX 76116 www.nchacutting.com

Desert Cowboy is a bi-monthly publication distributed throughout the West and on-line with Cowboy events, news and poetry.
56484 Onaga Trail, Yucca Valley, CA 92284 www.desertcowboy.com

Farmer and Stock Owner is the magazine of the South Australian Farmers' Federation, published bimonthly.
123 Greenhill Road, Unley, SA, 5061 Australia

Great Lakes Rodeo News has news, feature stories, results, upcoming events, and photography covering the professional, amateur and youth rodeo associations within the Great Lakes Circuit.
P.O. Box 382, Iron River, MI 49935 www.greatlakesrodeonews.com

Hoof and Horns is an Australian magazine, published bimonthly. Founded more than 50 years ago, they feature comprehensive coverage of Australia's horse sports.
PO Box 586, Ormiston, QLD, 4160 Australia

Horse & Rider includes coverage of horse-world news and events, profiles of legendary horses and horsepeople, and articles on training techniques, competitive strategies and horse-care.
1597 Cole Blvd., Ste. 350 Golden, CO 80401 www.horseandrider.com

Horses All is a monthly newspaper for horse enthusiasts across Canada and the northern United States with human-and-horse features, news and association reports, and expert equine columnists.
278-19th Street NE, Calgary, AB, T2E 8P7 www.horsesall.com/horsesall

Missouri Life is a bimonthly magazine that explores Missouri, its diverse people and places, both past and present.
P.O, Box. 421, Fayette, MO 65248 www.missourilife.com

Montana Magazine focuses on Montana history, natural history, outdoor recreation, and travel.
P.O. Box 5630, Helena, MT 59604 www.montanamagazine.com

Nevada Magazine is a complete guide to the Silver State, produced bi-monthly under the auspices of the Nevada Commission on Tourism,
401 N. Carson St., Suite 100, Carson City, NV 89701 www.nevadamagazine.com

New Mexico Magazine is published monthly and includes features on the state's multicultural heritage, arts, climate, environment and people.
495 Old Santa Fe Trail, Santa Fe, NM 87501 www.nmmagazine.com

North Dakota Horizons Magazine is a quarterly publication with editorial emphasis on North Dakota people, places, and events.
P.O. Box 2639, Bismarck, ND 58502 www.ndhorizons.com

Oklahoma Today is a bimonthly publication that explores the people, places, history, and culture of Oklahoma.
P.O. Box 53384, Oklahoma City, OK 73152-3384 www.oklahomatoday.com

Pacific & Prairie Horse Journal is a monthly magazine serving Western Canada's horse community.
P.O. Box 2190, Sidney, BC, V8L 3S8 Canada www.horsejournals.com/pphj.htm

Persimmon Hill magazine, published since 1970, is journal of the National Cowboy & Western Heritage Museum.
1700 N. E. 63rd Street, Oklahoma City, OK 73111 www.cowboyhalloffame.org

Pro Bull Rider is the official magazine of the Professional Bull Riders Association (PBR) published bimonthly.
1570 Corporate Drive, Suite A, Costa Mesa, CA 92626 www.pbrnow.com

ProRodeo Sports News (PSN) is the biweekly publication of the Professional Rodeo Cowboys Association (PRCA).
101 Pro Rodeo Dr., Colorado Springs, CO 80919 www.prorodeo.com

Pro Rodeo World is published monthly by the International Professional Rodeo Association.
P.O. Box 83377, Oklahoma City, OK 73148 www.iprarodeo.com

Range Magazine is devoted to the issues, people, lifestyles, lands and wildlife of the West, and includes regular features about Western art and poetry.
106 E. Adams, Suite 201, Carson City, NV 89706 www.rangemagazine.com

ReadTheWest.com is an on-line magazine with features including Western fiction, poetry, art, and music.
www.ReadTheWest.com

Reno.com is an on-line publication that covers the Reno Rodeo and other area Western cultural events.
www.reno.com

Rocky Mountain Rider is a monthly regional all-breed horse magazine, distributed throughout the Northern Rockies.
P.O. Box 1011, Hamilton, MT 59840 www.rockymountainrider.com

Rocky Mountain Roper and Rodeo News is a news source for the rodeo athlete, with feature articles and listings for all arena events.
P.O. Box 842, Laporte, CO 80535 www.rockymountainroper.com

Rodeo Illustrated Magazine provides comprehensive rodeo information and coverage of professional rodeo events throughout the country.
5601 Bridge Street, Suite 356, Fort Worth, TX 76112 www.rodeoillustrated.com

Rope Burns serves the Cowboy entertainment and trade industry with comprehensive and up-to-date listings and articles about Cowboy Poetry and music events.
P.O. Box 35, Gene Autry, OK 73436 www.workingcowboy.com

Roundup Magazine is a publication of Western Writers of America, sponsors of the Spur Award for distinguished writing about the American West.
1012 Fair Street, Franklin, TN 37064-2718 www.westernwriters.org

South Dakota Magazine is a bi-monthly South Dakota lifestyle magazine with feature articles and a statewide list of events.
P.O. Box 175, Yankton, SD 57078 www.sodakmag.com

Sunset Magazine is a monthly magazine "written by Westerners for Westerners," in publication since 1898.
80 Willow Road, Menlo Park, CA 94025 www.sunset.com

The Texas Cowboy Gazette is an on-line magazine dedicated to the life, legend, history and future of the Texas Cowboy.
www.texascowboygazette.com

Texas Monthly Magazine chronicles life in contemporary Texas and serves as a leisure guide for music, the arts, travel, restaurants, museums, and cultural events.
P.O. Box 1569, Austin, TX www.texasmonthly.com

Texas Highways is the official travel magazine of Texas, and tells the Texas story to readers around the world.
P.O. Box 141009, Austin, TX 78714 www.texashighways.com

The Tombstone Epitaph is a monthly publication of the newspaper founded in 1880, which calls itself "the Old West's most famous newspaper."
P. O. Box 1880, Tombstone, AZ 85638 www.tombstone-epitaph.com

The Virtual Texan, produced by the *Fort Worth Star-Telegram*, is a comprehensive depository of information organized in seven sections, The History, The Land, The Culture, Chuck Wagon, Reading Room, Hitching Post and Saddlebag.
www.virtualtexan.com

Western Horseman, published since 1936, covers all aspects of horses and equestrian life, includes features about ranching, Western culture, life and history, and usually includes a excellent example of western poetry.
Box 7980, Colorado Springs, CO 80933 www.westernhorseman.com

WildWest Magazine covers the true history of the people, places, battles, and events that led to the taming of the great American frontier.
741 Miller Dr. S.E., Leesburg, VA 20175 www.thehistorynet.com/WildWest/

The Wrangler is a twice-monthly publication with horse and rodeo news.
P.O. Box 6070, Riverton, WY 82501 www.thewrangler.com

The Wyoming Companion is a quality internet publication, with features on
Western literature and poetry.
www.wyomingcompanion.com

More

The Cattle Pages is an impressive network for small to medium-sized businesses in
the cattle industry—ranch owners, marketing managers, and entrepreneurs. Their
Publications listings range from Gene Autry's Ten Commandments to Cowboy Poetry.
www.cattlepages.com/pubs/

Cowboy Miner Publications publishes fine contemporary and classic poetry books,
including the works of Bruce Kiskaddon, S. Omar Barker, and Henry Herbert
Knibbs.
PO Box 9674, Phoenix, AZ 85068 www.cowboyminer.com

Gibbs Smith publishes a large number of some of the most popular Cowboy Poetry
and western books, including the two best-selling collections from Elko's National
Cowboy Poetry Gathering and *Cowgirl Poetry*, edited by Virginia Bennett.
P.O. Box 667, Layton, UT 84041 www.gibbs-smith.com

Hancock House publishes the work of classic and contemporary Cowboy and
Western poets, including Mike Puhallo and Bette Wolf Duncan.
1431 Harrison Avenue, Blaine, WA 98230-5005 www.hancockhouse.com

SilverCreekCowboy is a full service Western music and bookstore, and their Cowboy
Poetry offerings include hard-to-find contemporary poets' small press and self-pub-
lished books and recordings.
www.silvercreekmusic.com/CowboyPoetry.html

Westerns Movie Channel is a premium digital cable/satellite network that broad-
casts classic Western movies and television series, interviews with stars, and cover-
age of Western related festivals.
www.starzencore.com/se/westerns/index.html

MUSEUMS AND WESTERN HERITAGE SITES

Adams Museum Deadwood, South Dakota
The oldest history museum in the Black Hills, located in an elegant Victorian mansion built in 1892. The collection includes memorabilia associated with Wild Bill Hickok and Calamity Jane.
22 Van Buren Street, Deadwood, SD 57732 (605) 578-3724
www.adamsmuseumandhouse.org

The Alamo San Antonio, Texas
Representing nearly 300 years of history, three buildings house exhibits on the Texas revolution and Texas history.
P.O. Box 2599, San Antonio, TX 78299 (210) 225-1391
www.thealamo.org

Alberta Western Heritage Centre Cochrane, Alberta, Canada
A cowboy, ranch and rodeo interpretive facility located on the historic Cochrane Ranche.
Box 1477, Cochrane, AB, TOL OWO Canada (403) 932-3514
www.westernheritage.farmca.com

American Folklife Center Washington, D.C.
Part of the Library of Congress, the center carries out its congressional mandate, "to preserve and present American Folklife," through its collections, programs, and services. The center initiates fieldwork, maintains a public reading room and reference service, sponsors concerts and events, and produces print publications and published recordings from its collections.
101 Independence Avenue SE, Washington, D.C. 20540 (202) 707-5510
www.loc.gov/folklife/aboutafc.html

American Quarter Horse Heritage Center & Museum Amarillo, Texas
The versatility of the American Quarter Horse, from racing and rodeoing to ranching and showing, is documented in a research library and showcased through interactive exhibits, artifacts, video presentations, live demonstrations and works of art.
2601 I-40 East, Amarillo, TX 79104, (806) 376-5181
www.imh.org/imh/qhm/qhhome.html

American West Heritage Center Wellsville, Utah
A 160 acre living history facility that accurately interprets life from 1820-1920; the site of the annual Festival of the American West.
4025 South Hwy 89-91, Wellsville, UT 84339 (435) 245-6050
www.americanwestcenter.org

Amon Carter Museum Fort Worth, Texas
Expanding on philanthropist Amon G. Carter, Sr.'s original collection of 400 paint-
ings, drawings, and works of sculpture by Remington and Russell, the museum
encompasses a wide range of 19th and early 20th century American paintings,
drawings, prints, sculpture and photographs.
3501 Camp Bowie Blvd, Fort Worth, TX 76107 (817) 738-1933
www.cartermuseum.org

Astor House Museum Golden, Colorado
The museum and Clear Creek History Park's exhibits offer a look back in time to
Colorado life in the late 1800s.
822 12th Street, Golden, CO 80401 (303) 278-3557
www.astorhousemuseum.org

Australian Stockman's Hall of Fame Longreach, Queensland, Australia
Paying tribute to the men and women who pioneered the outback, exhibits explore
droving, bush crafts, Aboriginal stockmen, rough riding, transport, cattle, muster-
ing, campdrafting and other aspects of the outback heritage.
PO Box 171, Longreach, QLD, Australia 4730 +61 (0) 7 4658 2166
www.outbackheritage.com.au

Black American West Museum and Heritage Center Denver, Colorado
Historical artifacts, documents and other memorabilia tell the history and relate the
stories of the Black men and women pioneers who helped settle and develop the West.
3091 California Street, Denver, CO 80205 (303) 292-2566
www.coax.net/people/lwf/bawmus.htm

Bob Bullock Texas State History Museum Austin, Texas
"The Story of Texas" is explored through programs and exhibits themed Land,
Identity and Opportunity.
1800 N. Congress Avenue, Austin, TX 78711 (512) 936-8746
www.tspb.state.tx.us/tspb/tSHM/welcome/welcome.htm

Boot Hill Museum Dodge City, Kansas
Located on the original site of Boot Hill Cemetery, the museum employs audio-visu-
al programs, exhibits, reconstructions, restorations, living history demonstrations
and theatrical performances to interpret life in the 1800s.
Front Street, Dodge City, KS 67801 (316) 227-8188
www.boothill.org

Buffalo Bill Grave and Museum Golden, Colorado
Exhibits illustrate the life, times, and legend of William F. Cody; the Wild West
shows, Indian artifacts, Western art and firearms.
987-1/2 Lookout Mountain Road, Golden, CO 80401 (303) 526-0747
www.buffalobill.org

Buffalo Bill Historical Center Cody, Wyoming
The center houses the Whitney Gallery of Western Art's collection of paintings, sculptures and prints that trace the artistic interpretations of the West from the early 19th century to today, and the Buffalo Bill, Cody Firearms and Plains Indian museums.
720 Sheridan Avenue, Cody, WY 82414 (307) 587·4771
www.bbhc.org

Cattle Raisers Museum Fort Worth, TX
The museum houses Cowboy photos, artifacts, a talking-longhorn diorama, and is home to the largest documented branding iron collection in the world.
1301 W 7th St, Fort Worth, TX 76102 (817) 332-8551

Center for Folklife and Cultural Heritage Washington, D.C.
The center promotes contemporary grassroots cultures. It conducts research, maintains archives, and produces the Smithsonian Folklife Festival, recordings, exhibitions, documentary films and videos, symposia, and educational materials.
750 9th Street NW, Washington, D.C. 20560 (202) 275-1150
www.folklife.si.edu/index.htm

C. M. Russell Museum Great Falls, Montana
The collection includes 2,000 of Charles M. Russell's artworks, personal objects, and artifacts. Russell's permanent residence (built in 1900) and his original log cabin studio (built in 1903) reside on the museum grounds.
400 13th Street North, Great Falls, MT 59401 (406) 727-8787
www.cmrussell.org

Chisholm Trail Heritage Center Duncan, Oklahoma
The museum and visitor center relate the story of the famous Trail.
1000 North 29th Street, Duncan, OK 73534 (580) 252-6692
www.onthechisholmtrail.com

Coutts Memorial Museum of Art El Dorado, Kansas
The collection contains more than 1,000 pieces, including works by Remington and Russell.
110 N. Main, El Dorado, KS 67042 (316) 321-1212
http://skyways.lib.ks.us/museums/coutts/

Cowboy Artists of America Museum Kerrville, Texas
The museum's art features the hard-working Cowboys, women, settlers, mountain men and Plains Indians of the American West, and displays highlight the history of famous ranches and the diversity of Western culture.
1550 Bandera Highway, Kerrville, TX 78028 (830) 896-2553
www.caamuseum.com

Cowboy Memorial and Library Caliente, California
Located a few miles from the south entrance to Sequoia National Park, exhibits
include a chuck wagon, a buggy, a corral and other tools and trappings of western
trail life. Several giant vans house an extensive collection of branding irons, saddles,
spurs, hobbles, ropes and whips.
40371 Cowboy Lane, Walker Basin Road, Caliente, CA 93518 (661) 867-2410
www.tehachapi.com/cowboy

Desert Caballeros Western Museum Wickenburg, Arizona
The collections include Western art by Catlin, Remington and Russell, along with
exhibits of Cowboy gear, period rooms and dioramas from Arizona's territorial era.
21 North Frontier Street, Wickenburg, AZ 85390 (520) 684-2272
www.westernmuseum.org

Devil's Rope Museum McLean, Texas
A museum dedicated to preserving the history of barbed wire, and explaining its
impact on the development of the Old West.
100 Kingsley Street, Box 290, McLean, TX 79057 (806) 779-2225
www.barbwiremuseum.com

Eiteljorg Museum Indianapolis, Indiana
The American Western gallery includes paintings, drawings and sculpture that
explore artistic visions of the West from the early 19th century to the present.
500 West Washington St., Indianapolis, IN 46204 (317) 636-9378
www.eiteljorg.org

Fife Folklore Archives Logan, Utah
One of the largest repositories of American folklore in the United States, the
archives house over 25 folklore collections and projects, including a Cowboy
Poetry Library.
Merrill Library, 3032 Old Main Hill, Utah State University, Logan, UT 84322-3032
www.usu.edu/~folklo/folk.htm

Frederic Remington Art Museum Ogdensburg, New York
The collection includes 70 of Remington's oil paintings, 14 bronze sculptures, hun-
dreds of watercolors and pen and ink illustrations, 1,000 photographs, and many of
the artist's tools, personal possessions and sketchbooks. Remington is buried nearby
in Evergreen Cemetery.
303 Washington Street, Ogdensburg, NY 13669 (315) 393-2425
www.aam-us.org/frederic.htm

Fremont County Pioneer Museum Lander, Wyoming
The museum contains exhibits depicting the lives of pioneer families and settlers in
the area, along with early Indian artifacts.
630 Lincoln St., Lander, WY 82520 (307) 332-4137

Gene Autry Museum of Western Heritage Los Angeles, California
The museum is home to the Gene Autry Archive, a comprehensive collection documenting the career and business interests of the Western star, and is a major repository of western history and art.
4700 Western Heritage Way, Los Angeles, CA 90027 (323) 667-2000
www.autry-museum.org

Gene Autry Oklahoma History Museum Gene Autry, Oklahoma
The museum holds an extensive collection of memorabilia from Gene Autry, Roy Rogers, Rex Allen, Tex Ritter, Jimmy Wakely, Eddie Dean, and others who appeared in the musical Western movies of the 1930s and '40s.
P.O. Box 67, Gene Autry, OK 73436 (580) 294-3047
www.cow-boy.com/museum.htm

George Ranch Historical Park Richmond, Texas
This living history park celebrates Texas cowboy and ranch life from 1830 to 1930 using costumed re-enactors, cattle and horses.
P.O. Box 1248, 10215 FM 762, Richmond, TX 77406 (281) 343-0218
www.georgeranch.org

Gilcrease Museum Tulsa, Oklahoma
Treasures from this permanent collection of western art include galleries showcasing the works of Remington, Russell, Thomas Moran, George Catlin, and Olaf Seltzer.
1400 Gilcrease Museum Road, Tulsa, OK 41270 (918) 596-2700
www.gilcrease.org

Glenbow Museum Calgary, Alberta, Canada
This museum's exhibits focus on the development of the West from the earliest explorers who traveled across the continent in the early 1800s, including surveyors who captured images of the West in watercolor and on camera and professional artists who traveled West once the Canadian Pacific Railway was completed.
130 - 9th Avenue S.E., Calgary, AB, T2G 0P3 Canada (403) 268-4100
www.glenbow.org

Haley Library and History Center Midland, Texas
The Library houses more than 25,000 volumes of books, manuscripts and other printed material documenting Western history. Permanent exhibits feature the works of noted Western artists, and there is an extensive photographic archive of range and Cowboy life.
1805 West Indiana Avenue, Midland, TX 79701 (915) 682-5785
www.haleylibrary.com

Historic Fort Caspar Casper, Wyoming
The museum collects, preserves and exhibits artifacts concerning the social and natural history of Fort Caspar, the city of Casper, central Wyoming, and Westward migration.
4001 Fort Caspar Road, Casper, WY 82604 (307) 235-8462
www.fortcasparwyoming.com

Hubbard Museum of the American West Ruidoso Downs, New Mexico
The museum complex includes the Anne Stradling collection of 10,000 horse-related artifacts and is the home of the Lincoln County Cowboy Symposium.
P.O. Box 40, Ruidoso Downs, NM 88346 (505) 378-4142
www.zianet.com/museum

King Ranch Museum Kingsville, Texas
Highlights of the museum's collections include Toni Frissell's award-winning photographic essay of life on King Ranch in the early 1940's; saddles from around the world, guns, historic Texas flags, antique carriages and vintage cars.
405 North 6th Street, Kingsville, TX 78364 (361) 595-1881
www.king-ranch.com/main_museum.htm

Museum of the Cariboo Chilcotin Williams Lake, British Columbia, Canada
The museum is home to the B.C. Cowboy Hall of Fame and a special display area features photos, biographies and memorabilia of the province's outstanding Cowboys.
113 North 4th Avenue, Williams Lake, BC, V2G 2C8 Canada (250) 392-7404
www.cowboy-museum.com

Museum of Northwest Colorado Craig, Colorado
The Cowboy and Gunfighter Museum housed here showcases Bill Mackin's collection of nearly 1,000 "working cowboys'" artifacts.
590 Yampa Avenue, Craig, CO 81625 (970) 824-6360
www.museumnwco.org

National Cowboy and Western Heritage Museum Oklahoma City, Oklahoma
Visitors can view art by Prix de West Award winners as well as significant works by Russell, Remington, Bierstadt and others. The complex also contains Prosperity Junction, a 14,000 square foot turn-of-the-century western town, and the American Cowboy, American Rodeo and Western Entertainment galleries.
1700 N.E. 63rd Street, Oklahoma City, OK 73111 (405) 478-2250
www.nationalcowboymuseum.org

National Cowgirl Museum and Hall of Fame Fort Worth, Texas
The museum is dedicated to honoring and documenting the lives of women who have distinguished themselves while exemplifying the pioneer spirit of the American West. The honorees include Cowgirls, ranch women, writers, artists, teachers and entertainers.
111 West 4th St., Fort Worth, TX 76102 (817) 336-4475
www.cowgirl.net

National Ranching Heritage Center Lubbock, Texas
This outdoor museum was established to preserve the history of ranching and pio-
neer life and the development of the livestock industry in North America. More than
35 authentic furnished ranch buildings and structures have been relocated here to
show the evolution of ranch life from the late 1780s through the 1930s.
3121 Fourth Street, Lubbock, TX 79409 (806) 742-0498
www.ttu.edu/RanchingHeritageCenter

New Mexico Farm & Ranch Heritage Museum Las Cruces, New Mexico
This 47-acre site celebrates the role of agriculture in the Indian, Spanish and Anglo
cultural mosaic of New Mexico.
Dripping Springs Road, PO Drawer 1898, Las Cruces, NM 88004 (505) 522-4100
www.nmmnh-abq.mus.nm.us/frm/frm.html

Northeastern Nevada Museum Elko, Nevada
The museum's brand collection contains original brand patches filed in Elko County
in the early 1870s, and a permanent exhibit features historical artifacts, maps and
information about the California Trail and some of its emigrants. A themed exhibit
accompanies each National Cowboy Poetry Gathering.
1515 Idaho Street, Elko, NV 89801 (775) 738-3418
www.nenv-museum.org

Old Cowtown Museum Wichita, Kansas
An open-air, living history museum that interprets the history of Wichita and
Sedgwick County, and life on the southern plains circa 1865-1880.
1871 Sim Park Drive, Wichita, KS 67203 (316) 264-0671
www.old-cowtown.org

Old West Museum Cheyenne, Wyoming
The collection focuses on the reality of ranching, Western landscapes, rodeo and
Native American cultures. Artists represented include Bill Anton, whose "The Best
Laid Plans" is the cover art for *The Big Roundup*.
P.O. Box 2720, 4610 North Carey Avenue, Cheyenne, WY 82003 (307) 778-7290
www.oldwestmuseum.org

Panhandle-Plains Historical Museum Canyon, Texas
The largest history museum in Texas contains more than a million artifacts, ranging
from Comanche Chief Quanah Parker's eagle feather headdress to historic collec-
tions of Texas art. The Western heritage area includes a reconstruction of a late
1800s Panhandle town.
Located on the campus of West Texas A&M University at 2503 Fourth Avenue,
Canyon, TX 79016 (806) 651-2235
www.panhandleplains.org

Phippen Museum Prescott, Arizona
The museum houses an outstanding collection of Western paintings, drawings, bronzes, historic photographs and artifacts along with a section dedicated to the work of George Phippen, one of the original founders and first President of the Cowboy Artists of America.
4701 Highway 89 North, Prescott, AZ 86301 (520) 778-1385
www.phippenmuseum.org

Phoenix Art Museum Phoenix, Arizona
The museum's extensive Western American Collection includes the works of Remington and Russell. Howard Terpning, Robert Lougheed, Fritz White and other members of the Cowboy Artists of America are also represented.
1625 North Central Ave., Phoenix, AZ 85004 (602) 257-1222
www.phxart.org

Pro Rodeo Hall of Fame and Museum of the American Cowboy
Colorado Springs, Colorado
Rodeo's evolution, from its origins in 19th-century ranch work to its present status as a major spectator attraction, is documented in two multimedia presentations. There are also exhibits of historic and modern Cowboy and rodeo gear, a replica rodeo arena and a sculpture garden.
101 ProRodeo Drive, Colorado Springs, CO 80919 (719) 528-4764
www.prorodeo.com

Rockwell Museum Corning, New York
One of the most comprehensive collections of American Western art in the eastern United States, the museum contains paintings and sculpture by Remington, Russell, Bierstadt and many others artists.
111 Cedar Street, Corning, NY 14830 (607) 937-5386
www.rockwellmuseum.org

Roy Rogers-Dale Evans Museum Victorville, California
The treasures and personal memories of the adventures and lifetimes of King of the Cowboys Roy Rogers and Queen of the West Dale Evans are showcased here. Among the exhibits is the mounted Trigger as most remember him, rearing up on his hind legs.
15650 Seneca Road, Victorville, CA 92392 (760) 243-4547
www.royrogers.com

R. W. Norton Art Gallery Shreveport, Louisiana
The gallery's collection of American western art includes works by Russell and Remington. The collection of Russell bronze sculptures is one of the largest and most complete ever assembled.
4747 Creswell Ave., Shreveport, LA 71106 (318) 865-4201
www.softdisk.com/comp/norton

Sharlot Hall Prescott, Arizona
Founded by poet and historian Sharlot Hall in 1928, this institution continues to explore the rich diversity of its regional heritage with its exhibits, festivals, living history events, theater performances, library and archives. The museum hosts the Arizona Cowboy Poets Gathering.
415 West Gurley Street, Prescott, AZ 86301 (520) 445-3122
www.sharlot.org

Sid Richardson Collection of Western Art Museum Fort Worth, Texas
The collection is a permanent exhibit of 56 paintings by Remington and Russell, a legacy of the late oilman and philanthropist, Sid Williams Richardson.
309 Main St., Fort Worth, TX 76102 (817) 332-6554
www.sidrmuseum.org

Stockyards Museum Fort Worth, Texas
Located in the historic Livestock Exchange Building, the museum tells the story of the Fort Worth Stockyards and the meat packing industry in Fort Worth.
131 E. Exchange Avenue, Fort Worth, TX 76106 (817) 625-5087

Texas Ranger Hall of Fame and Museum Waco, Texas
The museum offers exhibits on history and material culture related to the Texas Rangers, Texas, and the American West.
100 Texas Ranger Trail, Waco, TX 76706 (254) 750-8631
www.texasranger.org

Waltzing Matilda Centre Winton, Queensland, Australia
The world's only center dedicated to a song (by "Banjo" Paterson) contains an interactive exhibition gallery, a sound and light show, and a vast collection of pioneering memorabilia from the region.
Elderslie Street, Winton, QLD, Australia +61 7 4657 1466
www.matildacentre.com.au

Wells Fargo History Museums California and Minnesota
The Wells Fargo History Museums display original Concord Coaches, Wells Fargo documents, artifacts and early photos, and a collection of fine art.
San Francisco, Los Angeles, Sacramento, San Diego, and Minneapolis
www.wellsfargohistory.com/museums/index.html

Western Folklife Center Elko, Nevada
The home of the National Cowboy Poetry Gathering and Western preservation projects, the center has an exhibition gallery and archives with documentation resulting from the center's fieldwork.
Western Folklife Center, 501 Railroad Street, Elko, NV 89801 (775) 738-7508
www.westfolk.org

William S. Hart Ranch and Museum Newhall, California
The museum is housed in the former home and ranch of William S. Hart, the silent film Cowboy star and director. The Spanish colonial Revival style mansion contains original furnishings and an impressive collection of Western art.
24151 San Fernando Road, Newhall, CA 91321 (661) 254-4584
www.hartmuseum.org

Will Rogers Memorial Museum Claremore, Oklahoma
The museum frames the family tomb in a sunken garden, and contains Will Rogers artifacts and memorabilia, a research library and archives, and original art works by Russell and others.
1720 West Will Rogers Blvd., Claremore, OK 74018 (918) 341-0719
www.willrogers.org/memorial

Women of the West Museum Boulder, Colorado
The museum's exhibits and programs explore the historic and continuing roles of women in shaping the American West.
1536 Wynkoop, Suite 400B, Denver, CO 80202 (303) 446-9378
www.womenofthewest.org

Woolaroc Museum and Gallery Bartlesville, Oklahoma
Located on 3600 acres, Woolaroc is a western art museum, wildlife refuge and nature trail. It includes more than 10,000 American and Western art and artifacts.
Rt. 3, Box 2100, Bartlesville, OK 74003 (918) 336-0307
www.woolaroc.org

XIT Museum Dalhart, Texas
The museum documents the history of the XIT Ranch, once a 3 million acre spread employing 150 Cowboys. Exhibits include a 1900 chapel, parlor, bedroom and kitchen, works of Texas artists, and American Indian artifacts.
108 E. 5th, Dalhart, TX 79022 (806) 249-5390

INDEX OF POETS

*Additional information and poetry for all poets is
available at www.CowboyPoetry.com*

INDEX OF TITLES

INDEX OF FIRST LINES